Introduction to
Computer Assisted Valuation

Introduction to Computer Assisted Valuation.

Edited by
Arlo Woolery
Sharon Shea

 A Lincoln Institute of Land Policy Book

Published by
Oelgeschlager, Gunn & Hain
in association with the
Lincoln Institute of Land Policy

International Standard Book Number: 0-89946-198-0

Library of Congress Catalog Card Number: 85-15545

Printed in the U.S.A.

Oelgeschlager, Gunn & Hain, Publishers, Inc.
131 Clarendon Street
Boston, MA 02116

Library of Congress Cataloging in Publication Data

Main entry under title:

Introduction to computer assisted valuation.

    "A Lincoln Institute of Land Policy book."
    Bibliography: p.
    Includes index.
    1. Real property—Valuation—Data processing.
I. Woolery, Arlo. II. Shea, Sharon.
HD1387.I55 1985   333.33′2′0285   85-15545
ISBN 0-89946-198-0

TABLE OF CONTENTS

FOREWORD

There are two kinds of people in this world: those who write books and those who read them. The people who write books usually know more about their subject than do their readers. However, their success as writers is best measured by how much of what they know is imparted to their readers. The authors of this book were chosen for their special tasks because of their demonstrated abilities to make complex subject material relatively easy to understand.

Introduction to Computer Assisted Valuation is intended for the property tax administrator who has the responsibility for valuing thousands or even hundreds of thousands of taxable parcels of real estate. But it is also targeted at the independent fee appraiser, whether part of a large firm or the operator of a one-man shop. Land data management for both private and public sector use is also covered.

In his chapter, Gene Dilmore was asked to include a section on beating the "but I can't do math" blues. As Gene would say, "You no more have to be a mathematician to use a computer in valuation work than you have to be an electronic engineer to enjoy watching color television." A few simple instructions, an on and off switch, and a few easily mastered controls, and you are all set to enjoy as much color television as your location, cable system, or backyard microwave receiving dish will bring you. Computers are like that too. A few simple instructions, an on and off switch, a few more controls than your color television set, and all of a sudden you are a player and not a spectator.

There's an old saying that you can tell a real craftsman by the way he uses his tools. If your craft is valuation, then the computer could be one of your most useful tools. No other tool will help you test as many assumptions in less time. Adding a printer may even make life easier for your secretary. Nobody gets put out of work by a computer, but nearly anyone can work more productively if the computer is put to its proper use.

Appraisers can be only as good as the data which supports them. Bob Kitchen was asked to write the basic chapter on data collection and data administration. Just as the basic recipe for rabbit stew starts with the phrase, "First catch the rabbit," the basic recipe for computer assisted valuation starts with, "First capture the data." Once the property characteristic data is captured, it can be put to a fairly wide variety of uses. Rich Almy explains how to use the same data in land management systems and computer assisted valuation.

The introductory chapter on hardware will give readers some idea of the tremendous range of options open to the beginning computer user. Cost is no longer a major constraint, and off-the-shelf equipment will do most of the jobs described in this book.

No printed material dealing with information technology and data processing is complete without lifting the curtain and taking a short peek into the future. Gene Carter does just that in his chapter, Artificial Intelligence and Beyond. Every appraiser in every appraisal is faced with a seemingly endless series of decisions. Gene Carter's thoughts on decision theory and expert systems provides some reassurance to the valuer who is constantly encountering new forks in strange roads.

The glossary and bibliographies are Committee efforts. In this case, the Committee hopes to put to rest the old saw about the camel being a horse designed by a Committee. The glossary was compiled with the thought that a new generation of terms is growing up around a new generation of microcomputer equipment. If the same words do not have the same meaning to different people, it is difficult to communicate, so we hope that there will be general agreement on the definitions of the terms included in our glossary.

The scribe in Ecclesiastes wrote, "Of the making of many books, there is no end," and that is why bibliographies are born. We have gone the scribe one better and included two bibliographies, one general and one on legal challenges to computer assisted valuations. While these do not claim to be a complete listing of all the writings on the topic of computer assisted valuation, they do include those writings most useful to our readers.

Since there are sixteen different authors for the chapters in this book, it is inevitable that there is some duplication and repetition. However, that is not all bad because a good thing bears repeating. Books are like drinks, some are meant to be quaffed, while others are meant to be sipped. This book is more of the sipping kind, since readers will be able to go to any chapter and extract a bit of information that may be required at a given moment. The predominance of Lincoln Institute people on the contributors list simply reflects the pioneering work of this organization in computer assisted valuation for ad valorem tax purposes.

In addition to the chapter authors, the list of people deserving thanks for their efforts in producing this book is a long one; far too long to list here. Our special thanks go to Mary O'Brien for her patient supervision of the compilation of the bibliographies and the glossary.

Arlo Woolery
Sharon Shea

CONTRIBUTORS

RICHARD ALMY is Executive Director of the International Association of Assessing Officers.

E. EUGENE CARTER is Professor and Head of the Department of Finance, University of Illinois at Chicago.

GENE DILMORE is President of Realty Researchers, Birmingham, Alabama.

JOSEPH ECKERT is Director of Education for the International Association of Assessing Officers.

ROBERT J. GLOUDEMANS is Head of the Computer Assisted Appraisal Unit of the Arizona Department of Revenue.

ROBERT H. GUSTAFSON is Chief of Operations of the Property Tax Department of the California State Board of Equalization.

JOHN S. KIRKWOOD is Senior Lecturer in Land Administration at Sheffield City Polytechnic, England.

T. ROBERT KITCHEN is Deputy Executive Director for Operations, New York State Division of Equalization and Assessment.

WILL KNEDLIK is Director of Intergovernmental Programs for the Lincoln Institute of Land Policy.

MATHEW E. MACIVER is Educational Coordinator for the Lincoln Institute of Land Policy.

BRUCE F. NAGEL is Vice President of Eastern Operations and Northern Marketing for Cole-Layer-Trumble Company.

DENNIS ROBINSON is Systems Manager for the Lincoln Institute of Land Policy.

BRUCE SAUTER is Director of Property Valuation Research for the New York State Division of Equalization and Assessment.

JAN SCHREIBER is Research Scientist at the Lincoln Institute of Land Policy.

MICHAEL WHEELER is Director of Education and Research for the Lincoln Institute of Land Policy.

TELESFORE P. WYSOCKI is Program Manager at the Waukesha County Technical Institute, Wisconsin.

Chapter 1

INFORMATION TECHNOLOGY: ITS IMPACT ON REAL ESTATE VALUATION AND MANAGEMENT

John S. Kirkwood

Information is one of our most valuable resources. It is a resource for which there is no substitute and without which we cannot function. Most other resources, in contrast, have substitutes. For example, if we ran out of coal we could use oil or nuclear power. But there is no such alternative for information—it is irreplaceable. Imagine you wished to travel from New York to San Francisco. Without fuel you might resort to horse-power, just as the early settlers did. But without information you would be lost—both literally and metaphorically.

Thus, we are all vitally dependent on information. In the extreme it enables us to survive, but less dramatically it is an essential part of professional and business activity. For instance, medical practitioners need to know about the latest drugs and lawyers have to keep themselves well informed about case law and statutes.

The real estate specialist is, of course, no exception to this. To undertake a property valuation, for example, it is necessary to have information about the size and location of the property in question; the valuer must also be well informed about current property values and the existence of any lease or planning restrictions. The better the quality of the information, the easier is the valuer's task. Similarly, the manager of real estate requires a wealth of information covering such matters as rents, leases, tenants, running costs and the supply of, and demand for, different types of real estate.

This need for information has always been an integral part of professional activity, but in the last decade we have witnessed a dramatic increase in our power to handle it. The arrival of the silicon chip has triggered what many have referred to as "an information revolution" and this is affecting all aspects of our lives, including the processes associated with real estate management and valuation.

THE NATURE OF INFORMATION TECHNOLOGY

What then is information technology? A typical definition is that it is the appliance of science to the collection, storage, processing and transmission of information. Unfortunately such definitions encompass everything from the inscription of the Ten Commandments on tablets of stone to the use of satellites. Indeed, in one sense it is quite reasonable to refer to the printing press, say, as a piece of information technology. However, for our purposes it is necessary to use a narrower definition restricted to those devices which handle information via the use of electronic or magnetic signals. Although this means that attention is focused on developments that have occurred since the arrival of the electronic digital computer, we should not forget in passing that some of the technology has been with us since the nineteenth century (e.g., the telephone).

In 1959 Ferranti created a computer called the Pegasus.[1] This was a first generation machine capable of undertaking 3,000 instructions per second. It required a special air-conditioned environment in which to run and, because of its high cost, only 40 were sold. Last year ICL introduced a personal computer costing 1/250th the cost of the Pegasus and capable of 1,000,000 instructions per second. What is more, the ICL machine will operate on a desktop anywhere and requires no preventative maintenance.

These examples help to illustrate how far we have come in less than three decades. Thanks to first the transistor and then the integrated circuit (i.e., the chip) computers have become smaller, cheaper, faster and more reliable and robust. Computing power is no longer in the hands of an elite minority—it is available to almost everyone.

However, information technology is not just about computing. It is also about communications. As Corfield[2] has stated:

"Without access to the data required—which may not even be in the same country—the value of processing power is strictly limited."

---

1. Watson, J.M., *The Technology That Makes It Possible: Computer Electronics and Power,* January 1985.
2. Corfield, Sir Kenneth, *The Technology That Makes It Possible: Communications Electronics and Power*, January 1985.

Hence, when considering the impact of information technology, it is important not to overlook such developments as satellite communications, fiber-optic cables and digital switching systems. It is the combined effect of computing and communications that is producing such exciting changes.

THE CONCEPTS

Information technology is founded upon a number of basic concepts, some of which are surprisingly old when one considers our propensity to regard computers as being modern. These concepts formed the building blocks of the early valve-based machines and have remained a central part of computer design, despite the arrival of the transistor and the integrated circuit. They determine how computers work, and consequently, an appreciation of their nature is important, because it fosters a greater understanding of the potential and the limitations of information technology.

Possibly the most significant concept upon which information technology is based is that of binary notation; that is, a numbering system which uses only the symbols "0" and "1" to represent all numeric values. This may be contrasted with the more traditional decimal notation based on the ten symbols "0" to "9". The former approach suits the computer, which is really just a complex switching system, whereas the latter approach suits humans, who can more easily read decimal notations. Compare for instance 3985 (decimal) and 111101101101 (binary), both of which represent the same numeric value but using different conventions. It is rather like saying that "gasoline" and "petrol" mean the same thing.

It is, of course, possible to create a numbering system to any base, other examples being hexadecimal (16 symbols) and octal (8 symbols). But binary notation is used on computers because "0" and "1" can be represented simply and unambiguously by either the existence or absence of electric current or voltage. In contrast, to build a decimal-based computer would require the use of a range of voltages, which would be subject to fluctuation, and hence inaccuracy. Thus, the significance of binary notation is that computers are extremely accurate and reliable, a feature which is vitally important for, say, the preparation of property management accounts.

Closely related to the idea of binary notation is the method known as digital representation; that is, the concept of representing information as discrete values. This may be contrasted with analog representation which shows information as part of a continuum. Thus, for instance, a digital clock shows a discrete value whereas the traditional analog equivalent shows time by the sweep of the hands past a continuous scale. The virtue of the former is its lack of ambiguity, and this characteristic is an essential feature of the electronic digital computer. Hence, numbers, characters and commands can all be represented with a precision that has created great faith in the technology that we use to store, process and transmit information.

One of the most fascinating and important concepts on which computers are based is Boolean logic—fascinating because the laws of logic were formulated in the 1850s, by the English mathematician George Boole, long before anyone had even thought of designing an electronic computer. And yet, without Boolean logic, it would be impossible to design versatile, accurate computers. To represent his ideas, Boole used special symbols and the two values, true and false, which have since been represented by the binary digits "0" and "1". In the 1940s, Claude E. Shannon, an American mathematician, applied this Boolean logic to the design of the telephone switching circuit, the immediate forerunner of the computer.

Boolean logic forms one of the basic building blocks in the design of the digital computer, particularly the arithmetic and logic unit, which is where most of the processing takes place. The ideas of logic are applied to enable the computer to undertake the four arithmetic processes of addition, subtraction, multiplication and division. These are greatly simplified by considering multiplication as repeated addition and division as repeated subtraction. Further, as subtraction consists of no more than the addition of a number's complement, the arithmetic of a computer can be reduced simply to addition.

Thus, ultimately everything is reduced to numbers within a computer: values, text and instructions. All of this data is dealt with according to a rigorous logic. Consequently, computers operate with great precision and can handle all those processes, such as word processing, which are capable of being reduced to mathematical representation. However, because computers follow instructions according to a rigid system of logic, they are incapable of making the kind of creative mental leaps that humans make. Computers simply follow our commands, even in the case of "expert systems" which create the illusion of the computer thinking for itself.

Computers are capable of holding their instructions internally and this concept, introduced by von Neumann, is known as "the stored program." All electronic digital computers store both data and programs within their random-access memories and this means that they are able to process information without user intervention. Consequently, computers operate at speeds which are beyond our comprehension. For example, the many personal computers can process data at one million instructions per second. Try doing that on an Abacus!

Taken together, the above concepts mean that information technology provides the following substantial benefits:

— High speed processing
— Rapid communication of large volumes of information

— Accuracy of a very high order
— Mass storage of data and programs

However, the impact of information technology must not be seen just in terms of the simple effect of the above benefits. As Barron and Curnow[3] emphasize, the advances that have occurred in recent years have provided us, for the first time, with "a closed system for handling information." That is, we can now treat information as a resource in much the same way as we treat electricity or gas as resources: we can store it, we can process it and we can pipe it into homes, offices, shops and factories. The implications of this are probably greater in the field of real estate than in any other field.

REAL ESTATE VALUATION

Niklaus Wirth, designer of the computer language Pascal, has suggested that today the computational ability of the modern computer is almost an irrelevance.[4] To understand what he means and the relevance such a statement has with respect to using information technology for real estate valuations, it is necessary to briefly examine the changing way electronic computers have been used since they were first developed.

The first generation computers were designed and ran for the purpose of undertaking high-speed computation; that is, they were used almost exclusively for scientific and mathematical purposes. The main characteristic of such applications was that large, complex programs processed relatively small amounts of data. Consequently, the computer's storage capacity played a supporting role, while "number crunching" was the central activity.

This arrangement changed during the 1960s with the growing use of computers for commercial and business data processing. Such applications are characterized by the storage of very large volumes of data which are processed using relatively simple programs. Hence, for the majority of computer applications today, data storage and retrieval is of paramount importance, whereas the computational ability of information technology is merely supportive.

The above distinction is a useful one to apply when examining the impact of information technology on real estate valuation. Some valuations involve calculations that are beyond the capabilities of humans and therefore fall into the first category. Development appraisal using the Monte Carlo method, for example, would not be contemplated without the com-

---

3. Kirkwood, J., "Information Technology and Land Administration," *Estates Gazette*, 1984.
4. Wirth, N., *Pascal: User's Manual and Report*, Springer-Verlag, 1975.

putational ability of the electronic digital computer. In contrast, many valuations rely on the storage and retrieval of large volumes of data, which are then manipulated by relatively simple programs. Portfolio valuations are an example of this latter type.

Of the two types of valuation, it is clear that the second category is the largest. Relatively few real estate valuations really exploit the computer's power as a "number cruncher." Most of the mathematics of valuation can be accomplished using a handheld calculator. Thus, it is mainly the need to process large numbers of properties, stored on disk, that warrants the use of a computer.

Techniques and applications which fall into the category of using the computational power of information technology include the following:

— Sensitivity Analysis
— Risk Analysis
— Multiple Regression Analysis

Whereas the following applications exploit the data storage and retrieval potential of information technology:

— Portfolio Analysis and Valuation
— Valuation Databases

The nature of these applications and the impact of information technology is considered below.

Sensitivity Analysis

For certain types of valuation, involving a large number of assumptions, the valuer creates a mathematical model which is then manipulated to gain greater insight into the problem being considered. The classic example of this approach is the use of a valuation model to determine the value of a development plot. The model is simply an abstraction of the real world conditions, intended to show the interrelationship between, and impact of, the constituent variables (e.g., construction costs, finance costs, and rental value).

Before the arrival of electronic calculators and computers, valuers had to rely on undertaking this process by hand. This, of course, was both tedious and prone to error. In addition, during periods of expansion (e.g., the UK real estate boom of the 1960s) the process is almost unnecessary because of the large margin for error. In contrast, when the market is more "tight" the valuer has to consider the impact on the valuation of changes in the constituent variables. This process is referred to as Sensitivity

Analysis or Sensitivity Testing, and may be undertaken with ease using information technology.

The main point to emphasize is that even though the mathematics of the model itself may not be unduly complex, the need to carry out repetitive computations, using a range of inputs, justifies the use of either a computer or a programmable calculator.

The author has developed a number of calculator programs to undertake Sensitivity Analysis which illustrate the computing power of modern programmable calculators. However, despite their capabilities, it is often preferable to use a computer for a number of reasons. First, computer programs may be designed to be more user-friendly than a calculator program. For instance, the user may be asked questions and may be provided with explanations. With a calculator, the user needs to know in advance which buttons to press to enter the variables. Second, the output from a computer is more suitable for showing to clients. Finally, the results of each analysis may be stored on disk.

One relatively straightforward way of harnessing the computer for the purpose of Sensitivity Analysis is to use a spreadsheet package. The first spreadsheet was introduced in 1978 and, since then, there have been dozens of imitations and developments. Many real estate consultants have realized the advantages of using such packages, not the least of which is that valuation models may be tailored to individual requirements.

The importance of developing and using models for Sensitivity Analysis is that they allow valuers to exercise their judgment freed from the tedium of calculation. Thus, technology often highlights, rather than eliminates, the need for sound professional judgment.

Risk Analysis

In common with many commercial activities, real estate investment and development involves risk taking. The risks arise from many sources, such as changes in the general economic climate or tenants becoming bankrupt, and developers and investors usually make some assessment of the risks attached to a particular scheme. Often this is done in a rather vague manner, but sometimes attempts are made to be more specific. One way of being more specific is to assign probabilities to given estimates in the way that odds are quoted in horse racing.

The concept of probability is one with which we are all familiar. For example, we know that when we toss a coin there is a fifty percent chance of it coming down heads and a fifty percent chance of it coming down tails. We know this from our experience, but we may also measure it objectively. That is, we could toss a coin one hundred times and record the results. This is referred to as an objective measure of probability.

In the case of real estate, because of its diversity, it is not possible to conduct such analysis and consequently it is necessary to rely on the professional experience and judgment of the valuer. This is known as subjective probability. Although this type of information is less accurate than objective probabilities, it is still valuable in that it forces the valuer to be more specific about the assumptions being made.

The importance of this approach is that instead of basing development decisions upon single estimates of the constituent variables, the valuer is required to show a risk profile for each variable. For example, as Morley has shown,[5] a valuer may expect rents to lie between $4 to $5 per square foot for two given industrial units and yet assign different risk profiles to each:

Estimate of Rent	Probability Unit A	Probability Unit B
4.00	.10 (10%)	.00 (0%)
4.25	.20 (20%)	.15 (15%)
4.50	.40 (40%)	.70 (70%)
4.75	.20 (20%)	.15 (15%)
5.00	.10 (10%)	.00 (0%)

In both cases the valuer's simple best estimate ($4.50) is the same as the expected weighted value:

Unit A: $(4 \times .1) + (4.25 \times .2) + (4.5 \times .4)$
$+ (4.75 \times .2) + (5 \times .1) = 4.5$
Unit B: $(4 \times 0) + (4.25 \times .15) + (4.5 \times .7)$
$+ (4.75 \times .15) + (5 \times 0) = 4.5$

The figures are somewhat distorted to prove a point, but they do show that by using the single estimate approach there would be no way of distinguishing between the two units. In addition, the above risk profiles assume a normal distribution, but in certain cases the simple best estimate may differ from the expected weighted value because of a skewed distribution. For example, if the probabilities were 5%, 15%, 40%, 30%, and 10% respectively, the expected weighted value would be $4.56 rather than $4.50.

Another factor to be considered is the effect of combining probabilities. This is achieved mathematically by multiplying them together. For instance, if there is a 40 percent chance of the rental estimate being achieved and a 30 percent chance of the building cost estimate being correct, then there is only a 12 percent chance of both occurring (i.e., $.4 \times .3 = .12$).

These two features, the risk profile and the effect of combining pro-

---

5. Morley, S., "Valuation and Investment Appraisal" (Chapter 9), Ed. Darlow, C., *Estates Gazette*, 1983.

babilities, are incorporated into a technique called Monte Carlo Risk Analysis. This technique has already been used widely outside the field of real estate, and there is now some evidence that it is gaining acceptance as an aid to development and investment appraisal.[6]

Using the Monte Carlo approach, the valuer has to supply a range of assessments for each of the major variables plus estimates of their probabilities. Numerous valuations are then undertaken using varying combinations of these estimates, which are chosen using a random number generator. The results are then plotted in the form of a probability distribution.

Because the Monte Carlo technique involves the generation of random numbers and the repetition of the basic valuation at least one thousand times, it is impractical to contemplate using it without the aid of a computer. In addition, as the final results are presented in the form of a probability distribution, it makes sense to use the graphic capabilities of information technology to the fullest extent.

The author has developed a program which enables the Monte Carlo method to be applied to real estate development. The program, called RISKANALYSIS,[7] was written in UCSD P-system Pascal and runs on an Apple II microcomputer. The program makes full use of a facility known as Turtlegraphics to display the final results in the form of a probability distribution.

Pascal was chosen as the language because of its emphasis on the structured approach to problem solving and because it enables a large complex program to be split into separate interrelated procedures and functions. By its nature, the Monte Carlo method involves the frequent repetition of instructions using a range of values for given variables. In Pascal, this is accomplished by passing parameters to self-contained procedures. Thus, a piece of code may be written just once but used numerous times.

The RISKANALYSIS program identifies four major variables for which the user has to supply three estimates of value plus associated probabilities. These are rental value, building cost, finance rate and building contract period. The user then enters the remaining data, including land cost, and the computer undertakes one thousand computations of developer's profit. These results are then plotted on a probability distribution which shows the likelihood of any given profit being achieved. The developer thus has more information on which to base a decision than by the single valuation approach.

This type of analysis would hardly be possible without the computational power of the modern computer. Indeed, the above program takes a full

6. Byrne, P. & Cadman, D., *Risk, Uncertainty & Decision Making in Property Development*, Spon, 1984.

7. Op. cit. 3.

15 minutes to process the data on the Apple II! Consequently, the program is being re-written to run on a faster machine.

The most interesting feature of the above technique is that rather than making life easier for the valuer, it actually makes it harder by forcing the valuer to be more specific. Hence, in this case information technology increases the need for good professional judgment.

Portfolio Analysis and Valuation

The potential for using information technology for Portfolio Analysis and Valuation is well illustrated by the experience of St. Quintin, a London-based real estate consultancy. Their system, COMPAS ON-LINE exploits all aspects of computerization: mass data storage, speed of computation, use of graphics, and telecommunications.

The COMPAS ON-LINE system was developed jointly by St. Quintin and Chase Econometrics/Interactive Data Corporation (CE/IDC). The chief system designer, Stephen Sykes,[8] set out to achieve the following objectives:

— Storage on disk of all investments, valuation and analysis details relating to the individual properties and sectors within a portfolio
— Rapid on-line valuation facilities
— In-depth analysis of properties and portfolios in terms of structure and performance

An interesting feature of the system is that although St. Quintin's headquarters are in London, the computer on which the property data is held is located in the USA. (St. Quintin also has an in-house system called COMPAS.) Thus, telecommunications must not be overlooked when examining the impact of information technology on real estate valuation. Satellite and telephone links provide extensive freedom regarding the location of databases, and enable us to make the most of centralized mass storage.

The data held on the COMPAS ON-LINE computer may be accessed at portfolio, property or tenancy level and valuations may be undertaken on whole portfolios, single properties or single tenancies. Among the wide range of valuation facilities the system provides are the following:

— Valuation of freehold and leasehold interests
— Identification of top slice situations plus option to value at a different rate
— Valuation of any combination of open and fixed rent reviews

---

8. Sykes, S., "St. Quintin Computerized Property Appraisal System (COMPAS)," *Journal of Valuation*: 1(3).

— Coefficients defining how sensitive the capital value is to changes in estimated rental value or capitalization rate
— Risk analysis to determine a likely range of capital values

In addition, COMPAS ON-LINE includes a wide variety of analysis facilities. The following examples may give some idea of the range of the system:

— Individual property statistics
— Sectors and aggregate portfolio sub-analyzed by geographical region, tenure and bands of capital value
— Sector bar chart analysis by capital value, estimated rental value and net rental income
— Estimated components of portfolio capital growth due to changes in rental values, changes in yield rates, and approach of rent reviews
— Ten year projected cash flows aggregate portfolio, single property and single tenancy

The attraction of the above features to investment institutions should be obvious. Pension funds and insurance companies, for example, regard real estate as merely one of a wide range of alternative investments. Their main concern is that real estate should perform as well as, if not better than, other forms of investment. Consequently, they need the facilities to be able to measure performance quickly and accurately in order to make investment decisions that will be to the benefit of their clients. As the above example illustrates, technology may be used to provide the information fund managers need as an aid to their professional judgment.

Valuation Databases

The process of real estate valuation is vitally dependent on information. Without accurate, up-to-date information, valuers are reduced to the role of fortune tellers, making educated guesses about the future. Hence, a large proportion of the valuer's time is spent collecting, storing and analyzing information.

The information valuers require is extremely wide-ranging. For example, as Dilmore states,[9] valuers may need to know about some or all of the following:

— Purpose of the valuation
— The client (e.g., tax position)
— Geographical and economic context of the property

9. Dilmore, G., *The New Approach to Real Estate Appraising*, Prentice-Hall, 1971.

— Finance available
— Rights attaching to the subject property
— Property type

In addition, valuers frequently require information about comparable properties. Where this is in abundance, it is possible to apply statistical methods (e.g., MRA—see below), but in other cases, valuers have to exercise their professional judgment based on experience.

The process of collecting real estate information is both time-consuming and costly. It makes sense, therefore, to make full use of it once it has been collected. However, traditional information storage techniques, which are paper-based, often prevent this from occurring. For many types of analyses, it is just too difficult or expensive to extract the material that the valuer requires. Consequently, attention has focused on the facilities provided by information technology and, in particular, on the establishment of property or valuation databases.

The term database has a layman's definition and a specialist's definition. The layman's version includes any large assemblage of information and is applied to all types of computer storage regardless of structure. In contrast, the term database conveys a very specific meaning to computer specialists. As Martin states,[10] in a database, information is stored as data items, rather than the traditional approach of using records and files, a data item being the most basic information that can be stored about an entity (e.g., a tenant's name).

The distinction between the two definitions is important because the true database offers considerable advantages over what is really just electronic file-handling. First, true databases help to reduce data duplication. Second, as a result, there is less data inconsistency. (Obviously, if attempts are made to store the same information more than once, discrepancies may arise.) Third, with true databases, programs and data are independent so that either may be changed without changing the other; this is not always the case with traditional information storage systems. Finally, users may interrogate databases using special query languages.

Both types of database present the valuer with opportunities that are not available using traditional paper-based information systems. The computer's power to search, sort, select, index and analyze can be utilized to great advantage. Once the information has been entered, it can be manipulated in ways that would never be contemplated using traditional methods of storage. Hence, if a valuer requires comparable evidence of retail properties located in the center of a given city, it can be available at the touch of a button.

---

10. Martin, J., *Principles of Database Management*, Prentice-Hall, 1976.

Unfortunately, progress toward such an ideal has been slow. In the UK, for example,[11] the Inland Revenue Valuation Office has only just decided to install microcomputers in 50 of their regional offices, and yet they have the most extensive property records of any agency in the country. Frequently, such a lack of innovation is excused by a shortage of finance—and this is not unreasonable. But often another less palatable explanation is the lack of realization of the potential of information technology. Unfortunately, no amount of written explanation can remedy this failure of imagination, unless valuers also have access to working systems—"Seeing is believing."

Multiple Regression Analysis

In all the above cases, information technology may be seen as supporting and enhancing the valuer's role. However, one technique that actually threatens that role, and which also relies heavily on the use of computers, is Multiple Regression Analysis (MRA). As the technique is covered more fully elsewhere in this book, my comments here are restricted to its use and impact.

The significance of MRA is illustrated by a study that the Inland Revenue Valuation Office undertook at Swindon in the UK in 1973.[12] In the UK, a form of property tax, referred to as Rating, is used to raise revenue for local authorities. An integral feature of this tax system is the regular revaluation of properties to determine their Rateable Values (i.e., letting values). Because of the paucity of rental evidence for residential properties in the UK, the use of capital values as an alternative has been actively considered. The purpose of the Swindon pilot study was to determine if capital values could be determined using automatic data processing involving MRA.

A representative sample of dwellings was chosen and these were valued by reference to patterns derived from actual sales. Where properties in the sample had been sold, the sales prices and valuations were compared. These tasks were undertaken both manually, by a Valuation Officer, and using MRA. The results showed that the Valuation Officer achieved 80% of his assessments within ±10% of sale prices, whereas the computer-based technique produced 84% within the same limits.

Clearly it would be unwise to argue the case for MRA from just one small pilot study. However, this is not just an isolated incident and there is evidence from many countries throughout the world of the successful use of this technique. For example, MRA has been used in the USA since the

---

11. Kirkwood, J., "Information Technology: Micros for VOs," *Estates Gazette*, 9 March 1985.
12. Enever, N., "The Valuation of Property Investments," *Estates Gazette*, 1981.

mid-1960s to value rural bare land, urban bare land, single-family residences and multiple-family residences.[13] And the technique has also been successfully implemented in Denmark and Australia.

The significant feature of this evidence is not just that computers are used for their speed, accuracy and data storage capacity, but that human valuers can occasionally be out-performed by technology, with respect to the aspect they most cherish—professional judgment!

REAL ESTATE MANAGEMENT

Many of the processes involved in the management of real estate are of a mechanistic nature. Indeed, because of this fact, real estate management has acquired, in the UK at least, a rather mundane image. Consequently, those preferring a more "glamorous" career have turned to real estate development and valuation. However, the impact of information technology is changing the image of management and is freeing the real estate manager from its day-to-day drudgery.

The processes of management are ideally suited to computerization. They include: rent and service charge accounting, lease management, taxation, and property maintenance. The computer's capacity to store large amounts of data and to facilitate high-speed, accurate computation is used to the fullest extent in undertaking these processes.

The value of using information technology for management is perhaps best illustrated in the case of service charge accounting. In the UK, the process of charging tenants for services provided by the landlord has become increasingly complicated in recent years as additional services have been included. Consequently, tenants have become increasingly suspicious and have required accurate management accounts. Computers can provide valuable assistance in preparing such accounts. First, every item of expenditure, from bottles of cleaning fluid upwards, can be stored on a central file. Next, this information can be analyzed by the computer and a resume produced for the tenant, under appropriate broad headings. Thus, all the tedious accounting work is alleviated.

In relation to management accounting generally, well-designed computer systems offer the user considerable flexibility. For instance, software can cope with different accounting periods (e.g., weekly/monthly/quarterly), different methods of payment (e.g., cash/check/banker's order), and varying taxation provisions. The deletion, amendment and addition of property and tenant records may also be undertaken with ease.

---

13. Bruce, R.W. & Sundell, D.J., "Multiple Regression Analysis: History and Applications in the Appraisal Profession," *The Real Estate Appraiser*, January/February 1977.

Finally, the diary facilities that are such an integral part of modern computers are an invaluable aid to the property manager. For example, reminder dates for statutory notices, lease renewals, rent reviews and inspection and redecoration cycles may all be included.

PROCESS CONTROL

Within the real estate sector, emphasis is usually placed on the use of information technology for data processing and, yet, an equally important area of application is that of process control; that is, the creation of automatic control systems for plant and machinery (e.g., central heating and air conditioning).

The way that process control works is that sensors are used to monitor such features as temperature, weight, and speed, and this information is then fed to a computer. The computer responds by sending signals which cause valves to close or motors to stop according to a previously entered program. In this way the environmental conditions within a building may be controlled automatically. This concept is sometimes referred to as "the smart building."

Using the approach outlined above may lead to considerable savings in fuel costs. For example, the Honeywell Delta 1000 Building Management System[14] includes an optimum stop/start program which activates heating the plant prior to occupation. The time for this varies each day, depending on outside and internal air temperatures, in order to achieve the correct temperature levels with the least energy usage. At the end of each day, the plant is switched off before closing time to make use of all the residual heat within a building.

Other systems have been designed which monitor fuel and utility bills to indicate where savings can be made. For example, Stark Associates in the UK market an energy saving package which identifies the most economic tariff for electricity, thus reducing costs. It is claimed to provide between 5%-15% savings in energy costs per year.

CONVEYANCING

Earlier in this chapter reference was made to the idea of information technology providing a closed system for handling information. Nowhere is this concept more relevant than in relation to the conveyancing of real estate.

14. Kirkwood, J., "Information Technology: Process Control," *Estates Gazette*, 12 January 1985.

Conveyancing involves a number of processes that could benefit significantly from the application of new technology: the storage of property details, the undertaking of searches (e.g., to establish property rights), the preparation of correspondence and contract documents, and the transmission of information to other parties. The burden involved in these processes may be reduced substantially by the establishment of property databases, the application of word processing, and the use of electronic mail.

In the UK, for example, Longman Professional Software (a branch of legal publishers Oyez Longman) has established a conveyancing system that runs on a wide range of standard equipment, from single-user microcomputers to powerful minicomputers supporting a number of terminals.[15] Their system prompts the conveyancer to collect all the necessary information, advises on action to be taken, produces the necessary documentation and links with other computers. It also links the conveyancing and accounting information so that duplication of input data is eliminated.

Developments such as this one will inevitably help to reduce the delays which are currently a much-criticized feature of conveyancing. They will also lead to greater accuracy and hence clients will be offered a much better professional service.

One final point, which applies to all the areas touched upon in this chapter, is that as the technology becomes more accessible and user-friendly, the role of the professional advisor will become demystified. Members of the general public will demand better service and may even resort to using the systems directly themselves!

---

15. Brookes, M., "Conveyancing: The Future is Here," *Lawbase Magazine*, 1984.

Chapter 2

HARDWARE AND SOFTWARE OPTIONS

Dennis Robinson

"The purpose of computers is not to make life easy, but to make it more imaginative."

— Dr. Alan J. Perlis,
Higgins Professor of Computer Science, Yale University

It is inaccurate to think of computers as extremely fast calculators or as immensely efficient information storage devices, although computers are very good at these functions. It is more accurate to see the computer as a tool, one of the most versatile tools mankind has ever invented. A computer is an electronic means for converting ideas into practical, working devices. There are as many uses of computers as there are imaginative ideas. Computer Assisted Valuation (CAV) is certainly one.

Familiarity with computer technology is necessary for understanding the specifics of CAV or hardware and software options. The next few sections of this chapter provide a quick summary starting at the invention of the computer and finishing at the current state of computer technology.

REMOTE HISTORY

Computers have a long and interesting history. The concept of a computer dates back to the mid-1600s when the French scientist Blaise Pascal developed a mechanical adding machine; it was too unreliable for practical use but did demonstrate the workability of such a machine. Two centuries later Thomas de Colmar produced a successful commercial "arithmometer." At the same time, mechanical sequencing devices were developing. Rotating cylinders with pegs were used to control the playing of musical instruments, for example. Another popular example of such a machine is the Jacquard loom, developed in the early 1700s, which used perforated cards that controlled the weaving mechanisms.

Charles Babbage brought these two ideas together in the late 1830s. He developed the so-called analytical engine; it was controlled internally by rotating pegged cylinders and contained a mechanical arithmetic unit. Conceptually it is similar to today's computers. In fact, in 1936 a British mathematician, Alan M. Turing, invented the concept of a now famous and deceivingly simple machine which uses some of these early ideas as fundamental building blocks. The Turing machine is pictured below.

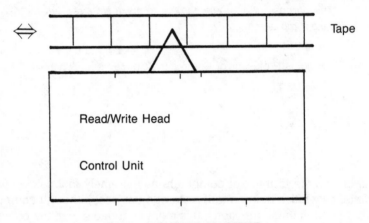

Figure 1: TURING MACHINE

This device contains a read/write head and a control unit which stores and retrieves a finite number of states (bits of information) on discrete squares of a tape. The tape can move in either direction. Remarkably, it has been proven that any digital computer can be simulated by a Turing machine.

RECENT HISTORY

Two of the most revolutionary and profound developments of mankind both emerged to prevalent use at the same point in history. One has unleashed an astounding creative force and the other an awesome destructive force: the electronic digital computer and the atomic bomb. During the late 1930s and early 1940s many attempts were made at applying notions of electronics to mechanical computers. Some notable pioneers in this field include Howard Aiken, then of Harvard University; John Atanasoff and Clifford Berry, then of Iowa State College; a German scientist named Konrad Zuse; and John Mauchley and J. Presper Eckert, then of the University of Pennsylvania. Mauchley, Eckert and their colleagues started out to develop a very fast electronic computer for large scale ballistics calculations. They succeeded in 1946 with the ENIAC. It contained 19,000 tubes for recording data and could perform 5,000 arithmetic operations per second. Significantly, through the use of interconnectable arithmetic operations, this made it the first *general purpose* electronic computer.

Just one more development was needed to create the modern computer. The U.S. Army Ordnance Department, which financed much of ENIAC, decided to also finance more computer research at Princeton's Institute for Advanced Study (where Albert Einstein was doing his work on relativity). John von Neumann, another famous mathematician there, was working on the hydrogen bomb as well as other projects. The bomb project required incredible computational ability; hence, von Neumann became interested in Aiken's Harvard Mark I (which incidentally was actually made by IBM) and the Eckert-Mauchley ENIAC. With his characteristic genius, he was able to perceive that not only data but the instructions themselves actually could be stored in the computer. In 1946, he explained these ideas in a paper which laid the foundation for the EDVAC. This was the first general purpose, electronic digital computer with an internal, *electronically stored program*. This type of machine, often called a von Neumann machine, is the prototype for all current computers. The electronically stored program, now referred to as *software*, is the innovation that allows the computer to be such a versatile tool, one that extends, if not surpasses, the human brain. New ideas for computer technology are now being generated at a dazzling rate. The current state of computer hardware will be discussed later in this chapter.

ELEMENTS OF COMPUTER PROCESSING

Almost all computers, no matter what size, are made up of the same basic elements: the central processing unit, routing circuitry, and input/output devices. The central processing unit (CPU) contains the arithmetic and logic unit (ALU) which is the part that does the actual "thinking." (The issues of whether or not a computer actually thinks like a human is beyond the scope of this book, but some interesting insights into this question are provided in another chapter.) That is to say, it is the ALU that adds, subtracts, multiplies, divides, compares, sorts, loops, branches, etc.

The central processing unit also contains the primary memory of the computer. The primary memory holds information on which the ALU can operate. For example, if the ALU needs to add two numbers together, the two numbers must be in primary memory so that they can be accessed by the ALU. If the ALU needs another instruction (of a program) so that it knows what to do next, that instruction must be in primary memory.

The third part of the central processing unit is the control unit. The control unit acts as a "traffic cop" between the ALU and other parts of the computer. For example, it instructs the ALU when to execute the next instruction or to the next element of data.

The input/output devices are the parts of the computer with which most people are more familiar. These are the devices through which the computer communicates with the outside world, such as a human, a manufacturing assembly line, or another computer. Examples include the computer terminal or screen, the keyboard, the line printer and the disk. The screen is the device which translates the computer's electrical signals into visual images which you can understand, such as letters and numbers. It resembles the screen of a television. The keyboard, usually attached to the screen, contains typewriter-like keys which, when pressed, transmit information to the computer. This information so transmitted could be instructions, answers to questions asked by the computer, or data such as property record cards. The line printer is the device which prints information from the computer onto paper providing what is often referred to as the "hard copy" of the information.

As described above, the computer primary memory also holds information, but in most computers, primary memory cannot store data when the computer is turned off; the computer's primary memory often has limited storage capacity. Storage capacity is greatly enhanced by the disk. The disk retains information even when the computer is turned off. The disk is sometimes referred to as secondary memory or as external storage. Other input/output devices that provide secondary memory include "floppy" diskettes, magnetic drums, cassette tapes, a non-removable "fixed" disk, etc.

Because the primary memory is limited in storage capacity, most information is stored on the disk, yet the ALU can act only on information that is in primary memory. The third main element of the computer — the routing circuitry — brings the information from secondary storage into primary memory when the CPU signals it to do so. There are many types of routing circuitry (such as the memory bus, input/output channels, direct memory access (DMA) channels, etc.) but the distinctions among them are not important for a basic understanding of computer operation. The schematic below pictures the three basic elements of what experts term "late third-generation" electronic computers.

HARDWARE, STATE-OF-THE-ART

Third generation technology refers to computers that are built with integrated circuits (often large scale integrated circuits) since about 1969.

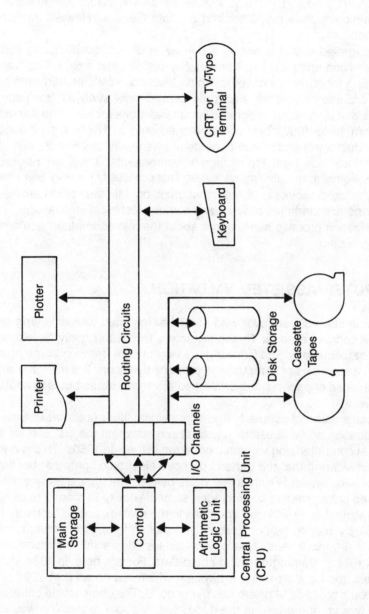

Figure 2: COMPUTER HARDWARE ELEMENTS

This includes such systems as the IBM 370, 3300 and 4300 series; Burroughs 6700 and 7700 series; Honeywell 6000 series; Digital Equipment Corporation PDP-10, PDP-11 and VAX series; as well as minicomputers and super-minicomputers manufactured by Data General, Hewlett Packard, Prime, etc.

An integrated circuit is simply a thin wafer of semiconductor material such as silicon enclosed in a hermetically sealed plastic case. The wafer and casing together are called a "chip." Microscopically etched onto the silicon are interconnected electronic components such as transistors, resistors and diodes. An integrated circuit wafer one inch in diameter may have from 10 to 1000 components etched onto it. These highly dense semiconductor integrated components are generally much more reliable and produce less heat than discrete components. They are not only drastically smaller but also much lighter. This process of making ever more densely packed circuits is called miniaturization. Miniaturization provides for enormous economies of scale and obvious technical innovations. The miniaturization process has brought about the microcomputer — a computer on a chip.

COMPUTER ASSISTED VALUATION

There is often debate over who should be credited with inventing any valuable concept or idea. This is especially true with rapidly developing computer technology. The following is a very brief narrative of some of the earliest applications of computers to property valuation. It is meant to suggest the types of applications developed at various times but is in no way definitive.

An examination of scholarly and professional literature in assessment administration and real estate appraisal suggests that the first serious attempts at computerizing valuation occurred in the late 1950s. This is quite early, considering that the general purpose electronic computer became commercially available only a few years before. The typical early system contained cost formulae but included some flexibility to modify rates applied to variables, to add new variables to the system, and to "update" the database by loading property record information through punched cards.

Essentially, those were replacement-cost-less-depreciation systems running on IBM or Remington Rand computers. For example, in 1964, John Cole described a state-of-the-art system which ran on an IBM 7094 and which could process 14 properties per second. The comparable sales approach was computerized in the mid-1960s. Multiple regression was still considered "experimental" in 1966, but only two years later Dr. William M. Shenkel of the University of Georgia described a model program which had been developed for computer valuation by multiple regression. Mass appraisal — a term almost synonymous with computer assisted valuation — emerged in assessment literature in the mid-1960s and relates to the use of computers to apply recognized appraisal techniques to numerous homogeneous properties.

In summary, most of the major ideas concerning the use of computers in valuation work that are prevalent today were developed in the decade before 1970. There have been, of course, many refinements and extensions of these techniques. Similarly, there has been a constant effort to keep the valuation applications up-to-date with ever advancing computer technology. The specifics of these techniques are discussed in subsequent chapters. The rest of this chapter discusses the current state-of-the-art in computer technology, basic operations of computers, and current hardware and software options available for computer assisted valuation.

HARDWARE OPTIONS FOR COMPUTER ASSISTED VALUATION — THE IMAGINATION IS BAFFLED BY THE FACTS

Computers are often classified into three groups: mainframes, minis, and micros, all of which are late third generation machines. CAV applications have been developed for all three classes. The supposed distinctions are that mainframes have much more general capacity than minicomputers and that minicomputers in turn have much more general capacity than do microcomputers (also called desktop or personal computers). These distinctions are not true now, and indeed, have not been true for some time. For example, the November, 1980 issue of *Datamation* compared the processing speed of many popular mainframes and minicomputers. The chart below shows the speed of several different kinds of computers, speed being measured in KOPS (thousands of operations per second; the higher the KOPS, the faster the computer).

Computer	KOPS	
IBM 370/148	425	
DEC PDP 11/70	600	
IBM 4341	758	
DEC VAX-11/780	831	
IBM 3031	1,045	
DEC 1099(2X)	1,160	
Cray-1	800,000	(the Cray-1 is widely considered the fastest computer)

All of the IBM machines listed are generally considered mainframes, whereas all of the DEC (Digital Equipment Corporation) machines listed are considered minicomputers. Contrary to common perception, some of the minis are clearly faster than their mainframe kin.

More recent testing of popular computers confirms this point. *Computerworld* rated the following machines in terms of MIPS (millions of instructions per second; the higher the MIPS, the faster the computer). Again, the listed IBM computers are considered mainframes and the others are minis or super-minis.

Computer	MIPS
IBM 4361-5	1.14
IBM 4341-12	1.20
AT & T 3B20D	1.80
DG MV/10000	2.50
PRIME Series 50, 9955	4.00

These makes and models were chosen to illustrate a point. It is easy to choose other examples where mainframes clearly outperform minicomputers in raw computing speed. There is no shortage of manufacturers and models to choose from. (A conservative estimate is that there are 300 different mainframes and an additional 300 different minis.) Price, moreover, is not a good measure of the performance of the computer, except in the very broadest sense. A $200,000 DEC VAX 11/780 is just slightly slower than a $500,000 IBM 4341-12, but is a lot slower than a $370,000 IBM 4381-1. These somewhat confusing numbers become all the more so when microcomputers are introduced into the picture. A February, 1984 issue of *Creative Computing* listed the results of a benchmark (a small program to test computational speed) executed on several computers. Listed below are a few examples (the lower the number, the better the computer performance; the time is expressed in seconds):

Computer	Time
Apple IIe	113.00
IBM PC	24.00
DEC VAX 11/780	1.00
Cray 1	0.01

The difference in times here is significant, but so is the difference in prices. The popular DEC VAX 11/780 is currently listed for just under $200,000; the IBM PC for just over $2,000! Although the PC is 24 times slower for this simple computational test, it is 100 times less expensive. A comparative price/performance ratio (100/24) shows that the PC is slightly over 4 times better — from a price/performance point of view.

Given this ratio, it may be acceptable for a computation (an MRA run, for example) to run 24 hours on the IBM PC even though it may only take an hour or less on the DEC VAX. In some applications, of course, a 24 minute response time may be far too slow, but a one minute response time may be very acceptable. In many cases, however, price/performance is important. Computer Assisted Valuation is an application where the price/performance ratio *is* a valid selection consideration.

A METHODOLOGY FOR CHOOSING CAV HARDWARE

Even experts have a difficult time choosing among the hardware options. In fact, computer experts cannot even agree on how to measure performance. Should raw computing speed be measured in MIPS or MFLOPS? Should the memory bus bandwidth be compared separately from the computing speed or in conjunction with it? Should I/O performance be part of performance evaluation? Should performance metrics be abandoned in favor of functional metrics? Technical questions like these can make a layman's head spin, and even the experts cannot agree on the answers. The primary reason for the lack of consensus on evaluating hardware is that the rate of technical change is just too fast and there is no end in sight. (Experts do seem to agree on that.) A super-minicomputer five years ago is an ordinary microcomputer today. In five years it will be obsolete. Significant changes in hardware options occur every three to six months.

Given all of these complexities, what is a prospective buyer to do? Perhaps the answer is suggested in Sir Arthur Conan Doyle's statement through Sherlock Holmes: "When you have eliminated the impossible, whatever remains, however improbable, must be the truth." If hardware options and prices are so quickly and constantly changing, choosing on those terms may be impossible. Instead, one should select a computerized valuation system based on the software, and then use whatever hardware is compatible.

It is easier to choose software intelligently. You can select the CAV software according to the specific tasks you want to perform and according to the size of the database it must support. This software selection process will simplify the hardware choice by eliminating most of the options. *After* this elimination process, other selection criteria can be applied to the hardware options that survive this first cut. One already mentioned is the price/performance ratio. Another very important one is availability of service. Others include compatibility with industry standards, availability of other compatible software and open-endedness of the hardware. The last refers to whether it can be connected to other computers, can be upgraded and can be expanded.

In short, the simple rule is to choose the software and then the hardware, yet it is a rule that is commonly violated for what people think are the best of reasons:

"We have an XYZ system and want software that will run on it."

"We want software that will run on an ABC because it has a good reputation."

"We have $60,000 in the budget for hardware so we want a computer for about that price or less."

Choosing the software before the hardware is putting the horse before the cart.

COMPUTER SOFTWARE

As mentioned earlier, von Neumann was responsible for the idea of the electronically stored program. A program is a set of instructions which tells the computer what to do and in what order. Typical instructions include the following: print information on the printer, get information from the keyboard, add some numbers together, store the result on the disk, display the color red on the computer screen, transmit some information to another computer, etc. All of these instructions have to be carefully ordered; just as in a recipe, frosting a cake must follow, not precede, the baking. Unlike a recipe, however, a computer program's instructions must be precise. Because most languages are far from exact, many special languages have been developed for programming or instructing the computer. A very exact, sequenced set of instructions is called an algorithm. The idea of an algorithm goes back at least 3500 to 5000 years ago. Tablets unearthed in Iraq by archaeologists and dated between 1500-3000 B.C. contain algorithms for solving algebraic equations. At the end of each ancient algorithm was the phrase, "this is the procedure", similar to the way we say STOP or END in some current programming languages.

Today, there are at least 170 programming languages with new ones being added all the time. The names of a few like FORTRAN (introduced in mid-1950s), COBOL (introduced in 1959-1960) and BASIC (introduced in mid-1960s) are familiar. Each language has its own unique set of commands for instructing the computer. Some are easier to use than others for certain applications, but in general, the same algorithm can be expressed in many of the languages.

The interface or connection between the hardware and software is a difficult concept to grasp. It can be described partially by the following diagram.

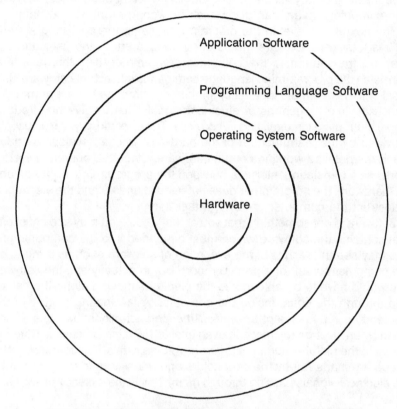

Application Software

Programming Language Software

Operating System Software

Hardware

Figure 3: COMPUTER HARDWARE AND SOFTWARE

The center circle contains the three major elements described above: the CPU, input/output devices and routing circuitry. All of the other circles are part of the software. The outer layer is the application package with which the user interacts. It contains the menu choices from which the user chooses functions, it contains the interactive dialogue by which the user enters his data or specifies certain options, and it often contains "help" information for guiding the user. In most well-designed systems, this outer level is all that the user has to understand in order to operate the entire computer system, other than pressing the ON switch.

The application level will actually be specified in a programming language. To display the menu of functions that the user sees on the computer screen (such as "print," "copy," or "delete," for example) may require dozens of instructions or commands expressed in the programming language. The entire application system may be modularized into hundreds of individual programs. They are stored on the disk along with data and brought into memory via the routing circuitry when needed — just like data. The computer system can distinguish between programs and data.

The next inner level in the diagram represents the operating system. This is a layer of software that is often transparent to the user and can even be transparent to the computer programmer. It is this level that translates the programming language commands into actual hardware electrical signals. A simple instruction in the programming language may get translated into thousands of electrical signals that involve hundreds of chips, the routing circuitry, and I/O devices. The operating system is usually provided by the manufacturer of the hardware whose developers understand the detailed workings of the hardware. Since the operating system works as a translating interface between the programming language and the hardware, the programmer does not need to understand the electronics to instruct the computer to perform tasks.

Software is not something that you actually see. You may see a diskette that contains the software which must be loaded into the computer, and you may see the results of the execution of software such as a menu on the computer screen or a printed report. But to actually see the software you would have to be able to see the electrons moving along the cables and through the chips inside the computer. A fascinating picture in the September, 1984 issue of *Scientific American* actually shows this. It was taken by an electron microscope of an Intel 80186 microprocessor. Different colors in the picture represent different voltage levels. The features of the image are made not by the conductors and transistors in the chip but by the electrical signals passing through them. This is the essence of software.

SOFTWARE, STATE-OF-THE-ART

Compared to changes in hardware technology, software technology develops much more slowly. Software, at the application level, lags many years behind the advancements in hardware. Often, the software advancements are developed only for the latest hardware and are not retrofitted to older hardware. In part this fact explains why some of the most recent revolutions in software techniques are available primarily on microcomputers and not minicomputers or mainframes. Another reason is that microcomputers are targeted at such a large market that it is more profitable to design software innovations for the microcomputer.

Generic software is an important innovation. It is software that provides great flexibility in a specific application category. There are currently only five categories of generic software: word processing, spreadsheet, graphics, database management, and telecommunications. Some argue that accounting constitutes a sixth category; others contend that accounting is not a well enough defined application area to constitute generic software; still others argue that a clever enough generic program has not yet been invented for accounting. The very terms of this debate elucidate the meaning of generic software. Another category of generic software that is just beginning to emerge commercially is "decision-modeling" software.

The proper question is not whether something is or is not generic, but how generic it is. A Computer Assisted Mass Appraisal (CAMA) software system that contains a set of factors that cannot easily be expanded or modified is not very generic. Likewise, a CAMA system that does provide for flexible factor manipulation, but does not provide all of the valuation methodologies is not fully generic.

Integrated software is another recent innovation. Integrated software means a simple software system in which the generic categories listed above can all share data and all operate in a similar and consistent manner. Usually integrated software employs a split-screen mode of operation in which the word processing, database management, spreadsheet, and communication software each share a section of the computer screen, as pictured below:

Database management	Communications
Word processing	Spreadsheet

The window sizes can be dynamically changed and repositioned for the convenience of the user. It is much easier to learn how to use a single integrated package than several separate packages, each with its own, often inconsistent, commands and terminology. Integrated software also allows more efficient operation. For example, the user can type a document in the word processing window, press a couple of keys to insert the name and address from the database into the document, and then with a few more key strokes transmit the whole document to another location through the communication window.

Ease-of-use is another ongoing improvement in computer software. It takes a smart programmer to make a smart computer (or so programmers like to say). As software developers become more sophisticated in their programming techniques, more "intelligence" is programmed into the computer. This makes them easier to use. Icons, which are pictures on the computer, are an example of this. The user operates the computer by pointing at the pictures; to delete a document the user points at the picture of the trash can, to file a document the user points at the picture of the filing cabinet. Voice communication with a computer represents another technique to foster ease-of-use. It is now available and inexpensive for limited vocabularies. Soon talking to your computer will be commonplace.

SOFTWARE OPTIONS FOR COMPUTER ASSISTED VALUATION

The ideal CAV system would be a fully integrated, easy to use, fully generic software package. In such a package the valuation subsystem would be fully integrated with word processing, database management, communications, and spreadsheets on a single computer screen employing window technology. It might appear as in the figure below:

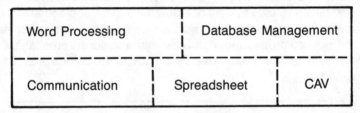

A fully generic CAV system means it would support private appraisal as well as CAMA methodology and it would support all methods of valuation for any set of factors. Ease-of-use means that the system should have all of these capabilities yet still be operable by the non-expert user. Although no system is currently on the market, the Lincoln Institute of Land Policy is working in this direction. The name of the system is SOLIR. It has been developed over several years as an experimental system for research and education. It serves as a very good model for software options available for computer assisted valuation.

SOLIR contains six major subsystems: database management, statistics, property valuation, land management, report generation, and an assessor/appraiser programming language. Database management provides data maintenance and display, sorting, dynamic record selection, importing data from or exporting data to other computers, backing-up the data and designing record layouts in a form of your choice. Statistics provide two-way frequency distributions, analysis of variance, histograms and scatter diagrams. The report generation subsystem allows any item of data to be printed on any form of your choice and allows for the creation of preprinted forms using any text and format. The property valuation subsystem supports the cost approach, comparable sales, multiple regression and feedback. The assessor/appraiser programming language allows the non-expert to write simple programs for data transformation (such as synthetic factors), inter-field edit checking, exception reports, etc. SOLIR operates on an IBM PC/XT or PC/AT. The recommended system is an enhanced PC/AT with 512KB of primary memory, 20MB disk, monochrome and/or color display and a printer. Such a system is currently priced at about $7,000. SOLIR has the capacity to support 32,000 parcels. Listed below are some approximate functional timing measurements (in this chart, unoptimized means that with minor program modifications the time could be reduced at least by ½):

Function	# Parcels	Minutes:Seconds
Compute and store the estimated sale price using MRA with 12 independent variables	5,000	50:00 (unoptimized)
Comparable sales with 10 factors	1,000	0:20 (optimized)
Feedback using 6 factors	200	3:00 (optimized)
Index (sort)	5,000	22:00 (partially optimized)
Plot boundaries of parcels	500	21:00 (unoptimized, using low cost plotter)

The valuation subsystem of SOLIR is fully generic. It supports all of the methodologies listed above and allows the user to define his own valuation factors. SOLIR is not fully integrated. All of the subsystems are integrated with each other, but these subsystems are not integrated with word processing, communication, spreadsheets nor accounting. SOLIR has not achieved the full measure of user-friendliness. For the non-expert to use it, two to three weeks of training and practice are required. Better documentation, computerized tutorials, and easy-to-understand menus and interactive dialogue are being developed to make it more user-friendly.

Both the hardware and software of SOLIR are representative of a state-of-the-art Computer Assisted Valuation system. There are many positive indications that the marketplace is moving in the direction of the SOLIR prototype. These commercially available programs will be generic, user-friendly and eventually fully integrated.

SUMMARY

This chapter has presented a methodology for evaluating computer assisted valuation hardware and software options. A primary rule of the methodology is to choose the software first, then the hardware. Hardware speed alone is not a sufficient performance measurement. The price/performance ratio is an important evaluation criterion. The functional timing measurements and general description of SOLIR provide a prototype for further evaluation of CAV systems. Finally, the imaginative, dynamically changing environment of computer technology has been described. Do not let this dissuade you from making the difficult choices. Do not keep waiting for a better system, because you may be waiting forever. There will *always* be better hardware and software options next year.

REFERENCES

Appraisal Journal, Vol.27, No.2, April, 1959; Vol.36, No.4, Oct., 1968; Vol.37, No.4, Oct., 1969; Vol.38, No.1, Jan., 1970; Vol.40, No.3, July, 1972; Vol.40, No.4, Oct., 1972; Published by American Institute of Real Estate Appraisers.

Birkhoff, Garrett and Bartee, Thomas, *Modern Applied Algebra*, McGraw-Hill, Inc., 1970.

Gotlieb, C.C., *The Economics of Computers*, Prentice-Hall, Inc., 1985.

Horowitz, Ellis, *Fundamentals of Programming Languages*, Computer Science Press, 1983.

International Association of Assessing Officers, *International Property Assessment Administration Proceedings* - 28th, 1963; 30th, 1964; 32nd, 1966; 33rd, 1967; 34th, 1968; 35th, 1969; 37th, 1972; 38th, 1973; Published by International Association of Assessing Officers.

Maisel, Herbert, *Introduction to Electronic Digital Computers*, McGraw-Hill, Inc., 1969.

Ralston, Anthony, *Encyclopedia of Computer Science*, Litton Educational Publishing, 1976.

Scientific American, Vol.251, No.3, Sept., 1984.

Many journals are generally worthwhile to the computer user. In particular see *Computerworld, Datamation, Computer Update*, and *Infoworld*. For particular background articles relevant to this chapter, the following issues are recommended:

Computer Update, March/April, 1985.

Computerworld, Apr. 2, 16, 1984; Jul. 23, 1984; Sept. 10, 17, 1984; Oct. 29, 1984; Nov. 5, 26, 1984; Dec. 24, 1984; Jan. 28, 1985; March 4, 1985.

Datamation, Apr., 1985.

Chapter 3

CHANGE AND TECHNOLOGY IN SOCIETY

E. Eugene Carter

INTRODUCTION

Speculating on the future course of technological change in the field of taxation is hazardous. In this book, the authors have been very concerned with suggesting how computer technology has evolved, and how such technology will become more commonplace in land-use deliberations, assessment, and the like in the coming years. Lincoln Institute's pioneering efforts with the CAMA system described later show how a commitment to a technical innovation by an organization with vision and funding can create a useful resource, which municipalities and states will find valuable.

In Chapter 17, I discuss CAESAR, the expert tax system which several of us are developing. Although this project may or may not become a valuable element in training, assessment, or tax planning, similar systems will be commonplace in industry, education, and government in my opinion. Thus, the characteristics of an expert system should be of interest to all of us.

Prior to that discussion, I should like to offer some brief comments on change, with emphasis on technological change. I have a particular perspective for viewing this process. I am a professor of finance and former

This chapter has benefited from the comments of Lutz Alt, Charlotte Boschan, Robert Hughes, Dennis Robinson, Rita Rodriguez, Ralph Westfall, and Arlo Woolery.

department head at the University of Illinois in Chicago, with a 1969 PhD from a technologically innovative management school, Carnegie-Mellon. I am also a director of an imaginative financial services/brokerage firm, among other firms. As a scholar, I was thus well aware of many computer and management techniques years ago: the computer on which I first learned to program in 1960, an IBM 650, is now on display at the Museum of Science and Industry in Chicago. As an administrator in the public sector, and as a consultant and a director in the private sector, I have seen how tardy and misguided some of the innovations from computer technology have been.

CHANGE

A model of the world (such as a model for change) is a simplification: any model as complex as the world would not explain very much. What one hopes to do is capture the relevant factors, to relate them in a sensible way, and to have insightful explanatory conclusions derived from the model. A model is an intellectual abstraction.

How do we explain the economics of the firm? Basically, it is built around some combination of land, labor, and capital. Among the more famous economists, Henry George and David Riccardo placed great emphasis on the value of land, Marx upon labor, and Schumpeter, Wicksell and Keynes perhaps emphasized capital formation and growth the most.[1] Each man had a model of the way the world worked, yet each emphasized different elements of the same land/labor/capital trilogy, in part because of differing assumptions about the underlying forces which drove the subcomponents of each element. One can understand why President Truman used to complain about his economists always saying, "On one hand . . . and on the other hand," wishing he had some one-armed economists. For us, the test is whether we have some useful insights, or can predict some results, knowing how to use our model.

I believe that the key to a model of change is to recognize that although technological capabilities are critical, the decisive variables are a *market need* (existing or awakened) which can be *served economically*, coupled with the *human intellectual capital* to use the technology. Wisdom (and luck) are what combine these variables effectively.

Let me offer some examples which in various ways illustrate my point. For at least ten years, we have heard about the advent of the checkless society, with emphasis on using debit cards at the point of purchase (which permits the customer to debit his/her account and credit the merchant's

---

1. These are obviously arbitrary judgments on the emphasis of each writer. Purists are welcome to substitute their own favorite.

account with the bank). Other ideas include paying bills by touch tone phone, crediting the merchant/mortgage holder/utility with a payment by punching in digits for the account number and the amount. Automatic payment of bills by programming the bank's computer to charge the account for, say, the mortgage payment each month is also suggested. The French "smart card" developed ten years ago has a small microchip inside it. Running the card through a card reader provides both greater security (it is hard to tamper with compared to the normal card with a magnetic strip) and a wealth of information. Encoded data such as medical data, emergency phone number, family, address, etc., could be read by one or more specialized decoders which might be available to all ambulance crews, for example.

Most of this collection of innovation has not developed, but not because the technology was not available inexpensively to offer it. Rather, determining what market benefit exists for a customer was something that bankers apparently never considered. Customers want the float, charging at one point and receiving a collated single bill later in the month. At that time, they can decide to pay it all at once or spread out payments. Customers want the option to delay a mortgage payment if needed, taking a ten-day grace period that most lenders permit (you can be sure the automatic payment system will take place no later than the 29th of the month, given who is in charge of determining payment dates!). Finally, some nervousness about immense computer foul-ups of accounts, plus a civil liberties issue of who would have access to the data in the bank accounts or encoded on the smart card are relevant. In short, the banks know what they will gain but have not considered until recently what the customer would get out of all this. Lower prices because the merchant gets his money immediately? Discounts for cash versus charge purposes seem to be largely a non-issue in most retail areas, gasoline notwithstanding. Thus, the need of the market is not recognized by the market promoters.

The ACE 3000 steam railroad engine is likely to be a reality in a few years. There are changing relative prices in oil versus coal. There is a technological evolution in the form of microprocessors (such are now in most new automobiles) which have sophisticated combustion models encoded to which the engine can respond. Finally, sophisticated buyers who understand the economics will probably create a market for this old technology in some areas of the country for particular types of hauls.

DSH (direct satellite to home) television transmission will probably be widespread. Addressable decoders (such as many new cable television systems have) coupled with much better distribution economics will probably permit this system to eclipse cable in most areas. Why? Cable offered the promise of a rapidly diversified television reception, plus better reception in some areas. Yet what has happened? First, the fixed costs to "wire" a community are considerable, both in getting the rights to wire the town and in physically stringing/burying the cable. Second, the economic pressures that have forced the networks to control program content (in order to hold viewers through an evening, whether or not the sponsor wants that particular show) and to sell time according to viewership have become obvious to cable operators. Programming is done to appeal to a wide audience, and the widest viewing audience is not the "average" American but the typical heavy viewer. There is a rapid number of disconnects in areas because of the lack of programming variety, coupled with a perception that one is paying for what once was free. High fidelity/stereo helps many cable operators with Music Television, and increasingly low-priced high fidelity video recorders such as Sony's BetaHiFi have had a feedback effect which reinforced the systems. However, the advantages of DSH seem to be a rapid ability to adjust to new transmitting technology (such as stereo sound) plus much lower costs per viewer in order to break even, largely because of lower costs of installation. Thus, it will probably offer greater specialized programming, which was the early promise of cable television.

Ultimately, then, the real benefit from having 40 million homes wired for cable television will come from the interaction which is possible. Simplified beyond the microcomputer-cum-modem discussed later, the home wiring will permit shopping, banking, etc., such as Columbus, Ohio's CUBE system has demonstrated to be technologically feasible. An enlarged democratic town meeting, so much a part of New England tradition, may be more practical electronically than it is physically today. In the absence of the feedback possible with the wired cable systems, television's "global village" is largely one-way interaction!

The typewriter and the telephone were both invented in the 1860s, yet it took time for people to recognize how they would change correspondence practices and business operations. Technology has obviously progressed in both areas, including electronic correcting memory typewriters with alternative typing elements as well as touch tone phones with abbreviated calling, call forwarding, and the like. But embedded human capital becomes a huge factor which cannot be economically overcome, in many cases. Part of the resistance to electronic mail has been the lack of paper, or an immediate hard copy. The original QWERTY typewriter was designed in part to prevent rapid typing which would jam the early machines. The highly efficient DVORAK keyboard, developed in the 1900s, never caught on both because the installed base of typewriters matched the old system and because operators were trained in a different way. Indeed, the need for "IBM compatibility" for twenty years in both mainframes and (now) microcomputers is an example of the same operation. There may be (are) better systems around, but one is caught in order to permit firms to have operators who can handle the existing system and to have machines which are interchangeable with the old dominant one. Again, one can see the interaction of a market awakened by a technological innovation, coupled with the positive and negative aspects of the human capital (knowledge) which permits the innovation to progress or to stifle something else.[2]

A philosophical issue is how much one designs for the world that is and how much one thinks about the world that can be. Bertrand Russell and others argue, in essence, that one should do some of both. Apropos the typewriter/computer transition, note that the more technically oriented designer of the Apple II wanted a separate numerical keypad and some other specialized keys. The more market-oriented partner argued (successfully) against them, noting that additional complexity would hinder the effort to sell the novel device. I believe he was correct, even though now, understandably, the more computer-familiar consumer criticizes the Apple II series for lacking those keys. On the other side, only recently have designers of word processing software for computers, the direct transition from a typewriter, taken much note of how people use typewriters. Thus, word processors are clumsy for quick entry of short items, such as addressing a single envelope. One creates a file, with margins, then saves it, goes to a print routine, and prints it. Now a few word processors finally have added a "typewriter" function which links the keyboard directly to the printer. Such flexibility from the first, which was technologically feasible years ago, would have eased the transition to the computer/word processor, much as today's memory/correctable electronic typewriters are easing the transition.[3]

Lest one doubt that markets are important, witness the change induced in the American auto market in ten years. With cheap gas, good highways over longer distances, rising real incomes, and management which accommodated wage demands (which ultimately made the auto workers' pay

---

2. Admittedly, the proliferation of sequential computerized calling machines which send their recorded irrelevances into your home in the order of telephone numbers is a debatable (deplorable?) form of progress.

3. Three impediments to innovation by manufacturers cited by a Governor are the bargain-mentality, technoid shock and the Dreadnought effect. The first term refers to the behavior of consumers who assume this year's innovation will be available at a much lower price shortly. This phenomenon gives competitors every incentive to avoid being first, using reverse engineering and other techniques to follow profitably. Technoid shock simply means that it takes time for consumers to understand what an innovation is about and the confusion about facts works to the benefit of all competitors rather than to the exclusive gain of the innovator. Finally, the Dreadnought effect refers to the destabilizing effect upon Britain's dominance of the seas by her introduction of the H.M.S. Dreadnought in 1906. This ship overwhelmed everything else which simply let other nations race to compete on a new basis. Hence, as the dominant naval power, Britain might well have been advised to not restart the game with this innovation. See Janklow (1985).

80% above the average wage level for all manufacturing), recall what happened. Productivity, measured by hours of labor required per car, fell behind other nations. With a closed market (i.e., no foreign competition), Detroit could concentrate on responding to creating market demands based on size, space, power, features, and annual style changes, coupled with attempts to move people upward in models and to increase prices overall. The major use of computers was probably allowing even greater variety of options to be readily assembled on the production lines in response to individual customer desires. In the end, an increased foreign competition came about in part because Japanese cars were available as the market shifted to a new requirement: efficient transportation. That meant inexpensive to buy and to operate, reliable, and easy to handle in a congested, fuel-conscious world. Hence, the computers became useful for design specification, robotics planning, and the like.

Hence, one can use technology (computers) in a creative way to respond to a market change. Sometimes, Americans in particular accept a change on a faddish basis ("it can be done, so we will do it"). Surely, profits can be made from fads alone, but ultimately one needs to *think*. Thus, the digital clock dropped to a less than significant market share after an initial surge. Why? People do not really want a clock to tell time, but to have guidance on time: how long until I must be there? How late is he? Many consumers consciously rejected the complex addition and subtraction of a digital mental calculation—and learned to simply visualize an old-fashioned analog clock face! (As one who purchased his last automobile primarily because it was the first production car in the world to have a full digital dash option, I am plainly out of step.) Similarly, I suspect the longer-term use of home telephone answering machines will not be accepting call backs (which, after all, places the burden on me to reach the other party rather than the other way around!) but, to permit people with very active lives to remain friends, "conversing" with each other several times a week one-way by using extended recording options which permit the caller to leave a thirty-minute message. An increasing frequency of answering machines on unlisted phone lines is consistent with this hypothesis.

Finally, language translators using computers have been proposed and tested for many years. At last, people are seeing that the way to use them is to make quick drafts of standard materials, such as many technical articles in particularly specialized fields. The crudely translated draft is then proofed and edited by an experienced human translator. This use of a machine saves time and is efficient. Efficiency has come about in part because the computer translators have improved a bit, looking at context, etc., but largely because the economics of large memory computer systems, including cost per unit stored and processing speed per thousand words, have dropped while the hourly cost of human translators has risen. Again, a specialized use is important. One can imagine what a machine translator of ancient Greek would have done with the exquisitely rendered lament of Sophocles' Oedipus, "Count no man happy until he has passed the furthest point of his life secure from pain."[4]

CHANGE AND COMPUTER TECHNOLOGY: RISK ANALYSIS

Within the chapters of this book, you will read about possible changes in the areas of computerization and land management. I will add some of my own prognostications below, prior to my discussion of artificial intelligence and CAESAR in Chapter 17. First, however, I should like to show how a technological/intellectual innovation I have studied in some detail has fared.

As an undergraduate, I had a good idea, ridiculed by a professor of accounting who stressed that management deals with solid, actual data, not guesses and probabilities. I was amused to see the idea now known as "risk analysis simulation" developed, written about, and ultimately popularized two years later in a leading management journal by a consultant. It became part of the standard literature in finance and management science; and like most good ideas, it seemed obvious once one thought about it. Eight years after that popularization, with the typical impatience of youth, I decided to see why a simple, obvious technique was not being used as widely as I expected. Casually interviewing four major oil companies whose technically sophisticated staff and management and large capital budgets made them natural candidates for the implementation of the idea, I learned a great deal about change in large organizations.

First, what is risk analysis? As noted in other chapters, one may often build a computer model which manipulates data to show some result. Large municipal databases may permit study of how changing property tax assessments will ultimately affect municipal revenues. This use involves What-If analysis: What if we change the personal exemption for a homeowner by $1000? What if we double the property assessment rate on businesses whose primary sales market is outside our municipality?

Such an analysis, often called simulation, does *not* involve probabilities. Essentially, one takes a judgment about some change and asks, given the data we have, what will be the result of this certain change in policy? There are uncertainties, of course: how much will the database change (firms/individuals move in or out, or change the category of their unit)? How accurate is the database to begin with? How effective will the enforcement

---

4. Translation by David Grene.

and hence the compliance be with the new policy? However, the formulation of the issue is deterministic, and the database is taken as given by the device: the What-if analysis.

In contrast, *probabilistic simulation* offers insights into risk which will not typically be given by simply adding up a set of variables. The most common use of risk analysis simulation in finance is in the analysis of capital expenditures. A typical firm (or public agency) has an investment which it can make and which will produce cash savings of varying magnitudes in future years. The manager wonders if it is wise to make the investment, given the cost of funds to the organization, the probable cost of investment, and the uncertain future cash savings. There are clearly probabilities involved, but they are not additive. Thus, knowing that there is a 90% chance that the future gross revenues (X) will be at least $1000, and there is a 90% certainty that future operating costs (Y) will be no more than $600 does *not* mean 90% certainty that the future net inflows (X−Y) will be at least ($1000−600=) $400. To recall high school probability, recall that on a roll of a die, there is a 5/6 probability that it will not be a four given that there are six equal sides of equal likelihood of turning up—unless you were shooting craps with some of my high school classmates. However, the probability that there will not be a four on either one of a pair of dice is not 5/6 (.833), or 5/6 + 5/6, but 5/6 times 5/6, or .694. Although the real example given about capital budgeting is much more complex, the important point is that probabilities are critical and results often counter-intuitive. Finally, knowing that the most likely values for a range of factors which are part of the capital expenditure under review are such and such does not mean that one can simply add them up to obtain the most likely return for the project, even though returns are obviously calculated from those factors.[5]

So, here was a technique which essentially let the computer roll the dice to figure out whole combinations of likely outcomes. The model builder would input the critical variables and would assign probabilities to the occurrence of different levels for each variable. These probability distributions could be of any shape, including the familiar bell-shaped normal curve, the uniform distribution of our die example (each numeral is equally likely), and so on. The computer would then use a random number generator to obtain a value for each variable for a single trial, or "pretend" investment. The outcome of each trial had a calculated return, and hundreds of trials could be made in a few minutes. The resulting distribution of returns gave management an idea of just how risky a given project was.

---

5. For more extensive discussion of capital budgeting and simulation, see any recent finance text, or see Carter, E. Eugene, *Portfolio Aspects of Corporate Capital Budgeting*, D. C. Heath and Company, Lexington, Massachusetts, 1974 or Rodriguez, Rita M. and E. Eugene Carter, *International Financial Management*, third edition, Prentice-Hall, Inc., Engelwood Cliffs, New Jersey, 1984.

With such a knowledge, management could then decide how high the return ought to be given the degree of risk.

As an example of what can only be derived from risk analysis simulation using the underlying probabilities of various factors, consider the manager whose criterion is rate of return. Suppose Project C and Project D are two mutually exclusive alternatives with a distribution of returns as shown in Figure 1. There is greater risk in Project D, which also has a higher median rate of return. Whether that is a better investment than Project C is debatable. The point here is to see how one might use the probabilistic information developed from a risk analysis simulation.

What did I find when I studied these firms? First, there were problems with this wonderful technological improvement, the technique of risk analysis. At that time, finance theory did not tell management what to do with the risk and return profile. More risk requires a higher return, as any Las Vegas bookie will tell us. How much? No one knew. There was a feeling that for a large corporation where any one investment was less than 3% of assets, it was not very important to worry about risk. There was a feeling that there was no way to get good input data. We might have some guess about the most likely value, but we did not know much about the form of the underlying distribution—how long were the tails? Was it symmetrical about the mid-point value? Was it lumpy? In the area of capital budgeting, if risk analysis simulation were considered a project, it would not pay its own way: gathering the data, creating the model, testing the results, and reaching a conclusion about rejecting/accepting projects that *otherwise* would have been accepted/rejected was not considered a profitable investment of time. Finally, risk analysis made evaluation and control *ex post* very difficult. How could one fry a manager with a bad outcome when he or she had noted that there was some chance that the project would bomb?

In the area of implementation, two of the four firms seem to be happily using the technique in some areas. In general, those firms which added the technique later seemed to be more successful; some awareness within business about the technique precluded some problems. Lesson: never be the innovator. Second, where top management facing a serious problem became committed to the technique, there was more likely to be successful implementation. Lesson: subordinates had to be convinced there would be a hearing for the innovation to spend time on it. Third, where there were in-house capabilities within a given division where the technique could be tried, there was more likely to be success. If a division manager had to call in technical staff experts whom he could not control and/or did not trust to not reveal sensitive data to other (competitive) managers or to superiors, there was less likely to be successful use of the technique. Fourth, there needed to be a commitment to educate the

Probability of return no
less than indicated rate

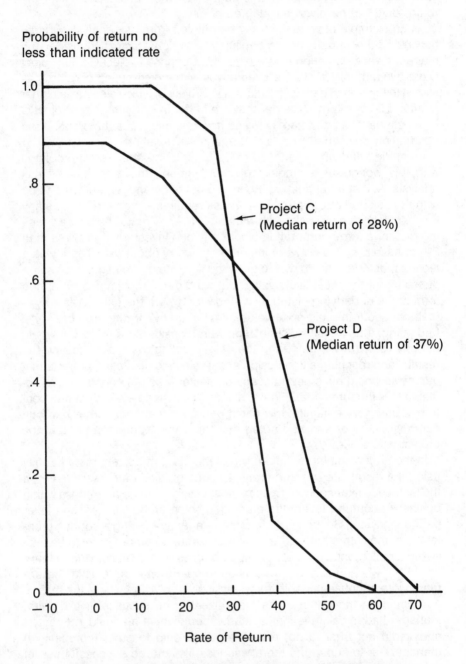

Figure 1: CUMULATIVE RATE OF RETURN DISTRIBUTION

users. Where everyone had to be taught the basics of probabilities and/or computers, there was too much time and effort wasted. Fifth, the model never seemed to meet the users' needs in the companies where it was not successfully used. Rather, the model builders insisted that the problem be made to fit their model rather than figuring out how to solve the problem at hand. (Indeed, many of us graduating from Carnegie were derided by some as being like a four year old with a hammer, determined to bash everything in reach whether it needed a screwdriver, a knife, or simply to be left alone.) One needed to make organizational and systems changes to take advantage of the technique, and the firms sometimes failed to recognize this fact. Thus, one needed a two stage management review, once to settle on the data and inputs and once to discuss the results, in contrast to the single annual shoot-out among divisions competing for scarce corporate resources. One needed machines and computer people who were responsible to the divisions whose budgets were being analyzed, rather than from a central staff computer operation.

Ultimately, then, the innovation had problems with the identity of the experts, with the typical human relations and organizational problems inherent in change, with early innovation being difficult to accomplish given ignorance and vested interest, and technical problems with the great solution. In some cases, of course, senior managers sabotaged the device: they were doing quite well in getting their piece of the corporate (money) pie without this technique, so why risk change?[6]

COMPUTER/MANAGEMENT TECHNOLOGY AND LAND POLICY

Given the caveats about technological change versus management change noted earlier, I should like to suggest the more likely ways in which I think certain types of technological change in the computer/information fields will alter land policy management. As noted, other chapters in this book cover many details of the current situation in these technical fields. In particular, see Dennis Robinson's Chapter 2, "Hardware and Software Options."

Microcomputers

Pioneered by garage products such as the Altair, popularized by the Apple II, and legitimized by the IBM PC, microcomputers have exploded from a non-existent market eight years ago to over $3 billion in 1984.

---

6. For more information on the risk analysis study summarized, see E. Eugene Carter, "Risk Analysis Revisited," *Harvard Business Review*, July-August, 1972, pp. 72-82.

Designated *Time* Magazine's "Man of the Year" in 1983, the machines have altered both the college classroom and the management suite. Stunning advances in speed and size coupled with price decreases have the machines eclipsing what even large mainframes could do five years ago. With hard disk drives, which in joint combinations can readily provide up to 40 megabytes of on-line storage coupled with 512 kilobyte internal memories (and larger), the machines provide a private user the ability to manipulate massive amounts of information with comparatively simple training.

Major advances have also appeared in software. First, spreadsheet (VISICALC-type) and word processing programs are almost a generic item. They cut horizontally across many fields. For the future, there may be more vertical packages used for diverse subtasks throughout an organization. Second, the emphasis today is on that mis-used and over-used term, "user-friendly." Often this term means screens with simple information to which the user responds by moving a blinking light with arrows, typing a single letter, or the like. These "menu-driven" systems are easy to start but often are very limited. Even when they are part of complicated systems, only a few seem to permit a transition to rapid operation by the sophisticated user using a single keyboard entry. Icons and screens are fine if you do not know what you are doing, but once familiar, you would prefer to move quickly to where you want to go. One problem with the mouse-driven software, for example, is that many of us do not like taking our hands off the keyboard to move an icon one space to correct an error. Finally, "integrated software" offers a way for a user to have a number of commonly used computer functions available at one time on the machine. This term means both that the functions (such as a spreadsheet program and a word processor) can freely transfer materials between themselves, as well as that common commands are used for most of the functions. An excellent example of this integration is Appleworks. A less desirable example is something such as the highly sophisticated Symphony from Lotus, which combines communication, database management, word processing, spreadsheet calculations, and graphics in one package. Think about what was said earlier in this chapter about change and technology. First, does anyone really care that much about combining all of these functions in one program? Second, even if one does, the program has over 600 commands, which does not imply that most users will have commonality across commands for different functions.

A redeeming feature of the video arcades so prevalent in theaters, grocery stores, gas stations and everywhere else is that most of this younger generation will grow up with some facility with screens, joysticks/keyboards and the like. The Apple Macintosh, using a mouse and high quality screen graphics, is designed to get even the novice moving rapidly with a computer. As a result, "user-friendly, integrated software" which can be readily available on cheap, powerful machines, coupled with a young generation of workers who are familiar with other forms of the device convince me that this micro boom is only beginning. How it will be used is discussed below after some other elements are surveyed.[7]

Database Managers

As discussed earlier, What-If analysis requires a specialized model or a database which can be readily used by a person with a computer. There are substantial issues here; the Federal government's miserable computer system for the Internal Revenue Service is in part the result of misguided zealots concerned about personal privacy testifying before appropriation committees. Civil liberties issues are important, and a concern about access to the data is not unwarranted. What is misplaced is forcing a major revenue agency to have obsolete equipment which cannot accommodate the data prepared for it by the private sector (1099's, asset transaction figures, and the like), nor can it combine geographically and financially diverse data for a given taxpayer identification number. The integrated software mentioned above will permit ready access to data easily manipulated by pre-trained operators, given the video arcade phenomenon. Start-up training costs will be small, the machines (microcomputers) will be readily available for other office tasks (word processing, for example), and the integrated, user-friendly software should permit an easy familiarization in the tax or municipal authority office.

Communications

Essentially, I believe there will be increased ability to link computers of all types together, coupled with access over standard phone lines, satellite systems, dedicated fiber-optics internal channels, and the like. Thus, a revenue office in Springfield can readily connect to a refund office in Peoria, a state revenue agent's terminal in Dekalb, and the like.

---

7. Notice I am not talking about home computers, even though many microcomputers (personal computers) are *used* in the home. Small capacity home machines did well in the market place initially, fueled by the Yuppie male suburbanite Cuisinart syndrome, as I called it: get the "in" thing whether or not you have any use for it. Guilt and advertising helped, of course: "How will Suzy (age 4) ever get into Brown unless . . ." As one computer manufacturer commented anonymously, "For any product to sell as a mass consumer item, you need mass distribution, cheap production costs, and a useful function. We've got two out of three with home computers." Balancing checkbooks or playing video games are not very useful functions; checkbooks can be handled more effectively with a calculator and pen or pencil while video games usually have better graphics on dedicated machines, such as the Atari XL.

Networks

Clearly linked to the whole communications area is the idea of microcomputer networks. Apple's new Appletalk network, which will cheaply link Apple and non-Apple micros to sophisticated laser printers at $50 per machine implies what can be done in this area. Modems, the devices by which a computer can talk over ordinary phone lines to other computers, are cheap and easily installed in most microcomputers. Coupling these networks and modems with the microcomputers and databases means that many operators in different locations can readily access the same secured database, using it for different purposes as they need to do so.

Hard disks, such as the Corvus 126 megabyte or the Odesta (Helix) system of one gigabyte (1000 megabyte) are available in a network system such as the Appletalk described above. A user accesses a file, copies it to his or her micro, and operates on it. Perhaps a revised version is then stored on the central hard disk to which others have access subsequently. The space is considerable. The Odesta system can probably hold the equivalent of 100,000 double-spaced, typed pages.

A major problem is that the largest databases typically need the huge memory of a mainframe computer which typically stores information in a way quite different from a micro or minicomputer. Thus, multiple users can update the files in a large mainframe only one at a time, though all can access the files simultaneously. In addition to this file sharing, secured pigeon holes (mail boxes) let each user have a unique secured spot of mainframe memory to which others can direct communications. Cullinet's Goldengate and Management Science of America's ExpertLink packages offer features such as these. On balance, though, the networks in general do not have good ability in handling this micro/mainframe connection. However, one can be optimistic that the features of the super-minis, such as Digital Equipment's VAX computer line, and the expansion of the micros mean that even minimal progress in networks may ease this problem.[8]

---

8. Many universities are working on this project. Programs include a Carnegie-Mellon program and MIT's Project Athena, both funded by huge grants from major computer companies. The problem is non-trivial. One worry is that the effort behind the grant is more derived from a desire to obtain massive amounts of funding for computer games for people to play with at the universities on one hand, and the manufacturers' thought that (1) if something turns up, at least they have first option on the rights to produce it, and (2) at least they are pre-empting their competitors' machines from being the ones on which the next generation of computer scientists are trained. Most great research breakthroughs come with hardworking people who enjoy their work, who have talent (a combination of training and brainpower in their area of research), who are committed, who are often able to defer gratification for long periods, and ultimately who are lucky. That is true in research as well as in corporate success. What should not be assumed is that people are doing great research just because they are having fun playing with toys.

Financial Theory

In recent years, developments in the theory of capital markets have given us new insights into the relationship between risk and return, the incentives for various parties to any contract to concur with the self-interest of others, and to the equilibration process in the capital markets. These areas (capital asset pricing, agency pricing, and arbitrage pricing) are but examples of what is being done in this area. Many will not work out well, yet the implications for financial management are profound. Moreover, I believe increasingly that insights from this area can be transferred to the non-profit area. Although we are still arguing about which discount rate to use in public projects, the general applications of looking at cash rather than some accrual income concepts, of considering the time value of money, and so forth are well accepted. Increasingly sophisticated uses of intellectual constructions from finance will be brought to the public sector and to land management in particular.

Optimization

Mathematical programming offers a way to find optimal solutions to many types of problems, and the theory has been around in basic form for forty years. The first industrial application of linear programming was with refinery operations in the early 1950s. Gradually, the wider use of computers and greater awareness by managers of the potential for the mathematical programming area have meant that it is used increasingly. The initial proponents of the field over-promised the results of it in the 1960s, and ignorance of human cognition (how we learn and think) coupled with tremendous problems of obtaining timely, accurate data limited the usefulness, as the earlier discussion of risk analysis simulation highlighted similar problems in that area. However, the application of mathematical programming techniques on microcomputers (and I currently run them on a small Apple II), coupled with a wider range of techniques, will bring much to bear in the public sector.

Essentially, mathematical programming approaches involve describing a problem in terms of a mix of variables. There is an objective function, which represents the value to be maximized or minimized, expressed in terms of these variables. In addition, there are various constraints, which are expressed in the form of equations placing restrictions upon the possible solutions which might be generated in response to the objective function. Thus, one might seek to maximize revenue from a property tax on commercial, industrial and private residential property (the objective) subject to a restriction on the possible mixture of rates, the relationship between rates, and some ceiling on one or more tax rates.

Today, there are readily available algorithms for mixed-integer programming, in which one can require that certain variables be integers; goal programming, in which multiple attributes of a commodity can be considered, and the objective is somehow to collect a package of commodities which collectively perform well against a variety of goal criteria; chance-constrained programming, in which a constraint is to be met with a given probability of being met, rather than a requirement that it must be met or no solution is possible; and quadratic programming, in which some of the variables can have exponents other than one (e.g., be squares). Many of these innovations, once applied to small personal computers and placed in the hands of reasonable users, promise benefits to the management of the public land use agency.[9]

Change is hard to accomplish, and once one learns how to use a given device in an effective way, one is reluctant to change. There is a perfectly good economic rationale for this result, of course. I happily operate on the eight-year-old design of an Apple II computer. The cost of upgrading to a newer machine is not the hardware or the massive amounts of new software; rather, it is the acquisition of revised knowledge about how to use what one has. It takes time to learn the idiosyncracies of a device, and one prefers the known problem to the unknown. It is why many people happily drive the old car . . . and perhaps retain the same friends.

One place where change will come and create a major impact, however, is in the area of expert systems, a subcomponent of the field called artificial intelligence. I often have seen both the resistance to change and the chaos from mandated change. However, this area is one in which I believe awareness of human cognition is so central that the change will be accomplished without the disruption of other experiences. Moreover, the rapid decrease in the cost of microcomputers means that the facilities will be available in the next few years to generate a wide range of sophisticated software packages in the expert system field. In Chapter 17, we turn to that topic, followed by a discussion of CAESAR, the Lincoln Institute's expert tax system.

---

9. For general background see Eppen & Gould, (1979).

REFERENCES

Brown, Harold I., *Perception, Theory and Commitment: The New Philosophy of Science*, University of Chicago Press, Chicago, Illinois, 1979.

Brownowski, J., *The Ascent of Man,* Little, Brown and Co., Boston, Mass., 1973.

_____, *The Origins of Knowledge and Imagination,* Yale University Press, New Haven, Conn., 1979.

Clark, Kenneth, *Civilization*, Harper and Row, New York, 1969.

Carter, E. Eugene, "The Behavioral Theory of the Firm and Top-Level Corporate Decisions," *Administrative Science Quarterly,* December, 1971, pp. 413-428.

Cyert, Richard M. and James G. March, *A Behavioral Theory of the Firm*, Prentice-Hall, Inc., Englewood Cliffs, N.J., 1963.

Eppen, Gary D. and F. J. Gould, *Quantitative Concepts for Management*, Prentice-Hall, Inc., Englewood Cliffs, N.J., 1979.

Hacking, Ian, editor, *Scientific Revolutions*, Oxford Readings in Philosophy, Oxford University Press, Oxford, England, 1981.

Hagen, E. E., *On the Theory of Social Change,* Dorsey Press, Homewood, Illinois, 1962.

Janklow, Governor William, "Cooperative R & D," *Issues in Science and Technology,* Spring 1985, pp. 10-12.

Lloyd, G.E.R., *Magic, Reason and Experience: Studies in the Origins and Development of Greek Science*, Cambridge University Press, Cambridge, England, 1979.

Mumford, Lewis, *Technics and Civilization*, Harcourt, Brace and World, Inc., New York, 1934.

Nystrom, Paul C. and William N. Starbuck, editors, *Handbook of Organizational Design*, Oxford University Press, Oxford, England, 1981.

Raiffa, Howard, *Decision Analysis*, Addison-Wesley, Reading, Mass., 1967.

Chapter 4

MODERN MODELING METHODOLOGIES

Joseph K. Eckert

INTRODUCTION TO MODELING METHODOLOGIES

Increasingly, mass appraisal practitioners are recognizing that considerable thought must be given to the structure of the housing market and available data before a mass appraisal valuation model is constructed and the variables specified if rational, decomposable, and explainable results are to be expected. Furthermore, from an education point of view, model building skills must be taught before the methods of calibrating models are explored; that is, model building should be separated from estimation methodology if maximum understanding of the model building process is to be expected. Far too often, the cost approach, and the use of a particular cost manual, is taught without any detailed explanation of the specific model implicit in the cost manual. Consequently, assessors who learn the cost approach this way are not able to construct a localized cost approach for their own jurisdiction, because they were not taught model building skills. Likewise, the various market approaches have been taught with too much reliance on statistical approaches that automatically select a set of factors and factor coefficients that, in a statistical sense, best explain sales prices (i.e., stepwise regression), but do not produce valuation formulae that can be easily decomposed into rational terms that could be easily explained to the public.

This chapter outlines the main features of good real estate model building for residential properties, and then discusses the unique problems and methods of calibrating CAMA models using construction cost data, as well as the various direct market estimating technologies available such as MRA and feedback.

MODELING AND APPRAISAL THEORY

Model building is a specialized application of appraisal theory. For instance, the fee appraisal process is a systematic method for collecting, analyzing, and processing data to produce intelligent, well-reasoned value estimates for a single property as of a certain appraisal date. The mass appraisal process accomplishes the same thing for a group of properties, and uses a model that is a mathematical representation of the housing market to accomplish this.

Good model structure develops from a clear understanding of how housing markets work. The appraisal principle of supply and demand provides an excellent framework for explaining market mechanics. Simply stated, the market value of any good is dependent upon the amount of effective demand there is for the good compared to the available supply of the good. The level of demand in a real estate market is related to population levels, mortgage rates, income levels, personal housing and service preferences, and the cost of alternative housing choices. The level of supply in a real estate market is related to size of the standing stock, construction costs, and the percentage of standing stock currently offered for sale. The interaction of these forces produces the selling price of a piece of property.[1]

If demand factors alone were to change such that the level of demand increased, housing prices would also increase. For instance, an increase in population in a market would result in higher real estate prices. Likewise, a change in supply factors, such as a decrease in construction costs, would increase supply and decrease prices at a constant level of demand.

There are several other appraisal principles that work in conjunction with

---

1. Selling price is also known as the value in exchange or market value only if the following assumptions about the operation of the market hold:

1. No coercion or undue influence over the buyer or seller in an attempt to force the purchase or sale;
2. Well-informed buyers and sellers in their own best interest;
3. A reasonable time for the transaction to take place;
4. Payment in cash or financing typical for the property type in the community.

It is market value in this context that the mass appraiser is trying to estimate.

supply and demand that the model builder must consider when construct-ing valuation models. They are discussed below.

Highest and Best Use

The demand for a certain property depends on the property's perceived utility to the buyer. The rational buyer will consider the most profitable likely use to which a piece of property could be put before deciding to bid on a property. The model builder, when considering the question of highest and best use of a property, must first assume the land is vacant and con-sider what new improvements could be constructed on the site that would maximize the return to the land. He would then compare this answer to his analysis of the optimal use of a property with the present improvement remaining in place. The decision to appraise the property as land and new improvement or land and existing improvement depends upon the estimated return from a new improvement compared to the cost of demolishing and constructing a new one. Typically, however, in a mature residential setting, the model builder considers the highest and best use of the property in the context of land and existing improvement.

Change and Balance

The principles of *change* and *balance* work together in the context of supply and demand. The principle of change holds that it is the future and not the past which is of prime importance in estimating value. In this con-text, economic and social forces are constantly changing and influence the factors that determine demand and supply for real estate. For instance, changes in the macro-economic environment that would lower interest rates will have a tendency to increase both the level of supply and the level of demand for housing.

The principle of balance works in the opposite direction of the principle of change. The principle of balance maintains that all markets have a tendency to move toward an equilibrium in their fundamental underlying forces. In real estate, the application of this principle states that an ideal interdependence exists between property types and land use which, when reached, creates and sustains value.

Substitution

The principle of substitution is related to the demand side of the market. It is related to the concept of opportunity costs in economic analysis. This principle states that the buyer will consider the costs of all reasonable alter-native properties before deciding to bid on a particular property. The rational buyer will pay no more for a property than the cost of a reasonably similar alternative. This principle is the basis for direct sales comparison analysis in the appraisal of real estate.

Competition

The concept of competition relates to both the supply and demand sides of the market. On the supply side, more individuals offering houses for sale or builders constructing houses will increase supply and lower house prices at a constant level of demand. In like fashion, many individuals interested in purchasing a particular type of property will increase the price of that type of property at a constant level of supply.

Contribution

The principle of contribution is related to the economic notion of marginal productivity. It is related to both the demand and supply side of the market. The principle states that the value of a part of the property is related to how much it contributes to the value of the whole property. From the supply side, this means that the costs of a new amenity, such as a new addition to an existing house, may not be recovered in the selling price of the house. Likewise from the demand side, the new improvement will be priced strictly on the principle of substitution. For instance, the addition of a fourth bedroom to a house located in a neighborhood with three- and four-bedroom houses will add to the value of the house only the dollar value currently prevailing between three- and four-bedroom houses. This price differential may or may not cover the cost of constructing the fourth bedroom. The use of land depth tables and other types of size adjustments in mass appraisal are founded upon this principle.

Institutional Forces Influencing Supply and Demand for Housing Services

When analyzing the principles of supply and demand outlined above to determine their impact on housing prices, it is helpful to consider four institutional forces that work continually through those principles to influence property values. These forces are broadly defined as social, economic, government, and environment.

Social Forces

Social forces work primarily through the principle of change on the demand side of the market and are manifested through the demographic composition of the population. The model builder, therefore, must properly analyze and interpret demographic trends, particularly as they affect total population growth, migration, rate of family formation, and population age distribution, in order to insure that these dynamic factors are built into the mass appraisal model structure.

Macro-Economic Forces

Economic forces influence both the supply and demand sides of the market. Macro trends in employment, income, interest rates, construction costs, and inflation rates work through the principles of change, substitution, and competition to change the levels of demand and supply in real estate markets. These dynamic macro trends must be monitored and measured when mass appraisal models are constructed, in order to insure that the sales are chosen during time periods when the real estate markets are in equilibrium.

Macro-Government Forces

Government forces influence real estate prices and are important considerations in highest and best use analysis. The rational buyer, when considering a piece of property, considers the level of public services, the extent of local zoning, building and health codes, national, state, and local fiscal policies, and special legislation that might limit ownership rights, such as rent controls or restrictions on condominium conversion. Public improvements, such as transportation corridors, drainage systems, etc., should also be taken into consideration.

Environmental Forces

Environmental forces are important considerations in consumer preference formation. Environmental forces are related to local conditions such as topography, size and shape of the lot, and soil conditions, as well as to broader locational issues such as the property's access to public transportation, schools, stores, service establishments, parks, cultural facilities, churches, and employment. Proper study of these considerations by the model builder is an important first step in developing the neighborhood delineations needed to measure the influence of location on sales prices.

THE GENERIC MODEL

In order to develop a workable model suitable for mass appraisal processing, it is necessary to develop quantitative measures for each of the above-mentioned categories that influence the supply or demand for real estate, formulated in a mathematical relationship to sales price.

For instance, the housing service stream (the supply side) can be quantitatively measured by the physical characteristics of the house and land. Income and preferences (the demand side) can be measured by developing land and building quality ratings, neighborhood ratings, as well as ratings for other important social, economic, and environmental forces that would influence preferences (e.g., schools, proximity to public transportation, etc.).

Careful delineation of the type of housing services, as measured by style, structure type, age, quality of construction, and condition could account for the possible substitutes available in the marketplace.

Elementary Models

The simplest model of real estate value might hypothesize that market value is a function of building value and land value:

1. $MV = BV + LV$

This model could be expanded to include a description of building and land value, where building value is a function of usable living area and a dollar-per-square-foot-living-area price, and land value is a function of land area and a dollar-per-square-foot-land-area price:

2. $BV = P_B \cdot ULA$
   $LV = P_L \cdot LSF$

A complete general model statement can be made that expresses market value as a function of the land and building components:

3. $MV = (P_B \cdot ULA) + (P_L \cdot LSF)$

Now, this simple model can be expanded to include other features of the site that the model builder expects will contribute to value in an additive manner. For instance, building value could be hypothesized to be related to usable living area, number of baths, and the square foot of additions.

4. $BV = (P_1 \cdot ULA) + (P_2 \cdot bath) + (P_3 \cdot additions)$

The P values are the unit values in dollars associated with a change in one unit of the physical characteristics. This building value model could be written as a general mathematical expression:

$$5.\ BV\ =\ P_{1\text{-}z}\cdot X_{1\text{-}z}$$

$X_{1\text{-}z}$ represents all possible building features that contribute to value in an additive manner, while $P_{1\text{-}z}$ represents the corresponding unit values of physical features of the building. Land value also might be related to several additive characteristics, such that land value could be written as:

$$6.\ LV\ =\ P_{1\text{-}z}\cdot Y_{1\text{-}z}$$

where $Y_{1\text{-}z}$ represents land features that contribute to value in an additive manner.

A general model statement can be made that expresses market value as a function of all of the possible land and building components:

$$7.\ MV\ =\ BV\ +\ LV$$
or
$$7A.\ MV\ =\ (P_{1\text{-}z}\cdot X_{1\text{-}z})\ +\ (P_{1\text{-}z}\cdot Y_{1\text{-}z})$$

Equation 7A expresses total value as a function of the physical characteristics of the building and land. Additional adjustments need to be made to this basic value definition in order to account for the economic, environmental, governmental, and social forces, as well as for other site factors such as style, age, and condition that influence consumer preference formation for housing services.

Value influences in these latter two categories can be thought of as qualitative adjustments, and should be made as percentage adjustments to basic building and land values whenever possible. For instance, market value can be specified to include qualitative adjustments for any of the above concepts:

$$8.\ MV\ =\ Q_{B\text{-}z}(BV)\ +\ Q_{L\text{-}z}(LV)$$

so that market value depends on building value plus land value as well as the qualitative adjustments made to each. For instance $Q_{B\text{-}z}$ may be a series of percentage adjustments made for quality of construction, age, and condition while $Q_{L\text{-}z}$ might represent percentage adjustments for topography and zoning.

It is important, in addition, to try to distinguish between qualitative adjustments that influence building and land individually from those that influence the entire parcel value:

$$9.\ MV\ =\ Q_G\{(Q_B\cdot BV)\ +\ (Q_L\cdot LV)\}$$

A model can be defined where Q_G, defined as general percentage adjustments, can be distinguished from the Q_B and Q_L percentage adjustments. For instance, a Q_G adjustment might be a general neighborhood qualitative adjustment, a qualitative adjustment rating nearness to public transportation, or a percent adjustment related to the dynamic factors in the market, like population growth, interest rate changes or increases and decreases in employment. All these factors influence both the land and building value simultaneously.

Finally, refinements can be made to this general model formulation to take into consideration certain non-linear or interactive effects in the housing market. For instance, in the cost approach, dollar-per-square-foot prices are usually adjusted downward as building size increases (a non-linear effect), while depreciation adjustments are developed using both age and condition (an interactive effect). These adjustments can be made as percentage adjustments, and can be treated just like percentage quality adjustments affecting land value, building value, or both simultaneously.

The general model format just outlined can be used as a starting point in the development of a table or formula driven cost approach, or as an initial structure for an MRA or feedback application. The principal differences that will result in the application of the model structure in the cost vs. the market approaches will be in the method of determination of the qualitative percentage adjustments and the additive factor prices. In the cost approach, those should be developed from construction cost information for your jurisdiction in conjunction with current sales in the jurisdiction. In the market approach, these will be developed directly from the market using the MRA or feedback processes to extract from the actual sales a set of percentage adjustments for qualitative factors and dollar values for physical property features that best explain existing property sales prices.

This is a model for market value that has the general structure outlined in equation 9 above:

$$MV = Q_G \cdot \{(Q_B \cdot BV) + (Q_L \cdot LV)\}$$

Building value (BV) is equal to usable living area times a square foot price, and land value (LV) is equal to land area times a square foot land price. Q_G is a neighborhood adjustment percentage; Q_B includes adjustments for age, grade, condition, and stories; and Q_L includes a percentage adjustment for topography:

$$10.\ MV = \text{Neigh. Adj.} \begin{bmatrix} \text{Age} \cdot \text{Grade} \cdot \text{Condition} \cdot \text{Story} \cdot P_B \cdot \text{ULA} \\ + \\ \text{Top. Adj.} \cdot P_L \cdot \text{LSF} \end{bmatrix}$$

Now, let's suppose we have developed, using construction cost or market data, appropriate percentage adjustments for each qualitative factor, as well as the square foot prices for land and building area. For a typical property in our community, this information might look like this property listing:

Characteristic Name	Characteristic Listing	% or Dollar Adjustment
Land Square Foot (LSF)	15000	$1 per square foot
Age	60	.6
Grade	Superior	1.2
Condition	Good	1.1
Stories	2	1.05
Topography	Hilly	.9
Usable Living Area (ULA)	2000	$25 per square foot
Neighborhood	Good	1.2

Now we can use the model described in equation 10 above to appraise this property, by simply substituting for the terms in the formula the appropriate percentage or dollar amounts and multiplying:

Total Value =
1.2 {.6 x 1.2 x 1.1 x 1.05 x (25 x 2000)} + {.9 x (1 x 15000)} = $66,069

The estimated value derived is a product of all the additive and percentage adjustments. Estimates of value can be generated for all of the properties in the population base using this method. These values must then be reviewed by the appraiser for reasonableness, and additional terms can be added to the model as needed to bring about optimum results. The final model can be easily decomposed and formatted as a set of tables that can be used to explain to taxpayers and other interested groups how individual values were computed.

ESTIMATION TECHNIQUES

The generic model described in the above section must be calibrated such that each term has a rational coefficient before the model can be used for appraisal purposes. In the most general sense, these coefficients can be estimated directly from the market using recent sales as the reference (sales comparison approach) or from a combination of construction cost and recent sales data (the cost approach).

Sales Comparison Approach

In mass appraisal model building, the sales comparison approach has been typically implemented using either linear multiple regression analysis, adaptive estimation procedure (feedback), non-linear regression, iterative correlative estimation, or Bayesian regression.[2]

Linear Multiple Regression is a curve-fitting technique that fits a linear multivariable model of the general form:

1. $y = a_0 + a_1 x_1 + a_2 x_2 + a_k x_k + u$
   where y = sales price
   $x_1 - x_k$ = represents k property descriptors
   $a_0 - a_k$ = represents the model coefficients
   u = error term

to a set of sales records such that the coefficients of the model are chosen so that the sum of the squared deviations of the model's predicted values subtracted from the recorded sales is minimized.

The model is then used to directly estimate the sales prices of unsold properties based on their individual property characteristics or indirectly the $a_0 - a_k$ estimates are used in conjunction with automated sales comparison software to compute the adjustments necessary to adjust the sales prices of selected comparable sales for the property characteristic differences between the subject property being valued and each selected comparable sale.

There are several options available when selecting multiple regression software that the potential user needs to be aware of when considering using this technique to implement the sales comparison approach. Broadly speaking, the potential user can select a non-stepwise regression package or a stepwise package. The non-stepwise routines require the user to specify all the candidate predictors (i.e., the model structure) which enter the model regardless of their statistical significance. Generally, only candidate variables that are highly correlated with one another or have zero variance would be automatically eliminated from the model when non-stepwise regression is used. The stepwise routines generally include the following options:

---

2. For a comprehensive mathematical treatment of these methods, see David L. Jensen, "Alternative Modeling Techniques in Computer-Assisted Mass Appraisal," unpublished paper, the Lincoln Institute of Land Policy, Cambridge, Mass., (May, 1983).

1. Forward selection regression

2. Backward elimination regression

3. Forward stepwise regression

4. Backward stepwise regression

These stepwise alternatives try to develop the best model from all the candidate variables based on the candidate predictor's statistical significance. The forward selection regression procedure enters variables until all of the significant candidate predictors have been entered. The backward elimination method starts with the full model (i.e., all potential model variables) and eliminates from the model repetitively the variables least significant until only significant variables are left in the model.

Forward and backward stepwise regression are refinements of forward and backward elimination. The principle difference is that forward stepwise allows the elimination of any variable that entered the model at an earlier step, but has become statistically insignificant while backward stepwise allows the re-entry into the equation of any variable that was insignificant at the time it was deleted, but which has since become statistically significant at a later step.

Both forward and backward stepwise regression are considered superior to the forward and backward elimination methods because they both allow the possibility that various candidate variables might change in statistical significance in subsequent stages of the stepwise procedure. In addition, backward stepwise regression considers interaction effects where multiple variables may be highly significant when considered jointly, but as individual candidates statistically insignificant. This last property of backward stepwise regression is what has made it the preferred alternative for practitioners using stepwise regression.

Since all of the stepwise procedures try to maximize predictive success with the minimum number of terms, the model structure arrived at with these procedures might not be acceptable from an appraisal standpoint. It is typical that important variables from a political or appraisal standpoint might be left out of the final model or that the estimated coefficients of one of several variables might have non-intuitive weights. This set of problems usually arises because of the extreme intercorrelation of housing data. For instance, if two highly correlated variables enter the model, then you have two variables that are measuring or explaining the same underlying influence. The estimated coefficient weights for the two variables then can be arbitrarily determined since each can compensate for the influence of the other.

If one or the other of the mutually correlated variables is eliminated in the stepwise selection process by automated procedures to eliminate highly correlated variables, it is not clear that in all cases the politically acceptable variable will remain in the equation. For instance, typically room and square foot of living area are highly correlated variables. If rooms enters the equation, but square foot of living area does not, then it might be hard to explain the model to the public, the courts and the general appraisal community even though the equation will have high statistical validity and good predictive power. The problems that have occurred because of the high degree of correlation in housing data have been dealt with principally using the following techniques:

1. Forced predictor insertion

2. Constrained regression

3. Ridge regression

Forced predictor insertion has been used in conjunction with any of the stepwise procedures to insure that a logical model structure is achieved. Typically, this procedure allows, within the stepwise procedures, a specific subset of variables to unconditionally enter the model. Other candidate variables may then enter relative to their particular statistical significance.

Constrained regression may be used with both stepwise or non-stepwise regression.[3] The simplest format requires the model builder to define acceptable upper and lower limits for candidate variables. This method involves a process that systematically sets the coefficient that is farthest away from its bounds equal to the closest limit, then the influence of the variable is removed from the sales price.

$$2.\ y - b_1X_1 = b_0 + b_2 X_2 + b_3X_3 \ldots b_ky_k + u$$

---

3. For a contemporary understanding of how constrained regression is used in mass appraisal, see Richard A. Borst, "Use of Constrained Regression by Non-Statisticians," a paper presented at the World Congress on Computer Assisted Valuation, the Lincoln Institute of Land Policy, Cambridge, Mass., (August, 1982); Joseph K. Eckert and Jeff Epstein, "The Use of Constrained Regression as an Update Methodlogy in Brookline, Mass.," a paper presented at the Colloquium on Stability of Annual Value Estimates as Related to Valuation Methodology, the Lincoln Institute of Land Policy, Cambridge, Mass., (May, 1983); John F. Thompson and Jack Gordon, "Constrained Regression Modeling in Conjunction with the MRA/Comparable Sales Approach," a paper presented at the Colloquium on Stability of Annual Value Estimates as Related to Valuation Methodology, the Lincoln Institute of Land Policy, Cambridge, Mass., (May, 1983).

and the remaining variables are regressed on the sales price residual ($y - b_1 X_1$). This process is repeated until all of the coefficients are within their predefined bounds.

Ridge regression is an operation that is done on the crossproducts matrix before it is inverted. The procedure involves inflating the respective sums of squares constituting the diagonal element of the correlation matrix ($X'X$) by a constant called a ridge factor (K).

3. $B = (X'X + KI)^{-1} X Y$

This procedure artifically reduces the intercorrelations of the candidate variables in the regression, and generally produces coefficients that are more intuitively appealing. There is one drawback to this procedure, however. That is, that it is extremely difficult to pick the K factor that will stabilize the coefficient while preserving a least squares solution.

Generally, the procedure must be repeated many times with increasing values of K until the coefficient stabilizes with reasonable values.

Model Formulations Using MRA

The generic model described earlier in this chapter is characterized as a hybrid additive multiplicative model. In this form, linear MRA cannot easily be used to estimate the generic model coefficient directly.[4] This is because MRA assumes a strictly additive model form. Strictly multiplicative models can be accommodated within MRA, however, by simply applying a logarithmic transformation to either the dependent variable (i.e., sales price) alone, or to both the sales price and all the candidate predictors. Under the first multiplicative option:

4. $\log_b y = a_0 + a_1 x_1 + a_k x_k$

the result is equivalent to a model where the individual terms represent a compounding percentage adjustment:

$$y = b^{a_0} \cdot b^{a_1 x_1} \cdot b^{a_2 x_2} \cdot b^{a_k x_k}$$

---

4. The hybrid additive multiplicative models can be reformatted into a linear form by expressing each simple percentage adjustment by the multiplier ($l + r_1 x_1$). Then each multiplicative expression can be expanded algebraically into a strictly additive set of terms. In this form the hybrid model can be estimated using linear MRA. However, the estimates of the coefficients, particularly of the higher interaction, may not be interpretable, thus the decomposability of the model is compromised.

Likewise, under the second arrangement where:

$$5. \; Log_b \; y = a_0 + a_1 \; Log_b \; X_1 + a_2 \; Log_b \; X_2 \ldots + a_k \; Log_b \; X_k$$

then the results are a model:

$$5a. \; y = b^{a_0} \cdot x_1^{a_1} \cdot x_2^{a_2} \ldots x_k^{a_k}$$

where the terms are scaled exponentially.

Neither the pure linear nor the multiplicative forms (log linear) of MRA can be used to estimate a hybrid additive multiplicative model directly. However, a multi-stage process using both the linear and multiplicative MRA form can be used to estimate a hybrid model. The process involves the following steps:[5]

1. Convert all qualitative categorical type data to a binary format, then use additive MRA to estimate the coefficients for each of the categorical dummy variables.

2. Use the estimated coefficients from Step 1 to linearize or recode each categorical value into an index that varies around 1.0 for each of the qualitative variables. This will produce a set of market-derived percent adjustments for the qualitative factors.

3. Estimate, using linear MRA, the coefficients for the additive part of the hybrid model, then predict and store a value for each case in the sales file using this model.

4. Use the type 2 multiplicative model to estimate the hybrid model that includes all the recoded qualitative variables as defined in Step 2 along with the value predictor from the additive terms developed in Step 3 as independent variables in the model.

A stepwise or non-stepwise procedure can be used to estimate the last step, depending on the preference of the model builder. Typically, a stepwise procedure that allows forced predictor insertion will maximize both model integrity and statistical validity. Additionally, if the model builder believes that there may be correlation between the additive and qualitative

---

5. For an example of how this process worked in an actual mass appraisal project, see Jerome C. German, "How an MRA Model Can Contain More than Fifty Terms Successfully and Provide Consistent Decomposition of Value," a paper presented at the World Congress on Computer Assisted Valuation, Lincoln Institute of Land Policy, Cambridge, Mass., (August, 1982); Patrick M. O'Connor, "Making One MRA Model Behave Appropriately Across the Whole of a Large County," a paper presented at the World Congress on Computer Assisted Valuation, Lincoln Institute of Land Policy, Cambridge, Mass., (August, 1982).

predictors in the model, he then should complete the following additional steps to eliminate this problem:

1. Use the results from Step 4 to develop a composite percent adjustment for all of the qualitative influences.

2. Divide sale price by this composite percent to create a sale price residual that is purged of the qualitative influences.

3. Re-estimate the additive components of the model using the sales price residual as the dependent variable.

4. Then re-compute Step 4.

Model Formulation Using Non-Linear Regression

Non-linear regression techniques were developed to estimate models that are intrinsically non-linear with respect to both variables as well as coefficients. This differs from a model that is non-linear with respect to variables. In this latter case, the model can be converted into ordinary linear models by a suitable transformation of the variables. The log transformations described in the discussion of multiple regression analysis are one example of this technique. Hybrid additive multiplicative models, however, are non-linear with respect to variables and coefficients and cannot be transformed into a linear form and estimated by linear multiple regression directly, without destroying the ability to interpret the results.[6]

Non-linear regression, however, can be used to estimate a hybrid additive multiplicative model directly. There are several non-linear regression techniques available that are generally categorized into those that are derivative based and those that are not. Those that use derivatives are the Gauss Newton, modified Gauss Newton and Lowenberg-Marquardt techniques. Those that are not derivative based are the Finite Difference Analogues of the Derivative Based Algorithms and the DUD (doesn't use derivatives) techniques.

All of the techniques require that the user specify the structure of the model as well as the starting coefficients of all of the variables in the model. Then all of the techniques compute adjustments to the initial set of coefficients. These adjustments are made iteratively until the improvement in fit as measured by the change in residual error becomes negligible. The Gauss Newton approach uses a first order Taylor series in the computation of the corrections to an initial set of coefficient estimates b_{1-k} such that:

$$Y - F(b_{1-k}) = \Delta b_1 \cdot \frac{dF(b_{1-k})}{db_1} + \Delta b_k \cdot \frac{dF(b_{1-k})}{db_k} + \varepsilon$$

---

6. See Footnote 4.

The residual $Y-F$ (b_{1-k}) can be regressed upon the respective partial derivatives dF $(b_{1-k})/db_1$, evaluated at the initial coefficient estimates such that the Δ b's can be estimated and added to their respective starting coefficients.

The successful use of these techniques are usually governed by a number of user-defined factors. These include: 1) the specific model structure employed; 2) the initial coefficient estimates and upper and lower bounds; and 3) the maximum iterations allowed. Non-user factors, such as the degree of correlation between candidate predictors in the model, as well as the possibility of several sub-optimal solutions for the predictor coefficients, can also affect the results.

Model Formulation Using Adaptive Estimation (Feedback)

Another alternative to linear multiple regression is adaptive estimation. This methodology is also a suitable method for estimating a hybrid additive multiplicative model. The procedure, which uses the engineering concepts of feedback and pattern recognition theory was originally proposed by Richard L. Longini[7] and Robert Carbone.[8] The process assumes a hybrid model form which is hard-coded into the software. In order to use the feedback procedure, property characteristics must be divided first into quantitative variables and second into qualitiative variables. The quantitative variables are assumed to contribute to value in an additive way. The qualitative variables are thought to make percentage adjustments. Quantitative variables must further be categorized as contributing to either land or building value, while qualitative variables must be categorized as influencing the land or building value or the sum of land and building value. The quantitative variables are generally continuous variables like square feet of living area, number of rooms, etc., while the qualitative variables are generally handled as binary variables with one representing each qualitative class. Binary qualitative variables can be developed from categorical type variables such as style or grade, as well as from ranges of continuous factors.

Once the variables in the models have been defined and classified, then an initial coefficient must be assigned to each variable. Generally, the qualitative factors are given a value of 1, while the quantitative factors are

---

7. Professor of Electrical Engineering and Urban Affairs, Carnegie-Mellon University, Pittsburgh, Pennsylvania.

8. Director, Department d'Operations et Systems de Decisions, University Laval, Quebec, Canada.

given dollar values. The model so defined is then used to make predictions of sales price for all records in the sales file or a case-by-case basis using the imputed initial coefficients and the listed parcel descriptors. The feedback procedure then computes the difference between the predicted sale price and the recorded sale price. This difference then is used to develop corrections for each coefficient so that a closer prediction would result if the model was reapplied to the same parcel.

The partial correction to the additive factors is made based on the following formulae:[9]

$$7.\ \Delta\ a_1 = \left[\ |a_1|\ \frac{X_i}{\overline{X}_i(t)}\ \right]\ \frac{\varepsilon}{\hat{y}}\ u_i$$

$$8.\ \overline{X}_i(t) = LX_i + (1\text{-}L)\ X_i\ (t\text{-}1)\ 0 < L < 1$$

The changes in the additive coefficients are computed as a percent of the residual error. The percent factor is a function of the current coefficient value and the ratio of the variable (X_i) to its exponentally smoothed mean $\overline{X}_i$.

The partial correction to the qualitative factors is made based on the formulae:[10]

$$9.\ \Delta\ Q_1 = \left[\ Q_1\ \frac{Z_1}{N_v}\ \right]\ \frac{\varepsilon}{\hat{y}}\ u_i$$

$$10.\ N_v = \Sigma_i\ Z_i$$

The changes in the qualitative coefficient are proportional to the percentage residual error, with the proportionality factor being a function of the current coefficient estimate and the ratio of the binary (Z_1) to the total number of binary variables. In both cases, the correction is also regulated by a damping factor which controls the adjustment to an individual sale.

The feedback routine processes sales one at a time, beginning with the sales of earliest date. The process continues until the residual error shows no improvement from one iteration to the next. Generally, the process is constrained to finish only on a forward pass through the data. This insures that the coefficients will reflect the prices of the current market.

---

9. Robert Carbone, "Notes on the Carbone-Longini Feedback Systems," presented at Course 208 Feedback Computer Assisted Mass Appraisal, Lincoln Institute of Land Policy, Cambridge, Mass., (April, 1982).

10. Ibid.

Iterative Correlative Estimation

The iterative correlation estimation technique was developed by Gerow M. Carlson [11] and can be used to estimate a hybrid additive multiplicative market model. The technique varies from the feedback or non-linear setup in that it requires all of the qualitative variables be defined as equally spaced percentage adjustments made from a reference classification rather than as a set of binary variables. Once the model is formulated and initial coefficients have been assigned from the quantitative and qualitative variables, sales price estimates and residual values are computed for every sale. In addition, the linear correlations are computed between each variable in the model and the residual error.

The linear correlation coefficients become the basis for the coefficient refinements of the quantitative and qualitative variables. The qualitative variable coefficients are adjusted directly in this procedure while the percent increment between categorical units are adjusted for qualitative variables. The adjustment coefficients are then used in another iteration. The process stops when the adjustment reaches a small user-defined level.

Bayesian Regression[12]

The Bayesian estimation technique is a methodology that is particularly useful in the process of model update. In Bayesian regression, the model coefficients are not based on the least squares solution applied to the latest sales, but are computed as estimates that are in part dependent upon a prior distribution of the coefficient estimates. For instance, an initial solution and associated covariance matrix of the following form:

11. $\hat{B}_0 = (X_0'X_0)^{-1} \cdot (X_0'Y_0)$

12. $W_1 = (X'X_0)^{-1}$

can be recast in the Bayesian format:

13. $\hat{B}_0 = \left[W_a X'X + W_0 W_1^{-1} \right] \cdot \left[W_a X'y + W_0 W_1^{-1} \hat{B}_0 \right]$

---

11. Director, Division of Property Valuation and Review, Vermont Agency of Administration, Waterbury, Vermont.

12. For a detailed discussion of the use of Bayesian regression as a model update methodology, see David L. Jensen, "The Application of Bayesian Regression for a Valuation Model Update in Computer-Assisted Mass Appraisal," a paper presented at the Colloquium on Stability of Annual Value Estimates as Related to Valuation Methodology, Lincoln Institute of Land Policy, Cambridge, Mass., (May, 1983).

where X´X and X´y are the sum of squares/sums of crossproducts derived from the new sales and B_0 and W_1 are the coefficient estimates and their scaled covariances obtained from a prior modeling effort. The W_a and W_0 are two weighting factors that allow the new sales to be emphasized relative to the old sales. Bayesian regression as outlined above shares some of the properties of both weighted regression and constrained regression. Bayesian regression is more efficient than weighted regression because it does not require the full recomputation of the sum of squares/sum of crossproducts matrix for both the new and old sales. It is also less subjective than constrained regression because the constraint on the new coefficient is based on the covariances of the coefficients derived in the previous model effort.

Bayesian regression is also potentially helpful when there is a need to modify a global model to subsets of the global surface. For instance, county models can be tailored to fit smaller communities within the county using this methodology. This application is particularly useful when there are not enough initial sales to produce reliable sub-global models for a particular jurisdiction.

The Bayesian regression approach can also be adapted to any of the Gauss Newton based non-linear regression approaches and thus estimate directly a model of the hybrid additive multiplicative variety.

Comparative Conclusion

Table 1 compares the principle modeling methodologies discussed above with respect to twelve characteristics. Readers making in-depth analysis of the table should consider the following important points.

First, both non-stepwise and stepwise MRA, while statistically rigorous methodologies, are capable of handling only strictly additive or multiplicative model forms. This characteristic limits the degree of appraisal realism and direct model decomposability that can be expected using these estimation techniques. The predictive power of these methods is excellent, however, and the output can be re-formatted into a base home approach[13] or directly used in an automated sales comparison program to aid in model decomposition and explainability.

When the stepwise techniques are used exclusively, it is recommended that the procedure be used with forced predictor insertion to insure that all important structural variables enter the model. In addition, it is desirable

13. For a complete discussion of the Base Home Approach, see Robert Gloudemans, "The Base Home Approach to Explainability in Mass Appraisal", a paper presented at the Colloquium on the Stability of Annual Valuation Updates, Lincoln Institute of Land Policy, Cambridge, Mass., (May, 1983).

TABLE 1

Method	Minimum Computer Requirements	Model Structure	Model Decomposition	Optimality	Convergence	Time Requirement
1. Non-Stepwise Linear Regression	Micro or mini with 100-200k internal memory 10-32 bit addressing	Strictly additive or strictly multiplicative	Difficult without 2 stage modeling or home base reformatting	Mathematically rigorous least squares solution	Automatic in one pass	Single pass
2. Stepwise Linear Regression	Same as Above	Same as Above	Same as Above	Same as Above	Same as Above	Same as Above
3. Non-Linear Regression	Save as Above	Additive, multiplicative or hybrid additive/multiplicative	Relatively easy	Same as Above	May converse on non-optimal solution; starting coefficient important	Multiple pass through data required
4. Adaptive Estimation (Feedback)	Can be run on micro with 64k internal memory and 8-bit addressing	Hybrid additive/multiplicative	Relatively easy	Heuristic	Same as 3	Same as 3
5. Iterative Correlative Estimation	Same as 1	Hybrid additive/multiplicative	Relatively easy	Heuristic	Same as 3	Same as 3
6. Bayesian Regression	Same as 1	Maybe hybrid if run in conjunction with non-linear regression	Easy if run in conjunction with non-linear regression	Same as 1	Same as 1	Same as 1

	Time Trend	Update Capacity	Input Requirements	Expertise	Programming Requirement	Statistical Tests	Intercorrelated between model variables
1.	Possible if time trend variable included in the model	Unstable except in conjunction with Bayesian regression	Variables in a specific model structure	Skilled model builder for initial setup	Not Complex	Goodness-of-fit and variance statistics provided	A significant problem with this technique
2.	Same as 1	Same as 1	All possible candidate variables	Same as 1	Complex	Same as 1	Intercorrelated variables are automatically eliminated but rational model structure not insured without forced predictor insertion
3.	Same as 1	Same as 1	Both variables and initial coefficient in specific model structure	Same as 1	Complex	Same as 1	Not a significant problem
4.	Same as 1	Stable update capabilities	Same as 3	Model builder with good appraisal skills	Not Complex	No goodness-of-fit or variance statistics provided	Same as 3
5.	Same as 1	Not known	Same as 3	Same as 4	Not Complex	Same as 4	Same as 3
6.	Same as 1	Stable update capabilities	Specific model structure and variable covariances from prior model run	Same as 1	Complex	Same as 1	Not a significant problem if run in conjunction with non-linear MRA

when the model builder is limited to using linear MRA to construct a model using a multistage process that uses both normal linear and log linear MRA in order to structure a hybrid additive multiplicative model that would more fully approximate the appraisal realities of the housing market.

The iterative correction techniques, non-linear MRA, adaptive estimation and iterative correlative estimation are all capable of estimating the hybrid additive multiplicative model directly. All of these techniques refine an initial set of coefficients in order to produce a reduction in the residual error. Adaptive estimation applies corrections after every case is processed, while non-linear MRA and iterative correlative estimation applies the correction at the end of each pass through the data. The result of this is that adaptive estimation may converge to its final solution faster than the other techniques. The corrections that are computed in non-linear regression, however, are mathematically rigorous while the corrections within feedback and iterative correlative estimation are heuristic. The consequence of this is that only the non-linear techniques provide direct, supportive statistics necessary to enable complete evaluation of the model.

All of the iterative correction techniques are, however, prone to find suboptimal solutions when the initial coefficients are not set near the global solution. This characteristic makes it necessary to have good prior information before using these techniques for modeling purposes. One strategy is to use a combination of stepwise MRA with one of the iterative techniques as the best modeling mix. Stepwise MRA could be used to determine:

1. Initial estimates of coefficients close to the global solution.

2. An estimate of the residual variance of the global solution.

3. Which variables are fully supported by the sales.

4. Which variables are additive and which are multiplicative in nature.

5. The degree of intercorrelation between model variables.

This information then could be used to structure a hybrid additive multiplicative model using one of the iterative techniques, as well as provide the information on approximate minimum variance of the global solution needed to monitor the convergence of the iterative techniques.

Calibrating the Model Using the Cost Approach

The steps generally considered appropriate when implementing the cost approach involve:

1. Estimating the value of land as if it were vacant and marketable.

2. Estimating the reproduction or replacement cost of all improvements to land as of the date of appraisal.

3. Estimating accrued depreciation from all causes and deduct this estimate from the estimate of reproduction or replacement cost.

4. Adding the current depreciated reproduction or replacement cost of all improvements to the estimated land value.

Estimating Land Value[14]

The estimation of land is probably the most problematic aspect of the cost approach particularly in well developed areas where there are few land sales. In areas where there are a representative number of varied land sales, land values can be calculated using the following steps:

1. Adjust all sales to the assessment date.

2. Sort sales by zone.

3. Divide sales by their respective land square foot or front foot to get a standard unit measure.

4. Plot unit prices on map and develop average rates for each neighborhood.

---

14. For a detailed discussion of estimating land valuation, see "Improving Real Property Assessment," Chapter 7, International Association of Assessing Officers, Chicago, Illinois, (1978); David L. Jensen, "The Use of Multiple Linear Regression in Residential Land Valuation," a paper presented at the Colloquium on Econometric Approaches to the Valuation of Vacant and Improved Land, Lincoln Institute of Land Policy, Cambridge, Mass., (January, 1983); Joseph K. Eckert, "Using MRA to Deal with Missing Data and Land Value Determination," a paper presented at the World Congress on Computer Assisted Valuation, Lincoln Institute of Land Policy, Cambridge, Mass., (August, 1982); Richard Ward, "Residential Land Valuation Techniques Developed in Ramsey County, Minnesota," a paper presented at the Colloquium on Econometric Approaches to the Valuation of Vacant and Improved Land, Lincoln Institute of Land Policy, Cambridge, Mass., (January, 1983); Anders Muller, "Separate Models for Computer Calculations of Land Values and Building Values of 1.3 Million Residential Properties in Denmark," a paper presented at the Colloquium on Econometric Approaches to the Valuation of Vacant and Improved Land, Lincoln Institute of Land Policy, Cambridge, Mass., (January, 1983).

5. Develop a size adjustment factor for parcels with land areas above or below the mean zone lot size.

6. Develop percent adjustment for properties with irregular size or abnormal topograph or location factors.

7. Develop a formula for land value where land value is equal to the neighborhood front foot or square foot price multiplied times the parcel front foot or square foot with the results modified up or down by the percent size adjustment and the other qualitative factors developed in Step 6.

The formula developed in Step 7 can be easily computerized and the formula applied to a property record file that includes information on lot size, shape, topography, neighborhood and zone. In the absence of abundant land sales, the model builder must develop estimates of land value from some other source. The two most common methods are the land residual method and the land ratio or abstraction method. The land residual method involves subtracting RCNLD from the sales prices of recently sold properties. The resulting residual is what then is used as a proxy for land value in Step 1 above. The abstraction method is based on comparative information from other neighborhoods or other communities that have plentiful land sales. For instance, it might be observed that the land values in a neighborhood in an area with plentiful land sales tend to average 20% of total property value. This information could be used to extract a land residual from sales in neighborhood B, an older area with no land sales activity. This residual would then be the proxy land value for Step 1 above.

Estimating Improvement Costs

When estimating improvement costs, the model builder first has to decide if it is reproduction or replacement cost that is to be estimated. Reproduction cost is the cost of reconstructing an exact duplicate of the existing structure while replacement cost is the cost of constructing a structure that has identical functional utility. Once this decision is made, then the model builder must decide the method of estimating improvement costs. There are four commonly accepted methods for doing this:

1. The comparative unit method.

2. The unit-in-place method.

3. The trended original cost method.

4. The quantity survey method.

The comparative unit method requires that all direct and indirect costs be summed and divided by a measure such as floor area to arrive at unit cost per square foot.

The unit-in-place method requires that all the direct and some of the indirect costs be expressed on the basis of unit measures. This results in a "replacement" unit cost for a single component such as the roof or plumbing.

The historical cost method requires that a structure's original or historical cost be trended using a factor derived from a construction cost index.

The quantity survey method involves a listing of all labor and material costs for the major construction components. This is added to an estimate of all of the indirect costs (architects' fees, permits, loan costs, etc.).

For mass appraisal purposes, the comparative unit method is the method most commonly used. This is because it can easily be structured in a formula or table format and generally does not require as much detailed cost data to implement the method. Generally, the method is augmented by some unit-in-place estimates for special features (i.e., fireplaces) in order to produce a complete RCN estimate. The steps necessary to calibrate the generic hybrid additive model described in the earlier sections of this chapter use the comparative unit method involving the following steps.

1. List the building types to be covered by the formula.

2. Study the design, style, size, type of construction and quality of construction of each building type in the taxing jurisdiction.

3. Determine the subclasses within each major building class from the analysis in Step 2.

4. For each subclass, establish within specifications for the class.

5. Determine building components for which unit-in-place cost data will be needed.

6. Collect cost data for all building types and their subclasses.

7. Analyze cost data to arrive at unit costs.

8. Derive appropriate multipliers to reflect qualitative differences for each subclass within a major building type.

9. Develop unit-in-place adjustment cost for the building components identified in 5 above.[15]

---

15. See "Improving Real Property Assessment," Chapter 6, International Association of Assessing Officers, Chicago, Illinois, (1978) for a detailed discussion of these methods.

After the data has been collected, it should be arrayed by class and subclass. This can be augmented with the use of a statistical package like SPSS[16] or a generic CAMA package like SOLIR. We will demonstrate this process for a hypothetical community that has just one property type, single family residential. Within this class there is a range of subclasses. The properties can be sorted by two grade designations, D4 and D5; 2 story levels; 6 exterior wall categories, A - F. In addition, living area varies from 1000 -2500 square feet for these properties. In this example we sorted the data initially by story and grade; then further broke it down by size and exterior wall type.

Table 2 shows the cost data distributed in the various categories. The cost data as shown is the sum of all direct and indirect costs minus items that must be priced using the unit-in-place method. These items must be added later in the process. Note that there is at least one representative cost for each of the major grade and story categories as well as cost information on all of the exterior wall types and several size categories for properties in the D4, 1 story category. For this example, this will be enough information to develop a formula driven cost approach for this hypothetical community. In a real modeling situation, cost data needs to be collected for the standard property for each sub-group heading.

Table 3 demonstrates the next stage of the process. First of all, total cost figures have been converted to a square foot price by dividing the appropriate square foot of living area listed in the vertical column into its associated cost in the horizontal column. Once this process is complete, then a reference property needs to be identified with its associated square foot price. In our hypothetical example, the 1-story, D4, 1000 square foot property with A type wall construction will be designated as the reference property. The next step is to divide the base rate for the reference property into all of the square foot prices for the property in all of the other categories. This process creates a table of percentages that then can be multiplied times the reference property's base rate to convert it into a square foot rate appropriate for any of the other categories. For instance, the base rate for a 1-story, D4, 1000 square foot property with F type exterior wall construction can be determined to be 25.2 (21.5 x 1.17). Likewise, the base rate for a 2-story, D4, 1000 square foot property with F type exterior wall construction can be computed as 24.1 (21.5 x 1.17 x .96). In each case the base rate of 21.5 for the standard property was multiplied by the appropriate percent adjustment to convert it to the rate for the desired class.

This process can be generalized as a formula that could be used to appraise a property in this hypothetical database. Table 4 illustrates this. The percentages for each of the sub-groupings listed in Table 3 have been listed

Table 2

1 Story D4

	A	B	C	D	E	F	Exterior Wall Type
SFLA							
1000	21500	22500	22800	23400	24100	25200	
2000	19100						
2500	18080						

2 Story D4

1000	20700						

1 Story D5

1000	22100						

2 Story D5

1000	21200						

as arrays by sub-group headings. The costing of any property would involve the multiplication of the base rate for the reference property times the square footage of the property times the percent adjustment appropriate for the grade, exterior wall type, size and number of stories. For instance, a 2-story, 2000 square foot property of D5 grade, with B exterior wall type would be priced by multiplying 2000 x 21.5 to get the basic building value of $43,000. This number would be multiplied by 1.027, 1.046, .88 and .962 to adjust that value for the appropriate grade, exterior wall, size, and stories listed for the property. The only additional information that would be needed at this point would be the pricing for the add-on items that use the unit-in-place method. These items could be expressed in dollars or as a percent of the base rate. Once the data has been arranged in array format like it is in Table 3 and a table of add-ons developed, it is easy to write the formula and create the database that can be used to compute replacement cost new. In our hypothetical examples, all of the properties to be appraised would have to be listed and the data for the key variables entered into the computer. A simple program then could be written in any of the popular programming languages like Basic or Cobol, or within any of the generic CAMA or statistical packages such as SOLIR or SPSS that would automate the manual process that we demonstrated above.

Table 3

1 Story D4

	A	B	C	D	E	F
SFLA						
1000	21.5	22.5	22.8	23.4	24.1	25.2
	(1)	(1.046)	(1.06)	(1.08)	(1.12)	(1.17)
	$\frac{A}{A}$	$\frac{B}{A}$	$\frac{C}{A}$	$\frac{D}{A}$	$\frac{E}{A}$	$\frac{F}{A}$
2000	19.1	19.73				
	(.88)					
2500	18.08					
	(.84)					

2 Story D4

1000	20.7	21.3
	(.962)	

1 Story D5

1000	22.1
	(1.027)

2 Story D5

1000	21.2
	(.985)

Depreciation

Once the model builder has completed a model for RCN,[17] then he must develop the appropriate depreciation factors to be applied to RCN to arrive at an estimate of current market value of the improvement. Estimates made for depreciation must be derived directly from the market.

There are several methods of estimating depreciation for mass appraisal purposes. In general, these methods produce lump sum estimates rather than a detailed breakdown of all of the various types of depreciation, as is done in fee appraisal work. The most common method of estimating accrued depreciation is the sales comparison method. There are six steps

___
17. Replacement cost new.

Table 4

Simple Cost Formula

		Grade X	Exterior Wall Type X	Size Adj. X	Story
Square Foot X Street Price	X	D4	A	1000	1st
		D5	B	2000	2nd
			C		
			D	2500	
			E		
			F		

		Grade X	Exterior Wall Type X	Size Adj. X	Story
SFLA X 21.5	X	1.0	1.0	1.0	1.0
			1.046		
		1.027	1.06	.88	.962
			1.08	.84	
			1.12		
			1.17		

Subject:

SFLA	2000
Grade	D5
Exterior Wall Type	B
Size	2000
Story	2

$2000 \cdot 21.5 \cdot 1.027 \cdot 1.046 \cdot .88 \cdot .962$
(43000)
$= 39104$

---

involved in this method to produce an estimate of accrued depreciation suitable for use in the cost approach. These steps involve:

1. Stratify all arms-length sales adjusted to the appraisal date by building type, age, quality of construction, type of construction and location.

2. Subtract land value from the sale price to estimate a residual building value. Use only sales with one improvement on the land in this step.

3. Divide the residual building value by RCN to find the "percent good" factor.

4. Graph the percent good against effective age.[18] You will probably want to create graphs that correspond to the data breakdown in Step 1 above.

---

18. The estimate of effective age is a critical part of estimating depreciation. Effective age is the typical age of structures that are equivalent to the one in question with respect to utility and condition. If the structure has generally undergone typical depreciation and maintenance, then the effective age is the same thing as actual age. Likewise, a structure

5. Fit a curve that best describes the pattern revealed by the data points. This process should be done using a simple linear regression procedure. If the graph reveals a non-linear pattern, logs of both effective age and percent good should be taken before the regression model is estimated.

The formulae estimated in Step 5 then can be added to the formula estimated for land and RCN to complete the formula driven cost system. A final algorithm can be coded into the system that multiplies for every property the estimate of RCN times the estimate of percent good and adds the resulting RCNLD[19] to the estimated land value to produce a total parcel value.

Fine Tuning the Cost Model (Basics)

Considerable refinement may be possible after this stage if a field check of values discovers that there is still depreciation unaccounted for or that location adjustment needs to be made to values. For instance, the basic method outlined above can be used to estimate additional depreciation that is not related to effective age. The main difference would be that in Step 3 above, the residual building value is divided by RCNLD instead of RCN. The percent good derived in this way might then be plotted against floor area or qualitative class to approximate functional obsolescence associated with other improvements. Likewise, the percent good could be plotted against distance from traffic or some other negative environmental influence in order to measure economic obsolescence. In any event, additional equations could be estimated that could be added to the cost model outlined above.

Finally, location adjustment should be made as a global adjustment to both totals of RCNLD and Land. These adjustments can be estimated in the following manner:

1. Compute RCNLD plus land for all arms-length sales.

2. Divide the estimate of total parcel value by actual sales price to produce a sales ratio.

---

with less than average maintenance may be effectively older than actual age, while a structure subject to better than average maintenance may be effectively younger than actual age. See *Improving Real Property Assessment*, Page 185, for detailed discussion of how to estimate effective age empirically.

19. Replacement cost new less depreciation.

3. Sort the ratio by location factors and compute the mean ratio for each grouping.

4. Measure the distance of the mean ratio from 1.0 for each grouping and use this information to create percent adjustment factors that can be used to raise or lower values in each location grouping.

5. Apply the factors to all estimates of value, recompute the sales ratio, and again sort by location factors. The mean overall sales ratio and the mean ratio within any location grouping should now be close to 1.0. If it is not, create new adjustments and repeat the process.

Fine Tuning the Cost Model (Advanced)

Much of the process of determining depreciation and the fine tuning for location factors in the cost model can be done with the aid of linear and non-linear multiple regression or feedback. The use of these techniques can cut down on many of the computational steps that would have to be made without their use. For instance, the feedback methodology could be used to estimate the percent adjustment for neighborhood influence in the following manner. A model could be defined with RCNLD as the building qualitative variable and the land value as the land quantitative variable. The neighborhoods could be entered as a set of binary variables entered as general qualitative adjustments. All of the initial coefficients would be set to 1 and the feedback process started.

14. $y = N_1 \cdot N_2 \cdot N_3 \cdot N_x [\text{RCNLD} + \text{Land}]$

Feedback would then refine the neighborhood coefficient until no improvement in the residual error resulted from additional passes through the data. At completion, the N values would have been market calibrated to the appropriate percent needed to be applied to RCNLD + L, for each neighborhood, in order to insure that the assessment sales ratio was 1.0 for each neighborhood. Variations of this same model could be estimated using linear and non-linear MRA to accomplish the same end.

Likewise, log linear MRA is often used to automate the calculation of depreciation. These models require that:

1. A residual value be created by subtracting land value from sales price for all of the sold properties.

2. That a general percent good factor be assigned to each property

based on its effective age. For instance, the model builder could simply let each year of additional effective age be equal to a one-half percent depreciation factor, such that property with a 10-year effective age would be assigned a 95% percent good factor.

3. That grade and relative condition codes be recoded as continuous percent adjustments that vary around one. This process has generally already been completed when the formula for RCN was created.

4. Logs of sale price, the percent good index, the grade and condition index, and RCN be computed for each sale.

5. A log linear regression model be estimated:

$$\text{Where 15. SP} = X_1^A \cdot X_2^B \cdot X_3^C \cdot X_4^D$$

$X_1 = \%$ good index
$X_2 = $ grade index
$X_3 = $ condition index
$X_4 = $ RCN

$A = $ the power to which X_1 is raised
$B = $ the power to which X_2 is raised
$C = $ the power to which X_3 is raised
$D = $ the power to which X_4 is raised
$SP = $ sales price

With log linear MRA it is the value of A-D which is being estimated by the regression procedure. Generally, with this process the value of D turns out to be a number near 1, indicating that the RCN estimate will be processed with no modification in value. The values of the other variables usually vary around 1, indicating that the procedure has recalibrated the initial percentage factors for each variable to conform to actual market influences.

For instance, if initial percent good was .71 for a particular property, but the regression estimate for A, the power to which that factor was to be raised, was estimated to be .5, then the market calibrated percent good for that property would be .84. Generally, when the value of any of the powers is estimated to be less than 1, then the starting percent distribution for each factor is pulled toward 1. The reverse is true if the estimated coefficient is greater than 1. Likewise, a negative power would reverse the initial distribution of the percent factors. For instance, for the case cited above, .71 raised to the -.5 power would be 1.19.

The estimation of a model of this type will automatically market calibrate a generally defined percent good factor, and then adjust it for the grade of the property and the relative condition. The estimated formulae can be used to estimate replacement cost new less depreciation with the knowledge that the depreciation percentage is market derived in a mathematically rigorous manner.

Chapter 5

BASE HOME METHODOLOGY

Robert J. Gloudemans

The base home approach addresses the important issue of explainability in mass appraisal. It involves "repackaging" a valuation equation derived through multiple regression analysis (MRA), adaptive estimation procedure (AEP or "feedback"), and other statistical procedure into a tabular format. The method complements and enhances other model building techniques.

This chapter will discuss the development of the base home approach in Arizona, the methodology of the approach, the evaluation and fine-tuning of models utilizing the approach, and its use in condominium and townhouse valuation. The chapter concludes with a summary of the advantages, limitations, and possible extensions of the base home approach.

BACKGROUND

Arizona was one of the first states to make extensive use of modern, sales-based mass appraisal techniques. In the early 1970s, the State began

The author wishes to acknowledge the great help and support of a colleague, Alex J. Chizewsky, who produced the models and reports illustrated in the chapter, and Seth L. Franzman, Administrator of Assessment Standards, Arizona Department of Revenue, whose continual encouragement and support have permitted implementation of The Base Home Approach and other mass appraisal enhancements referenced in the chapter.

annual reappraisal of all property. For most single family residences, this was accomplished through use of MRA.

Initially, a single MRA model was developed and recomputed annually in each county. While these models tended to produce statistically good and, indeed, much improved results in comparison with the previous cost-based system, the models suffered from various technical problems, as well as serious explanatory difficulties. Support for the new system began to erode until, in 1979, the State initiated a series of reforms. A cornerstone of these enhancements, designed to improve understanding and utilization of the system, was introduction of the base home approach.

Since its introduction for the 1980 tax year, the base home approach has undergone various changes and extensions.[1] The following discussions reference several of these changes for illustrative purposes, but focus primarily on current use of the approach in Arizona.[2] The approach has also been tested and adopted in various forms by several other assessment agencies in the United States and Canada, as well as Denmark.[3] The approach is now part of the International Association of Assessing Officers' CAMA Model Building Workshop and an adaptation of the approach is included in the Lincoln Institute of Land Policy's SOLIR assessment/appraisal system for microcomputers.

METHODOLOGY

The base home approach involves the conversion of an MRA or other statistical equation into tabular format. There are four steps in the process:

1. Optional stratification of properties subject to a single valuation model into groups for which separate base homes will be specified. This will result in a series of base homes that are more similar to the subject parcels with which they are compared.

---

1. In the most recent tax year the approach was used to develop valuations for single family parcels in 12 of the states' 15 counties and condominium/townhouse valuations in six counties. Maricopa County (Phoenix) does not use the approach.

2. The original base home approach, along with a more detailed discussion of the evaluation of mass appraisal in Arizona, is described in Robert J. Gloudemans, "Simplifying MRA-Based Appraisal Models: The Base Home Approach," *Property Tax Journal* (December, 1981). For a more technical discussion of the base home methodology, see Robert J. Gloudemans, "The Base Home Approach to Explainability in Mass Appraisal," paper prepared for Colloquium on Mathematical Methods in Computer Assisted Valuation sponsored by the Lincoln Institute of Land Policy, May 18-19, 1983.

3. See Anders Muller, "Separate Models for Computer Calculation of Land Values and Building Values for 1.3 Million Residential Properties in Denmark," paper presented at Colloquium on Land Valuation Methods sponsored by the Lincoln Institute of Land Policy, January 24-26, 1983.

Arizona's mass appraisal system initially involved only one MRA equation per county. Until further geographic stratification could be achieved, single family residences were stratified by construction class within county for base home purposes. Since there are seven single family residential construction classes in Arizona, this resulted in seven base homes per county. In contrast, counties are now divided into "market areas" for both model building and base home purposes, so that there is one MRA model and one base home per market area. Nevertheless, further delineation of base homes by construction class or other criteria are still easily imagined.

It should be emphasized that the degree of stratification is solely a matter of preference.[4] Values computed by the base home approach will always equal those yielded by the statistical equation from which the base home values and other required table entries are derived. Multiple base homes per statistical equation entail a corresponding increase in the number of base home tables that must be maintained. However, greater stratification increases the comparability between subject and base homes and thereby reduces the number and magnitude of required adjustments.

2. Specification of the base home characteristics. These characteristics must include all those used in model development (e.g., square footage, age, type of construction, location, etc.). Values for the base home characteristics should be representative of the stratum and can be computed as the median, mean, or other representative number. Valuations of subject parcels will not depend on the values specified for the base home characteristics. However, proper specification of the base home characteristics both enhances the credibility of the approach and minimizes the magnitude of adjustments between the base and subject homes.

3. The value of the base home is estimated by applying the valuation equation (e.g., MRA in Arizona) to the base home characteristics.

4. Conversion of the regression or other model coefficients to dollar amounts to be added or subtracted for differences in characteristics between the base home and subject properties. Technically, these "component adjustments" are the first order derivatives of estimated

---

4. Strata created for base home purposes, however, must not overlap strata used in model development.

value with respect to the property characteristics used in modeling. That is, they represent the NET change in value associated with a unit change in a particular property characteristic (e.g., one square foot, one year of building age, one garage, or one patio). Depending on the form of the valuation model, the component adjustments may be expressed in dollars, dollars per square foot, or other per unit amounts. The model coefficients can be converted to component adjustments manually or by computer program. In Arizona, this process was initially performed manually but is now automated.

FORMAT

The format of the base home approach as currently used in Arizona is illustrated in Exhibit 1. One valuation model and base home is developed for each market area. Exhibit 1 applies to the Bullhead City market area in Mohave County, which is a growing community on the Colorado River with a current population of approximately 15,000. The top of the report shows the base home characteristics: construction class of R3-Fair, 1200 square feet, type A (forced air) heating, RF cooling (refrigeration), one covered patio, a one-car garage, no pool, and an effective age of 10 years, which, when plugged into the regression model, yields a physical depreciation allowance of $3,000. The base home is located in subarea (neighborhood) 03, which has an average residential land value of $13,787. Applying the regression equation to this statistically typical property yields a base home value of $55,240.

The second part of the report shows the component adjustments. Notice that there is one set of adjustments for each improvement class (LM through R6). This is because several characteristics in the valuation model are interactive with improvement class. The component adjustment for square footage is $25.00. This means that $25.00 is added for each square foot above the base of 1200 and $25.00 is subtracted for each square foot below 1200. Only a single, constant adjustment is required for square footage, even though it appears in the MRA model (not shown) for the market area as part of four interactive variables. This is because the component adjustments represent only the net effect of a particular property characteristic upon value (all other characteristics held constant). Hence, if a subject parcel were identical to the base home in every respect except that it were 100 square feet bigger, its value would be $57,740 (the base home value of $55,240 plus $2,500).

The next set of component adjustments relates to construction quality. No adjustment is required for an improvement class and grade of R3-Fair,

FEB. 28, 1985   ARIZONA DEPARTMENT OF REVENUE PHOENIX DATA PROCESSING CENTER   PAGE 21

REPORT NBR: PS4029-01   MARKET MODEL BASE HOME DESCRIPTION AND COMPONENT ADJUSTMENTS FOR THE COUNTY OF MOHAVE   VERSION: C
FOR THE 1985 TAX YEAR
LAST UPDATE 02/28/85

MARKET AREA 02-BULLHEAD

* BASE HOME DESCRIPTION *

IMP CLS	GRADE	SQFT	HEATING	COOLING	RATIOS TYPE NUM	GAR/CPT NUM	POOL NUM	EFF AGE	SQFT AGE	PHY DEP	SUB AREA	BASE LAND FCV	BASE HOME FCV
R3	FAIR	1200	A	RF	COV 1	GAR 1	1	0	10	3000	03	13787	55240

* COMPONENT ADJUSTMENTS *

IMP CLS	SQFT ADJ	TYPEGRADE ADJ			TYPE ADJ	HEATING ADJ	COOLING TYPE ADJ	COOLING ADJ	PAT-SLAB NUM ADJ	PAT-COV NUM ADJ	PAT-BOTH NUM ADJ	PATIO ADJ	GARAGES NUM ADJ	CARPORTS NUM ADJ	GAR/CPTS NUM ADJ	NO GAR/CPTS	POOL ADJ	DEPR ADJ
LM	25.00	MIN -15.13 / FAIR -14.35 / GOOD -13.65			A / B / NO	0.00 / 0.21 / -0.15	RF / EC / NO	0.00 / 0.53 / -1.33	-218	-1 / 2 / 4+	382 / 764 / 1147	191 / 491 / 792	-546	1 / 2+ / 3+	1950 / 3900	1 / 2+ / 3+	-1170 / -390 / -390	2+ / 3+	780 / 1560	-1950	7.80	0.25
R1	25.00	MIN -9.40 / FAIR -8.25 / GOOD -7.09			A / B / NO	0.00 / 0.33 / -0.83	RF / EC / NO	0.00 / 1.45 / 2.07	-218	-1 / 2 / 4+	382 / 764 / 1147	191 / 491 / 792	-546	1 / 2+ / 3+	1950 / 3900	1 / 2+ / 3+	-1170 / -390 / -390	2+ / 3+	780 / 1560	-1950	7.80	0.25
R2	25.00	MIN -1.07 / FAIR -4.54 / GOOD -3.01			A / B / NO	0.00 / 0.40 / 1.09	RF / EC / NO	0.00 / 1.91 / 2.93	-218	-1 / 2 / 4+	382 / 764 / 1147	191 / 491 / 792	-546	1 / 2+ / 3+	1950 / 3900	1 / 2+ / 3+	-1170 / -390 / -390	2+ / 3+	780 / 1560	-1950	7.80	0.25
R3	25.00	MIN -2.18 / FAIR 0.00 / GOOD 2.18			A / B / NO	0.00 / 0.62 / 1.56	RF / EC / NO	0.00 / 2.73 / 3.60	-218	-1 / 2 / 4+	382 / 764 / 1147	191 / 491 / 792	-546	1 / 2+ / 3+	1950 / 3900	1 / 2+ / 3+	-1170 / -390 / -390	2+ / 3+	780 / 1560	-1950	7.80	0.25
R4	25.00	MIN 3.54 / FAIR -6.37 / GOOD --			A / B / NO	0.00 / 0.81 / 2.03	RF / EC / NO	0.00 / 3.57 / 5.03	-218	-1 / 2 / 4+	382 / 764 / 1147	191 / 491 / 792	-546	1 / 2+ / 3+	1950 / 3900	1 / 2+ / 3+	-1170 / -390 / -390	2+ / 3+	780 / 1560	-1950	7.80	0.25
R5	25.00	MIN 10.57 / FAIR 14.77 / GOOD 17.77			A / B / NO	0.00 / 2.57 / 4.44	RF / EC / NO	0.00 / 4.44 / 6.44	-218	-1 / 2 / 4+	382 / 764 / 1147	191 / 491 / 792	-546	1 / 2+ / 3+	1950 / 3900	1 / 2+ / 3+	-1170 / -390 / -390	2+ / 3+	780 / 1560	-1950	7.80	0.25
R6	25.00	MIN 24.70 / FAIR 29.87 / GOOD 35.03			A / B / NO	0.00 / 1.48 / 3.70	RF / EC / NO	0.00 / 9.24 / --	-218	-1 / 2 / 4+	382 / 764 / 1147	191 / 491 / 792	-546	1 / 2+ / 3+	1950 / 3900	1 / 2+ / 3+	-1170 / -390 / -390	2+ / 3+	780 / 1560	-1950	7.80	0.25

FEB. 28, 1985   ARIZONA DEPARTMENT OF REVENUE PHOENIX DATA PROCESSING CENTER   PAGE 22

REPORT NBR: PS4029-01   MARKET MODEL BASE HOME DESCRIPTION AND COMPONENT ADJUSTMENTS FOR THE COUNTY OF MOHAVE   VERSION: C
FOR THE 1985 TAX YEAR
LAST UPDATE 02/28/85

MARKET AREA 02-BULLHEAD

* SUBAREA ADJUSTMENT VALUES *

01= -3445   02= -5375   03= 0   04= 0

* SUBAREA AVERAGE LAND FCV *

01= 10722   02= 8409   03= 13787   04= 11237

EXHIBIT 1

as this is the construction class and grade of the base home. An upward adjustment of $2.18 (per square foot) is made to an R3-Good, $3.71 to an R4-MIN, and so forth, while negative adjustments are made when construction quality is below that of the base home.

Heating and cooling adjustments appear next. No adjustments are made when the type of heating and cooling is equal to that of the base home. The magnitude of the adjustments for alternative heating and cooling types varies with the improvement class. For example, lack of refrigeration will subtract more value per square foot in a higher quality home than in a lower quality home.

Adjustments for patios, garages, and carports are self-explanatory. The magnitude of these adjustments does not vary with quality class since the items are not interactive with quality class in the MRA model. The pool adjustment is $7.80 per square foot, with no pool assumed in the base home characteristics. The depreciation adjustment is $.25 per square foot per year and explains the $3,000 physical depreciation included in the base home: 1200 × 10 × .25 = 3000.

Subarea adjustments represent differences in value associated with location in subareas (neighborhoods) different from the base home subarea. In the MRA equation these were included as "dummy" variables (1 if the subject property is located in the subarea and 0 otherwise) with the base subarea serving as the reference and therefore excluded. The subarea adjustment for the base subarea (03 in the present case) is always 0. The figures in Exhibit 1 indicate that the market tends to assign a $3,445 decrement to subarea 01, a $5,375 decrement to subarea 02, and to regard subarea 04 as comparable to the base subarea (03).

Subarea average land values represent the average land values of single family residential parcels in the various subareas. In the Arizona system, differences in locational desirability *within* subareas are computed as the difference between the land value of the subject parcel and the average land value of the subarea. If, for example, the average land value of residential property in a subarea is $10,000 and the land value of a subject parcel is $15,000 (perhaps because it is larger or commands a premium view), then $5,000 will be added in valuation of the subject property.

VALUE CALCULATION

Exhibit 2 illustrates the calculation of value for a subject parcel in the Bullhead market area by the base home approach.[5] The subject parcel is assumed to be located in subarea 01, have 1,450 square feet of living

---

5. Items IV.B, V, and VII can be ignored; they apply to homes maintained on a separate data file and valued through a base home format somewhat different than Exhibit 1.

area, a construction class and grade of R4-MIN, type A heating, refrigerated cooling, one covered patio, a one-car garage, and no pool, be 15 years old and in average condition for its age, and have a land value of $16,000. The base home characteristics and component adjustments are all obtained from Exhibit 1.

An advantage to the base home approach illustrated by the worksheet is the identification of the value added or subtracted for each physical difference between the subject property and base home: $6,250 for the extra 250 square feet of living area, $5,380 for the better construction quality, and so forth. In explaining the valuation on the property, the appraiser would note that the subject property is in market area 02, that the typical property in that market area has the characteristics described for the base home and a value for tax purposes of $55,240, and that the indicated adjustments (e.g., $6,250 for size) have been made for physical differences between the subject property and the base home.[6] The worksheet serves to document the figures and calculations.

EVALUATION AND FINE-TUNING

While the primary advantage of the base home approach is to enhance the understanding and explanation of mass appraisal models, the technique also facilitates the review and fine-tuning of models. The base home approach identifies the net impact of each property characteristic upon value. Hence, the appraiser/analyst can review the market component adjustments for reasonability in a straightforward manner. This stands in contrast to the analysis of multiple regression equations or alternative statistical models, in which the appraiser/analyst must work with interactive terms, variable transformations, and the like.

Exhibit 3 is an example of a summary report of the mass appraisal model developed for the Safford market area in Graham County for the 1985 tax year. Among other things, the report shows the number of sales, median sales ratio, and coefficient of dispersion for the market area, as well as for each subarea, improvement class, five size groupings, and three age categories. In this case, the pattern of results shows general consistency and uniformity among these various categories. If this were not the case, however, further fine-tuning would be suggested and easily accomplished.

---

6. If pressed on the derivation of the base home value and component adjustments, the appraiser might simply state that they are based on an analysis of sales in the area. This should generally suffice in that these values, by nature of the base home approach, should appear realistic. Note also that conversion to the base home approach relieves the need to explain the regression constant (which is included in the base home value)—certainly the base home value makes a more intuitive starting point in the explanation of value!

SALES-BASED CALCULATION FORM: SINGLE-FAMILY PROPERTY

I. MARKET AREA: **02**   SUBAREA: **01**   BASE HOME VALUE: _____ = **55240**

II. SIZE ADJUSTMENT: SUBJECT **1450** − BASE **1200** = DIFFERENCE **250** × ADJ.FACTOR **25.00** = **6250**

III. QUALITY (PER SQFT) ADJUSTMENTS:

COMPONENT	SUBJECT	BASE	DIFFERENCE	ADJUSTMENT PER SQFT
1. CLASS/GRADE	R4-M	R3-F		3.71
2. HEATING	A	A		-
3. COOLING	RF	RF		-

TOTAL ADJ. PER SQ FT = **3.71** × TOTAL SQFT **1450** = **5380**

IV. ADDITIONAL FEATURES ADJUSTMENTS:

A. "MARKET" METHOD:

COMPONENT	SUBJECT	BASE	DIFFERENCE	ADJ.FACTOR
1. PATIOS	Cov-1	Cov-1		
2. GARAGES/CP	GAR-1	CP-1		= -1170
3. POOL SQFT	0	0	0	= 0

B. "COST/MARKET" METHOD

COMPONENT	SUBJECT	BASE	DIFFERENCE	ADJ.FACTOR
ADD ITEMS	N/A	-	0	= 0

V. FULL BASEMENT (IF NONE, ENTER ZERO)

TOTAL SQFT **N/A** × ADJ. FACTOR **N/A** =

PARCEL NO. _____

EXHIBIT 2

VI. PHYSICAL DEPRECIATION ADJUSTMENT:

ACTUAL AGE   PHYSICAL ADJ.*   EFFECTIVE AGE
15   × 1.0   = 15
*GOOD=.7   AVERAGE=1.0   POOR=1.3

EFFECTIVE AGE   DEPR. ADJ. (PER SQFT)   SQFT   SUBJECT DEPR.
15   × .25   × 1450   = 5438

BASE DEPR.   SUBJECT DEPR.
3000   − 5438   = −2438

VIII. MOD, OBS, PART COMP ADJUSTMENTS: (IF NONE, ENTER 0)

SUBTOTAL (I-VI)   BASE LAND FCV   IMP SUBTOTAL   ADJUSTMENT PERCENTAGE
N/A   −   =   ×

VIII. SUBAREA (NEIGHBORHOOD) ADJUSTMENT (16000 − 13787)   = −3445

IX. SITUS ADJUSTMENT (LAND FCV − AVE LAND FCV OF SUBAREA)   =

X. ADDITIONAL IMPROVEMENTS (ENTER FCV OR ZERO)   = 0

XI. TOTAL FCV (TOTAL OF I − X ABOVE)   = 62030

DPST FORM 820 (Rev. 12/83)

JAN 31, 1985

REPORT NBR: PS4037-05

TAX YEAR: 1985

ARIZONA DEPARTMENT OF REVENUE PHOENIX DATA PROCESSING CENTER

PAGE 1

VERSION IND: C

** SINGLE FAMILY PROPERTIES **
** COST/MARKET MODEL **

SUMMARY STATISTICS FOR THE COUNTY OF GRAHAM

* BASED ON PS4029 DATED / / AND PS4031-01 DATED 1/28/85 *

	NUMBER OF PARCELS	MEAN CALC FCV	MEAN LAND FCV	MEAN IMP VALUE PSF	MEAN PCT OF INCREASE PREV FCV	NUMBER OF SALES	MEDIAN SALES RATIO	COEF OF DISP
MARKET AREA								
01 SAFFORD	2,719	37,201	8,258	20.91	6.58	262	.805	.099
SUBAREAS								
01-CENTRAL SAFFORD	559	33,361	7,070	19.80	4.22	35	.817	.101
02-N SAFFORD/T-BRD V	394	34,786	4,855	18.36	6.29	29	.785	.160
03-S SAFFRD/HLCRST	878	45,384	10,916	23.10	8.19	117	.805	.095
04-THATCHER	528	40,466	8,695	22.56	9.92	61	.827	.095
05-PIMA/SOLOMON	359	31,909	7,032	17.67	1.97	20	.765	.131
IMPROVEMENT CLASSES								
CLASS-I R1	31	13,004	5,560	11.34	5.51	2	.885	.108
CLASS-II R3	254	15,024	5,238	12.27	17.66	16	.756	.197
CLASS-III R4	2,224	35,115	18,238	23.59	1.26	231	.804	.092
CLASS-IIII R5	172	67,857	162,062	25.37	5.68	2	.842	.089
CLASS-IIIII R5		177,037	20,305	30.44	4.33	1	.818	.081
SQUARE FOOTAGE								
-1200	1,103	26,286	6,669	19.95	7.07	120	.798	.111
1201-1600	961	37,763	8,460	21.36	6.58	100	.804	.078
1601-2000	457	47,834	9,687	21.29	6.12	25	.793	.127
2001-2400	183	82,098	13,273	24.18	4.27	15	.831	.081
2400+							.844	
CONSTRUCTION YEAR								
1965 TO PRESENT	1,243	43,970	9,507	23.81	7.55	166	.802	.080
1941-1964	504	34,714	6,454	19.57	5.64	65	.817	.109
PRE-1940				16.37	6.06	31	.794	.175
ADDITIONAL CATEGORIES								
CLASS 87 PARCELS	3	74,447	24,059	23.69	-9.66			

NOTE: SALES ARE FOR 1984 AND 2 PREVIOUS YEARS AND INCLUDE SALES FOR WHICH (I1) SALES YEAR MINUS CONST YEAR GE 1,
(2) FCV/SP RATIO GE .25 AND LE 2.00. SALES ARE ADJUSTED BY MONTH OF SALE TO JANUARY OF TAX YEAR.
ANNUALIZED ADJUSTMENT FACTORS FOR PREV. YEAR 1.000, 2 YRS AGO 1.000, 3 YRS AGO 1.000.

EXHIBIT 3

Assume that there were a large number of R1 improvement class sales (rather than only two), so that the appraiser/analyst decided to apply an adjustment to bring the median sales ratio for R1 parcels (currently .885) more in line with those of the other improvement classes. This can be accomplished by simply changing the market component adjustment for R1s, even though improvement class constitutes part of three variables in the MRA equation for the market area.

The base home approach also tends to impose a degree of rigor or restraint in the design of mass appraisal models. Complicated models are relatively difficult to convert to the base home format and the decomposition of ill-chosen models into component adjustments will readily reveal property characteristics with an unreasonable or unintuitive net impact upon value. Well-designed transformations, including exponents and crossproducts, however, can be easily accommodated. In addition, component adjustments can be compared between models and over time for consistency and stability, even though the supporting equations may be different.

APPLICATION TO CONDOMINIUMS/TOWNHOUSES

The base home approach is particularly well-suited to condominium/townhouse appraisal. In the Arizona system, subareas for such parcels are comprised of complexes or groupings of similar complexes. In contrast to single family properties, multiple regression equations are developed at the subarea (rather than market area) level. This has the important advantage of avoiding the need to model neighborhood desirability, common areas, and many other value-influencing characteristics that tend to be constant for all units in the subarea. In fact, the only variables that generally need to be considered are square footage, "add items" such as patios and fireplaces, and land value. The paucity of required variables, in turn, minimizes the number of sales required for model development.

Exhibit 4 shows the base home description and component adjustments developed for the Yuma market area for the 1985 tax year. The base home descriptions appear on the left side of the report and the component adjustments on the right side. The most important component adjustment is for square footage. Add items include patios, garages, carports, fireplaces, and other such amenities. The cost of these items is obtained from the Department's cost manual and the 1.52 adjustment factor represents the adjustment required to convert manual costs to current costs. The system will also accommodate cooling and age adjustments, but none of these were required for the Yuma subareas.

Exhibit 5 illustrates the calculation of value for a subject parcel in the

FEB 7, 1985   ARIZONA DEPARTMENT OF REVENUE PHOENIX DATA PROCESSING CENTER   PAGE 11
REPORT NBR: PS4031-02   CONDO/TOWNHOUSE BASE HOME DESCRIPTION AND COMPONENT ADJUSTMENTS FOR THE COUNTY OF YUMA   VERSION: C
FOR THE 1985 TAX YEAR
LAST UPDATE 01/23/85

MARKET AREA 01-YUMA

| | | | | * BASE HOME DESCRIPTIONS * | | | | | | | * MARKET COMPONENT ADJUSTMENTS * | | | | | |
SUBAREA	UNITS	IMP CLS	GRADE	SQFT	COOL	HEAT	AGE	ADDS	LAND FCV	TOTAL FCV	SQFT ADJ	COOLING ADJ REF	EVAP	NONE	ADDS ADJ	AGE ADJ
50	72	R4	FAIR	1200	REF	TP-A	10	1700	8400	37111	15.95	.00	.00	.00	1.52	0
52	60	R4	FAIR	700	REF	TP-A	19	1950	8500	34500	30.25	.00	.00	.00	1.52	0
53	64	R3	FAIR	950	REF	TP-A	10	1345	6943	31800	15.00	.00	.00	.00	1.52	0
54	100	R4	FAIR	1240	REF	TP-A	5	4250	10900	51900	21.28	.00	.00	.00	1.52	0
55	12	R3	FAIR	1200	REF	TP-A	3	1665	6400	31200	7.03	.00	.00	.00	1.52	0
57	30	R3	FAIR	1200	REF	TP-A	5	5600	9600	45100	11.89	.00	.00	.00	1.52	0
58	78	R4	FAIR	1300	REF	TP-A	6	5000	10400	48130	18.32	.00	.00	.00	1.52	0
59	40	R3	MIN	900	REF	TP-A	18	950	7200	36500	9.18	.00	.00	.00	1.52	0
60	16	R3	FAIR	1300	REF	TP-A	5	6500	12500	57000	15.00	.00	.00	.00	1.52	0
61	40	R3	GOOD	1250	REF	TP-A	5	4600	8800	40225	20.00	.00	.00	.00	1.52	0
62	35	R5	GOOD	1700	REF	TP-A	1	5000	14200	124188	50.00	.00	.00	.00	1.52	0
63	18	R4	FAIR	1500	REF	TP-A	6	4500	12500	60000	29.82	.00	.00	.00	1.52	0
64	72	R3	GOOD	1250	REF	TP-A	7	3900	10100	48335	20.00	.00	.00	.00	1.52	0
65	83	R4	FAIR	1550	REF	TP-A	16	3000	18200	75000	20.00	.00	.00	.00	1.52	0
66	60	R4	GOOD	1700	REF	TP-A	7	6115	15400	73060	42.61	.00	.00	.00	1.52	0
67	40	R3	GOOD	1300	REF	TP-A	4	6800	11600	47060	31.11	.00	.00	.00	1.52	0

FEB 7, 1985   ARIZONA DEPARTMENT OF REVENUE PHOENIX DATA PROCESSING CENTER   PAGE 12
REPORT NBR: PS4031-02   CONDO/TOWNHOUSE BASE HOME DESCRIPTION AND COMPONENT ADJUSTMENTS FOR THE COUNTY OF YUMA   VERSION: C
FOR THE 1985 TAX YEAR
LAST UPDATE 01/23/85

MARKET AREA 01-YUMA

| | | | | * BASE HOME DESCRIPTIONS * | | | | | | | * MARKET COMPONENT ADJUSTMENTS * | | | | | |
SUBAREA	UNITS	IMP CLS	GRADE	SQFT	COOL	HEAT	AGE	ADDS	LAND FCV	TOTAL FCV	SQFT ADJ	COOLING ADJ REF	EVAP	NONE	ADDS ADJ	AGE ADJ
68	59	R4	FAIR	1900	REF	TP-A	3	8950	18000	79684	20.00	.00	.00	.00	1.52	0
70	30	R4	FAIR	1364	REF	TP-A	4	6400	9100	72500	30.00	.00	.00	.00	1.52	0

EXHIBIT 4

Yuma market area based on the information in Exhibit 4. The subject parcel is in subarea 50, which has a base home value of $37,111. Adjustments are made for size, add items, and land value, yielding a valuation of $34,229.

The models can be easily evaluated and fine-tuned by focusing on sales ratios by subareas. Differences in appraisal levels between subareas can be addressed by simply adjusting the base home values. Coefficients of dispersion obtained by this approach average about 10% per market area.

CONCLUSIONS

The base home approach enhances the explainability of mass appraisal models by converting statistical equations to table format. This facilitates understanding by appraisers, as well as explanation to the general public.

The base home is, in effect, a "supercomparable" representing the typical characteristics of parcels in an area or other property group. The computed base home value tends to be very reliable since MRA and other statistical techniques produce highly reliable results for typical data. Market component adjustments for physical differences from the base home are extracted from the regression equation. This process is best automated, although it can also be done manually by a person competent in mathematics. The result is a table of base home values and component adjustments which produce the same result as the statistical equation but which is less imposing and more easily analyzed.

A particular advantage of the base home approach is that the component adjustments represent the pure or net effect of each property characteristic upon value. This permits the model builder or appraiser to evaluate the reasonability of the models in a straightforward manner and to more easily fine-tune the models.

The base home approach is most easily developed for relatively simple statistical models, although its advantages for "simplifying the complicated" can be particularly useful for more complex models. Application of the base home approach will reveal unreasonable or questionable model results that may be buried in interactive terms in the raw statistical model.

Adaptations of the base home approach are limited only by the imagination. For example, one can stratify parcels subject to a particular valuation equation to his or her choosing and develop separate base home values for each. Base home value tables can be set up in any number of formats and the conversion process can be applied to equations generated by most statistical procedures and can be applied to most common types of property.

EXHIBIT 5

CONDO/TOWNHOUSE CALCULATION SHEET FOR THE COUNTY OF: Yuma

PARCEL NUMBER: _____

I.   MARKET AREA: __01__   SUBAREA: __50__   BASE HOME VALUE: __37,111__

II. SIZE ADJUSTMENT:
SUBJECT __1080__ - BASE __1200__ = DIFFERENCE __-120__   FACTOR × __15.95__ = __-1914__

III. PER SQUARE FOOT ADJUSTMENTS:
SUBJECT _____ BASE _____ TOTAL SQFT _____ FACTOR × _____ = __1__

COOLING

IV. ADD ITEMS:
SUBJECT __2050__ - BASE __1700__ + DIFFERENCE __350__   FACTOR × __1.52__ = __532__

V.   AGE ADJUSTMENT:
BASE _____ - SUBJECT _____ = DIFFERENCE _____ FACTOR × _____ = __1__

VI. PART COMP ADJUSTMENTS (IF NONE, ENTER 0):

SUBTOTAL (I-V)   BASE LAND FCV   IMP. SUBTOTAL
_____ - _____ = _____

IMP. SUBTOTAL   ADJ. PER.   ADJ.IMP.FCV.   BASE LAND FCV
_____ ÷ $(6,900 = 8,400)$ = _____ $-1,500$

VII. SITUS ADJUSTMENT (LAND FCV - BASE LAND FCV):   =

VIII. FULL CASH VALUE (TOTAL I-VII):   = 34,229

IX. OTHER ADJUSTMENTS: =

X. ADJUSTED (ASSESSOR OVERRIDE)
FULL CASH VALUE (TOTAL OF VIII AND IX ABOVE):   =

DPST 820-A (Rev. 12/83)

## Chapter 6

Computerized Cost Approach

Telesfore P. Wysocki

INTRODUCTION

For those of us who attended the First World Congress on Computer Assisted Valuation in 1982, we had the opportunity to focus on issues relating to the use of the computer—hardware and software—as a tool in the real estate valuation process. Those presentations that dealt with the methodologies of the appraisal process in the context of computer use generally accentuated the favorable effects of the statistical methods utilized in regression techniques and modified market approaches. Much of this emphasis on the credibility and reliability of the use of these techniques seemed to be at the expense of the alleged inadequacies of the cost approach. Perhaps this tendency by some to leave behind the traditional cost approach as outdated or inappropriate in estimating market value was due to a confusion between the purpose of an appraisal and the concepts of the approaches. Or perhaps there was a lack of understanding that a relatively sophisticated system design could be programmed on a microcomputer to allow for an expansion in the dimensions of the cost approach analysis.

APPROACHES TO VALUE

As regards the potential for confusion between the purpose of an appraisal and the concepts of the three approaches to value, it appears that we in the appraisal profession, by gradually labeling the approaches with one word descriptors, such as market, cost, and income, have conceptually limited an estimate of market value to only one apparently *legitimate* approach, the market approach. In effect, we are distorting the fact that if the purpose of the appraisal is to estimate market value, then market information should be applied in all three approaches when available. The approaches really are, as described in the not so distant past, the *sales comparison* approach, the *summation* approach, and the *economic* approach. It is recognized that each approach utilizes market-derived information in applying required valuation techniques unique to each approach. Sales information and value adjustments relate to conditions of the market environment as of the date of the appraisal for the sales comparison approach. Construction costs and depreciation analysis, with appropriate land values, are market-derived as of the date of the appraisal for the summation approach. Financial forecasting and capitalization techniques are relevant to the economic conditions as they relate to the date of the appraisal for the economic approach. The quality of the information that is most reliable will obviously guide the appraiser to a reliance on one or more of the approaches.

The point is that with the abbreviated descriptions of the valuation approaches used today in real estate, we have, to a degree, limited our own insight into the usefulness of these approaches. On a broader scale, we have confused those who rely on our estimates, particularly in the mass appraisal application. The lack of a clear perception of the nature of the data used in each approach has demonstrably confused taxpayers, attorneys and judges. We have unwittingly painted ourselves into a corner when trying to relate the validity of the cost approach analysis to an estimate of market value. After all, it appears that there is only one approach to market value—and that is *the* market approach. Some of this confused thinking seems to have carried over into the original development of software applications for computer assisted valuation systems. Until recently, computerized cost approach application software primarily consisted of an inventory of descriptive information (database) and computing power limited to mathematical manipulations, with little or no system development that allowed for an individualized and intuitive analysis of available data. Any considerations of selective component adjustments or unit-in-place build-up were thought to be limited to mainframe applications so that general cost estimating became the standard.

In truth, perhaps back in August 1982, such capabilities were limited due to hardware and software. But the attitude of appraisers/assessment officers seemed to limit even the consideration of this application development. Today, however, both the hardware and software have made component adjustments and unit-in-place build-up possible in the microcomputer environment. Perhaps just as importantly, system designs are available that allow easy update to file databases and hardware computing power eliminates time delays in processing the analysis. What may be more revolutionary as a result of a more sophisticated system design is the ability of the system to achieve credible results with a property description database that can vary. It can range from minimal building information, through accepting additional information for other building features, accepting selected building component changes, or even accepting an entire build-up by units. And the system can be flexible enough to deal with any of these requirements whether or not individual properties possess the same features or building details.

If one acknowledges the benefits of having available three different approaches to real estate valuation, and if it can be demonstrated that the effort in collecting and analyzing the appropriate data is relatively the same to apply in each approach, then why would one want to close an additional window through which a view of market value may be achieved? Whether the subject property is residential, commercial, industrial or agricultural, the approach should be considered and with the use of the computer can be addressed in an effective and efficient way.

REVIEW OF THE COST APPROACH APPLICATION

Before illustrating one way of developing a computerized cost approach system, a basic review of the cost approach application should be addressed as it relates to estimating market value. Simply stated, the cost approach involves the following three steps:

Step 1   Estimate and justify reproduction or replacement cost new of the improvements.

Step 2   Estimate accrued depreciation and subtract from cost new.

Step 3   Estimate land value as though vacant and available for development to highest and best use, and combine with cost new less depreciation.

What is critically important to understand and observe is what is meant by the term cost. There are two generally accepted types of construction cost—reproduction and replacement. Reproduction cost is, as it implies, the cost of building an exact replica of the existing structure using the same materials and same specifications as the original, except that prices reflect the costs as of the date of the appraisal. Replacement cost is the cost of building the structure using materials, methods and design as well as costs that are typical as of the date of the appraisal. The distinction as to which type of cost is used is critical to the integrity of the analysis. If reproduction cost is used, then the probability of outdated materials or lack of functional adaptation to styles and uses exists, resulting in excessive costs that must be accounted for in the depreciation analysis. Whereas, if the replacement cost is used, these types of obsolescences are not built into the cost and the cost then represents the utility of the building as expected in the market as of the date of the appraisal. This observation is basic and obvious, yet understanding the distinction gives credibility to the concept of the cost approach reflecting market conditions as of the date of the appraisal. Replacement cost is based on market conditions reflecting fees, materials, styles, and workmanship as of the date of the appraisal.

Conversely, if a segment of the market were, for some reason, to place a value on original materials or workmanship for a unique structure or use, the cost approach could recognize that preference. The approach could also measure, as best possible, such value beginning with the reproduction cost estimate. In a mass appraisal assignment, this flexibility is often needed and, with the appropriate system design and comprehensive cost data file, the computer can accomplish the reproduction cost computation as quickly and routinely as the replacement cost estimate.

Understanding and recognizing the differences in these cost terms may also provide a clearer insight into the accounting for and measuring of depreciation. It is in the first step of the cost approach, listing the subject property and computing the cost estimate, where the appraiser/assessment officer determines what major physical or functional features of the structure are outdated and, therefore, should be listed or described instead with materials and practices that are consistent with the market periods as of the date of the appraisal. In theory and practice, the professionally-applied judgment can lend considerable confidence and credibility to the final estimate of value. Unless there is evidence that the market considers those features to be valuable, in which case the reproduction cost new would be estimated, the replacement cost new estimate can account for a substantial amount of obsolescence that otherwise is difficult, at best, to estimate in terms of value loss. It might also be true that the theoretically knowledgeable buyers utilize this process intuitively when considering the purchase of the subject property.

Not all accrued depreciation in all its forms can be accounted for in the cost new selected. Measurement for depreciation loss comes from demonstrated experience in the market place. Once again, where the purpose of the appraisal is to estimate market value, the cost approach application relies on market information as the basis for estimates of depreciation. In a Computer Assisted Valuation (CAV) system used by a fee appraiser, it would probably be appropriate for the program to utilize a menu selection of formula applications used within the observed method for measuring accrued depreciation. Once the appraiser identifies the type of depreciation or obsolescence existing in the subject property, the formula used to measure the loss or the cost to cure can be selected and the required data entered into the formula for computation. Also the program can be designed to "manage" this computed information so as to apply this loss in value in the appropriate place within the final computations of the cost approach estimate.

In the Computer Assisted Mass Appraisal (CAMA) system utilized by assessment officers, perhaps there should be greater consideration for the use of a combined rating and building age guideline table. A rating of excellent to unsound of the subject property based on an inspection would be combined with a judgment of the remaining economic life of the improvement. These two estimates compared to each other on a type of grid table would identify an amount of normal depreciation as a result of normal physical deterioration and normal obsolescence. Obviously, this practice of estimating depreciation assumes increments of value loss that are bracketed by a range within which the subject property lies. It is not an estimate unique to the subject property, but is a *representative estimate* by comparison of the subject property to typical depreciation of the average property in a sampling of similar properties. Again, considering the fact that this appraisal process deals with thousands, or tens of thousands, of properties, the application of this practice has a practical result of making the process *manageable*.

Also, it should be mentioned that with a base of market information that most likely would involve hundreds of sales, the identification of relationships between rating and age could be narrowed and the number of brackets expanded. At the same time, the value loss within those relationship brackets would be further refined. The theory and practice of this method is commonly identified and utilized in a variety of cost manuals and software applications. The tables generally look something like this:

RATING	AGE				
	0-3 years	4-6 years	7-10 years	10-12 years	etc.
Excellent	0%	0-3%	3-5%	10%	
Good	3%	6%	10%	15%	
Fair	15%	20%	25%	30%	
Poor	-	35%	45%	60%	

Very often, the logic and research that applies to this method of accounting for normal physical deterioration and typical obsolescence is not well understood. Nor is it appreciated so that often the practice is rejected out of hand as not being precise enough or scientifically justified. However, with the computerization of the valuation process for a mass appraisal application, the significant amount of time saved in the routine work of grinding out numbers can be better spent in market research for the data needed to develop this method of measuring normal depreciation. In fact, the use of a CAMA system would allow time for the assessment officer to develop expertise and confidence in the application of all the methodologies for estimating an assessed value.

Either system, CAV or CAMA, should allow for additional consideration of economic obsolescence which typically does not lend itself to "normal" experiences. Overrides or additional entries should be allowed for exacting depreciation analysis when it is required.

In the cost approach methodology, land valuation requires the application of direct market information within the sales comparison approach or use of residual techniques. A complete CAV or CAMA system that incorporates database management would permit the transfer of the subject land value from another analysis like the sales comparison approach or a residual application. At this point, one should have an appreciation of the credibility of the cost approach application and its viability in the appraisal process to determine market value.

COMPUTERIZATION OF METHODOLOGY

The computerization of this methodology requires familiarity with computer hardware and a proficiency in programming application software. If this proficiency is lacking, the appraiser/assessment officer can develop an understanding of basic computer concepts. With this knowledge, the appraiser/assessment officer could profile the entire appraisal process in terms from which a computer technician would document and write the application software. The *CAMA Basics* course offered by the Lincoln Institute of Land Policy provides such an educational opportunity for the appraiser/assessment officer with little or no computer background. Also, the International Association of Assessing Officers (IAAO) recently initiated a CAMA membership section which will provide that group with the opportunities to learn more about computerization of the valuation process. The IAAO also offers a course in the *Fundamentals of Mass Appraisal* which provides additional insight into the appraisal process as it specifically applies to the requirements of ad valorem valuation. Perhaps in the near future, this course will incorporate, as a course objective, the practical use of computerized analysis as it is used in the mass appraisal environment.

If the effort and cost of designing, documenting, writing, and testing an entire system are prohibitive—and it can be expensive even in a microcomputer application—there now are available generic software packages. They are generic in the sense that they are designed on the basis of textbook appraisal application procedures and specific information requirements. The problems most often associated with generic CAV or CAMA systems is that the purchaser relies on the *appraisal expertise* of someone else— whoever designed the system. Very often, this is an uncomfortable feeling if for no other reason than the designer and the purchaser may have developed their appraisal expertise from different textbooks or have different levels of expertise. Obviously, the results in using the system under these circumstances can create more problems than are solved. Additionally, it is no small problem to recognize that the information requirements of the generic CAV or CAMA system may be different than the current property information recorded on cards or available in machine-readable format. The solutions to this situation are a complete re-inventory of all property information collected in the required format or an attempt at "interpreting" existing information into the required format. In either case, this time and effort at collection or conversion also adds to the expense of the system. As long as one looks for an entire generic CAV or CAMA system, these concerns will most probably persist. However, there is another alternative whereby one purchases a particular computer valuation application and builds an entire system around that program. Because there are a variety of generic cost approach software applications available for mini and microcomputer hardware, this option is feasible.

MICROCOMPUTER APPLICATION PROGRAMS

Recently the E. H. Boeckh Division of American Appraisal Associates and Marshall and Swift have made their cost data available in microcomputer application programs. As national construction cost data services that have been extensively used in their manual formats, most appraisal and assessment offices have their improvement data recorded as required by either service. The computerization of the cost approach application by each of these services allows the appraiser/assessment officer to utilize available improvement data based on one or the other service. Along with the construction cost and depreciation information of each improvement transferred into a database, the addition of land/site information is needed to complete the computerization of the cost approach application. The construction cost data file and the rating/age depreciation tables are completed and updated by the services. Access to the cost data files is not available to the user since it is proprietary information and is identified with the research of the individual service. Local adjustments, if not accurately reflected in the local modifiers provided by the service, must be made by additional market adjustment factors which are developed and entered by the user. Adjustment of the depreciation table files is currently not allowed. Perhaps, if the service is formally released from any liability for the validity of the final value estimate based on user depreciation data, access to the depreciation data files could be arranged.

Both the Boeckh and Marshall systems allow for different detail levels of required input data to develop a cost new estimate. Boeckh, in particular, provides a unique optional feature which allows the user to redefine any one or all building components in a model in the commercial and industrial valuation programs. Computerized microcomputer residential valuation packages are soon to be available that will allow cost new estimates based on a unit count method. No square footage information is required. Rather, the system relies basically on an identification of the class of construction or style, exterior wall material, number and identification of rooms, and additional improvement features. The depreciation analysis apparently requires the standard rating/age data. Appraiser/assessment officers who intend to rely more on regression or feedback modeling analysis would find this cost approach data requirement convenient and compatible with those application data requirements. Integrating these systems would require technical computer expertise and probably consent of the vendors providing the packages. If an appraiser/assessor were to choose to develop one's own computerized cost approach application system, the most difficult and demanding part of the system would probably be the cost data file structure and its correlation to the amount of required improvement data input.

By experience, one learns that there is an inverse relationship between the simple use requirements of the user of the program and the sophistication of the program operation. The easier the program is to use, the more sophisticated the system design and programming has to be. In this case, it is more than the typical "user-friendly" description of a program use. In the instance of CAV and CAMA applications, the ease of use refers more often than not to limiting the amount of individual descriptive improvement data that is needed to develop a credible value estimate. Particularly in a CAMA environment, the time and expense to gather and *keep current* a property description base is perhaps the single most expensive part of the appraisal/assessment process. If the CAV or CAMA system, in particular the cost approach module, is to require as little descriptive input data as possible *but still develop credible value estimates*, then the program must be designed and written to make effective use of file structure and data. The major characteristics of construction should be base-modeled and then identified by class of construction or style, number of stories, and type of occupancy (for residential construction) or use (for commercial or industrial construction). These are some of the major factors that impact the appropriate element cost in the build-up of an accurate cost new estimate.

DATA FORMULAE

Developing formulae for manipulation of data is a relatively easier task in the cost approach application if the cost data file is structured to "compensate" for the above-described construction features. One could start with the equation that cost new equals total square footage times the cost per square foot. However, one must identify what class or style of construction is being measured. Therefore, the equation must now read cost new equals total square footage times the Class 1 (or Ranch style) cost per square foot. And, if the structure is a two story model, then the formula must read cost new equals total square footage times the Class 1, two story cost per square foot. And, if the structure is a two-family dwelling, then the equation must now read cost new equals total square footage times the Class 1, two story, two-family occupancy cost per square foot. And so on, depending on what other characteristics of the improvement impact a change in the square foot cost calculation. If one follows this example of developing a cost approach system, it becomes clear that the development of individual models by construction features is a necessary procedure if a credible and accurate cost new estimate is to reflect the subject improvement. The model *costing* calculation can be efficiently done through the use of appropriate factors that reflect the differences in cost between different construction features.

As more and more variations are considered with the design of the program to allow for additional features and/or changes to the model, a more realistic and accurate estimate of value is achieved by the application of the cost approach.

CONCLUSION

As we enter this Second World Congress on Computer Assisted Valuation, no doubt other viewpoints may be expressed that have an impact on this discussion on computerized cost approach applications. It is not hard to imagine a discussion that brings into question why the value to be estimated for property tax purposes must be a market value. Couldn't it be a taxable value based on a pure cost approach analysis? Is ownership of real estate, primarily residential real estate, truly a measure of wealth as it had once been? Isn't the public focus of property tax liability centering on the perceived fairness of the sharing of the tax burden, as opposed to a requirement that it measure market value? And, if public perceptions are important, of what help are unfamiliar applications to a public understanding of the valuation process?

The cost approach has a "comfortable" logic and perceived realistic accountability that can be understood by the least sophisticated individual. If it were not constrained to the whims and fictions of a non-existent typical buyer/seller, it could be, by itself, the basis for an equitable standard to determine property tax liability for the residential class of property.

Chapter 7

MULTIPLE REGRESSION MODELS

Robert H. Gustafson

Almost every phenomenon we observe has a relationship with other phenomena occurring in nature if observed closely enough. The depth of the snow pack at certain locations and at certain times of the season relates to the amount of water available in the spring or summer; the number of continued days of warm weather is related to the size of crops that will be harvested later; and the size of homes is related to the age of homes. Some of these relationships are largely "cause and effect" as with the number of warm days and the size of crops or the snow pack and subsequent water supplies. Others are coincidental as with the size and age of homes; that is, size did not cause age, nor did age cause size, rather, their pattern developed reasonably independent of each other. Nevertheless, one may observe, in individual cases, a strong relationship, either positive or negative.

Some of these relationships are strong in that as one phenomenon changes so does its related phenomenon, while others are quite weak with small movement of one in response to the other. Some of these relationships are positive in that both parts move in the same direction and some are negative, as when one gets larger the other gets smaller (i.e., age vs. percent good). Some are quite simple as with the amount of liquid flow vs. the size of the release valve, while other relationships are quite complex as with the sales price of properties vs. their property characteristics.

Simple or complex, causal or coincidental, these are all relationships that can be studied and, in many cases, measured. By measuring the relationship, it is possible to utilize that relationship in predicting the possible outcome of one event given the results of related events or better understanding how one characteristic moves relative to other characteristics.

SIMPLE RELATIONSHIPS

The simpler relationships are easier to deal with since they can usually be reduced to a two-dimensional diagram and readily visualized. Figure A depicts on a scatter diagram of observations such a relationship using sales price and size of house as the two characteristics studied. The purpose of studying this relationship is to see if sales price can be estimated given only size or to study changes in sales price for given changes in size.

As tradition would have it, the sales price is plotted and measured on the vertical scale and it is the "unknown" variable[1] in a predicting mode or the "dependent" variable. Size as used here is the "known" or "independent" variable and is plotted and recorded on the horizontal scale. From the plot (each dot represents a separate observation), it is apparent that a relationship exists between sales price and size. Further, it can be observed that the relationship is positive (both variables increase or decrease together).

This observation can be strengthened by overlaying a straight line (linear fit) to the data. The one drawn on Figure A clearly shows that as size increases by 100 square feet, sales price increases by about $3,500. Further, it is possible to estimate the probable sales price of a single property by first locating the size on the horizontal scale, reading up until the freehand line is intersected, then reading to the left to read the sales price from the vertical scale. This can be illustrated by selecting a home of 1,400 square feet. The reading from the sales price scale is about $54,000.

Once the freehand line is drawn, it is easier to observe whether the relationship is strong or weak. The scatter of the observations about the line represents the power of the relationship. If the observations are quite closely clustered about the line, then it would follow that the estimate made by using that line would be expected to be fairly reliable; greatly dispersed observations would suggest poor predictive abilities.

Fitting the line of sight is not a very precise method of curve fitting, especially when the patterns are more dispersed than that shown in the illustration. Many different curves could be drawn to fit these data, yet only one would have the desired characteristics of minimizing the scatter about

---

1. The term "variable" refers to a characteristic that takes on a range of values throughout the problem as contrasted to a "constant" which is a characteristic that takes on the same value throughout the problem.

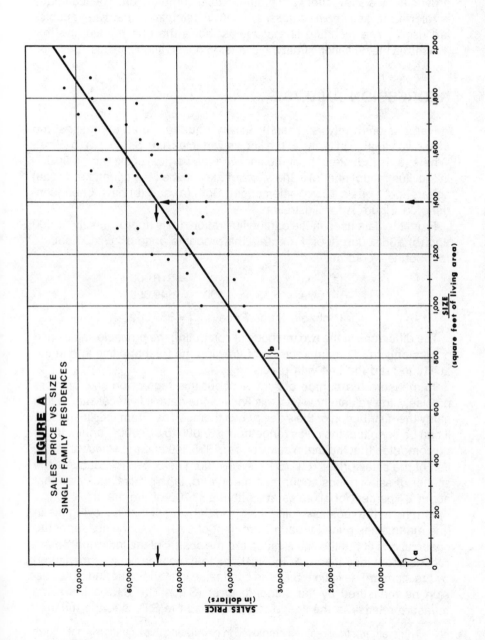

FIGURE A

SALES PRICE VS. SIZE
SINGLE FAMILY RESIDENCES

the line. This particular fit is referred to as the "least squares fit" and is arrived at by a straightforward mathematical computation. The technique is referred to as *simple regression analysis* (simple in that two variables are used). The resulting line of *regression* is the one unique line that minimizes the deviations from the scattered observations, that is, "best fits."

REGRESSION ANALYSIS

Regression analysis[2] results in an equation that expresses the unknown variable in terms of the known variables, i.e., S.P. = a + b (Size). Where (a) is the intercept of the line with the vertical scale (about $6,000 in the illustration) and (b) is the slope of the line (i.e., the change of 1 (one) square foot equals $35 of sales price). Both (a) and (b) have been identified on Figure A for illustration.

From the data used in the earlier illustration, (a) is approximately $6,000 and (b) $35/square foot. From this the probable price of a 1,400 square foot house would be:

$$
\begin{aligned}
\text{(a)} &= \$\ 6,000 \\
+\text{(b) size} = \$35 \times 1,400 &= \$49,000 \\
\hline
\text{Probable Sales Price} &= \$55,000
\end{aligned}
$$

The difference in the two methods of computing the probable sales price occurs only from the imprecision of drawing the freehand line and in the ability to read the line with precision.

To measure the degree of scatter about this regression line, or more precisely, to evaluate how well this line fits the data, it is necessary to first study the distribution of the sales prices themselves. From the illustration, it can be seen that the sales range from $37,000 to $72,000. Further, it can be computed that the mean sales price is $55,340 and the *standard deviation* of the sales prices (S.D./S.P.) is ±$8,700. The S.D./S.P. measures the scatter of sales prices about their mean and, in this case, indicates that about 67 percent of all sales are within ±$8,700 of the mean.

Turning to the regression line itself and thinking of it as a moving mean (the mean sales price for each increment of size), then the scatter of the observations about the line is much like the scatter of the individual observations about their mean. As the scatter about the mean can be measured by the standard deviation (S.D.), so can the scatter about the line of regression be measured by the standard error (S.E.). The S.E. is the same measure relative to the line of regression as the S.D. is to the mean.

---

2. The mathematical method employed in generating this equation is not shown but can be found by the reader in most elementary statistical texts.

CORRELATION ANALYSIS

This relationship permits us to introduce an additional measure that is most useful in regression analysis. By comparing the scatter about the regression line (S.E.) relative to the scatter about the mean (S.D.), one can measure the ability of the regression line to predict or to measure the strength of the relationship. This comparison is called the coefficient of correlation and is derived from the following formula:

$$\sqrt{1 - \frac{(S.E.)^2}{(S.D.)^2}}$$

In cases where the scatter is quite small about the regression line (S.E.) relative to the scatter about the mean (S.D.), the ratio of $(S.E.)^2/(S.D.)^2$ is quite small resulting in the answer approaching the square root of 1, which is 1. If the scatter about the regression line is larger (it cannot exceed S.D.) relative to S.D., then the ratio of $(S.E.)^2/(S.D.)^2$ approaches 1 (one) and the answer approaches the square root of zero, which is zero. Thus, we can see that when the scatter is small around the regression line, the coefficient of correlation is closer to 1 (one) and visual observation will verify a "good fit." As the scatter gets greater, and the goodness of fit gets less, the coefficient of correlation approaches zero, or there is little to no relationship.

MULTIPLE REGRESSION

The two-dimensional relationship between sales price and size used above is easily observed and readily understood by all. It does not, however, serve the purpose of estimating sales prices except in the most extreme situations. This is so due to the fact that sales prices of even single-family residences are not a function of size alone. The age of the structure, its quality and condition, the room distribution, the amenities of the home, the land and its characteristics on which the residence is located, and location itself are all added factors that must be considered to properly understand sales price.

This can best be seen by entering into the previous analysis a third variable, age of dwelling, in addition to size. Now the variable "sales price" will be evaluated relative to both size and age. A three-dimensional sketch is required to illustrate this adaption. However, it can best be visualized with the vertical scale still being sales price and having two horizontal scales, one for size and one for age. Fitting a line by sight is no longer possible. However, the mathematical derivation[3] of the plane of regression can be found much as before. The adding of a second variable (age) to relate to sales price advances the technique to multiple regression analysis (MRA) where *two or more* known variables are used to relate to the unknown variable (sales price).

By adding the second known variable to the analysis, the equation takes on the form of:

$$\text{Sales Price} = a + b_1 (\text{size}) + b_2 (\text{age})$$

Where (a) is the intercept of this linear plane on the vertical (sales price) scale, (b_1) is the slope of the plane due to changes in size, and (b^2) is the slope of the plane due to changes in age. The coefficients, (b_1) and (b_2), can be either positive or negative depending upon whether there is a positive or negative relationship between the individual known variable and the unknown variable. In this illustration, one would expect size to be positive and age to be negative (i.e., sales price declines as age gets older). The resulting equation could be as follows:

$$\text{Sales Price} = \$10{,}469 + \$45.62/ \text{Square Foot} - \$315/\text{year}$$

MULTIPLE CORRELATION

Since this equation utilizes two property characteristics, size and age, to estimate sales price one would expect an improvement over the simple regression equation developed earlier. To test that, one need only analyze the scatter about the regression plane. This study of how the regression equation predictions depart from the actual sales prices is performed as with simple regression; that is, the standard error (S.E.) is computed. If the new equation is an improvement over the earlier one then the S.E. should be less than when using size alone. Further, the coefficient of multiple correlation should be higher than earlier. The term multiple correlation, like multiple regression, refers to the fact that there are two or more independent (or known) variables as compared to simple correlation and simple regression.

The computation of the coefficient of multiple correlation is computed as before given the S.E. about the regression plane.

After the simple adding of one more variable to the equation, it can be

---

3. The mathematical equations used in this calculation are not shown but can be found in most elementary text books on statistics.

seen that additional variables may be accommodated in exactly the same way. The general form of the final equation is:

$$\text{Sales Price} = a + b_1 x_1 + b_2 x_2 + \ldots + b_n x_n$$

where (a) is the intercept of this plane on the vertical axis, (b_1) is the slope due to variable (x_1), b_2 is the slope due to variable (x_2), and (b_n) is the slope due to the last variable (x_n). Using this regression equation the standard error can be computed as well as the coefficient of multiple correlation (R^2).

STEPWISE MULTIPLE REGRESSION

The introduction of additional variables raises problems in determining which variables make significant contributions in estimating sales prices and in what combination should they be entered into the equation. One technique that has been invaluable in solving this problem is the statistical procedure referred to as stepwise multiple regression. This procedure sorts out from all available variables those making a significant contribution from those that do not and assembles them into a final equation with weights (coefficients) assigned each selected variable in accordance to its added contribution to sales price. The steps followed are somewhat as follows:

1. A correlation matrix is formed where the dependent variable and each of the independent variables in the entire data set are compared and a simple correlation coefficient is computed for each combination. The correlation with the dependent variable (sales price) that best assists in evaluating which single variable is best in explaining (related to) sales price. The correlation of the independent variables on each other helps measure the degree to which characteristics compare with each other. Some will have high intercorrelations like room count, bedroom count, and square footage of living area as they all measure somewhat similar characteristics. Others will show little or no relationship with each other as they are truly unrelated but may still contribute to explaining sales price.

2. From this matrix, the one variable is selected that best correlates with (has the highest value of r) with sales price. Using that variable alone, a simple regression equation is developed where sales price is expressed as a function of only that variable. For illustration purposes, let us assume the best single variable turned out to be "number of square feet of living area" (size). An equation is then

derived using size only from that simple equation, the standard error (S.E.) and the coefficient of correlation (r) are computed.

3. The correlation matrix is now recast entirely. Rather than relate each variable to sales price, as in the first step, the relationship is to that portion of sales price not explained by size. That is, the equation from Step 2 is applied to each sale and the amount each equation estimate differs from the actual sales price is used to replot against each of the remaining variables.

4. The best single variable (highest r) from this new matrix is selected and a new equation is developed using both variables to explain sales price. That is, the variable from the first step and the one added in this step are used to develop the new equation. Both the standard error (S.E.) and the coefficient of multiple correlation are computed to see if this equation does a better job of explaining variations in the sales price.

5. The process is then repeated in that the new equation is used to estimate the sales price in each sale, the amount by which that estimate differs from the actual sales price is computed, and the residuals are related to the remaining variables to develop a new correlation matrix.

6. The variable (not yet selected) with the best fit with the residuals at this point is selected and added to the equation.

This process is continued until one of three events occurs:

1. All of the variables have been entered into the equation.

2. None of the remaining variables makes a significant contribution to explaining variations in the sales price.

3. The number of variables entered equals the number of sales observations less one. That is, if there are 15 observations (sales) no more than 14 variables can be used in the final equation.

Generally, the equations use considerably less than all variables available and the process terminates under condition 2 as described above. The variables remaining after termination of the process with the best possible equation usually fall into three classes. First, there are those characteristics that either do not exist in the area under study or are common to all properties in the study area. These are generally dropped out early in the analysis depending upon the specific set of computer procedures and programs employed. Secondly, there are those characteristics that occur in the study area but appear to have no relationship to changes in sales price at that point in time. Thirdly, there are those characteristics which, on their own, may relate to sales price, but because they are highly correlated with variables already entering into the equation are unable to add anything additional to the relationship with sales price. For example, there may be several variables that measure size in one way or another (square feet, room count, etc.). One of these size variables will probably enter into the equation at an early stage. Its presence in the equation will generally explain most of the variation in sales price attributed to size leaving little, if any, explanatory power for the remaining size-related variables.

This description oversimplifies the process and fails to describe most of the tricks of the trade needed to effectively utilize an MRA system as an aid to the appraiser. Rather, it was intended to describe the procedure in its general form, pointing out its general application, and leaving the subsequent chapters and technical staff the specifics of applying such a system.

The important point is that MRA is in fact a generalized procedure that permits the researcher, analyst or appraiser to study relationships of one or more variables as they relate to another variable or characteristic. The end result is a mathematical statement that combines the individual relationships into a composite statement. Because it is a composite statement, the equation should not be taken apart. That is, because many of the components making up a home are interrelated with each other, the coefficients (or weights) assigned each variable may actually relate to the combined contribution of two or more characteristics. If one wishes to study the effect of one simple characteristic on sales price, then perhaps a simple regression equation should be used wherein only the one variable is used to relate to sales price.

Regression analysis, as employed here, is identical to the thought process employed by most appraisers when utilizing the sales comparison approach. Numerous factors must be considered in evaluating why one home sold for a price different from another. The principal difference, however, is that the computerized process permits the isolation of one variable from the others to judge whether it is making a contribution to sales price in this particular situation. The relationships are there, its just that MRA, if utilized properly, assists in detecting and measuring these relationships, thus extending the analytical abilities of the appraiser.

## Chapter 8

A FEEDBACK PRIMER

Jan Schreiber

BACKGROUND: THE IMPOSSIBLE PROBLEM AND THE LEAST BAD SOLUTION

All designers of valuation methodologies face the same general problem: how can the known characteristics of a collection of parcels be quantified and expressed in dollars so as to produce reasonable estimates of the value of each parcel? We usually assume that a reasonable estimate is one that does not differ too greatly from the selling price of the parcel at a particular point in time. While this assumption begs the question whether the real estate market truly behaves in a reasonable manner, it does give us a criterion—actual sales transactions—against which to measure estimates of value produced by one method or another.

In order to automate the process of valuation and to make it objective, it is useful to have an equation that expresses the relation between observable characteristics of a parcel and its value. A simple version of such an equation might say, for example, that the total value of a developed parcel is a function of the value of the land (expressed in dollars per square foot) and the value of the building (expressed in dollars per room):

$$\text{Total Value} = V_1 L + V_2 R$$

where L is the number of square feet of land, R is the number of rooms,

V_1 is the dollar value of a square foot of land, and V_2 is the dollar value of a room. Our problem then would be, on the basis of empirical information, to come up with values for V_1 and V_2 that would produce estimates matching the known sale prices of the parcels in question.

If only two properties were involved, there would be little difficulty. We would simply have two simultaneous equations with two variables. Suppose one parcel had a six-room house, 10,000 square feet of land area, and a recent sale price of $70,000. Suppose the other had an eight-room house, also 10,000 square feet of land area, and a sale price of $90,000. Using our very simple model, we would get the following two equations:

$$V_1 \times 10,000 = V_2 \times 6 = 70,000$$
$$V_1 \times 10,000 + V_2 \times 8 = 90,000$$

It is easy to determine that a value of one (dollar per square foot) for V_1 and 10,000 (dollars per room) for V_2 satisfies both equations. We could graph the resulting model equation (Total Value $= 1 \times L + 10,000 \times R$) on two axes showing actual and estimated values, and the resulting line would pass through points representing the values of both our sample properties (Figure 1). If all parcels in our sample obeyed this model exactly, the line would pass through all of them.

In principle, as long as there are as many equations (i.e., individual properties with sales data) as there are variables to be found, we can solve them together and produce an exact model accounting for the estimated value of each property. The resulting model might or might not have value as a predictive device, but it would be mathematically precise. The problem arises when an equation is "overdetermined"—that is, when there are more cases than there are variables, and not all of the cases fit the model.

Consider what happens when we discover a third parcel, one having ten rooms and 12,000 square feet of land area. We can apply our model to it and estimate its value at $112,000. But we discover that the parcel sold for only $105,000. Clearly it does not fit the model. If we add it to the graph (Figure 2), we see that the solid line fails to pass through it. We might try to revise the model, but we will soon find that no linear equation yields a line that will pass through all three parcels. (And if we developed a higher-order equation producing a curve that passed through all three points, we would very likely find that parcels 4, 5, and 6 lay outside the range of that curve.) Strictly speaking, the problem has no solution.

So we must compromise. We must be willing to settle for a model producing points that come as near as possible to the line showing equivalent actual and estimated values, though none of these points may lie directly on the line. Such points might look like the ones in Figure 3. Statistics is

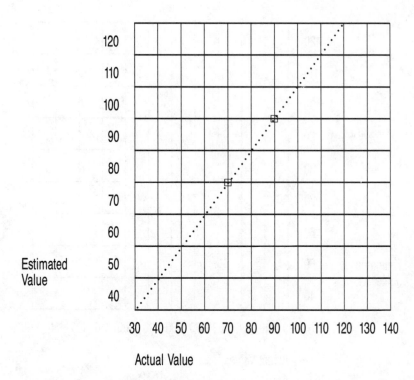

FIGURE 1: ACTUAL VS. ESTIMATED VALUES FOR TWO PARCELS

the science of dealing with inexactitude. We now seek what might be called the *least bad solution*.

Elsewhere in this book there is a discussion of the mathematically rigorous way of finding such points, known as multiple regression. It produces coefficients in the valuation model such that the net distance from each point representing estimated vs. actual value to the line of equivalence is minimized. The process is known as the ordinary least squares method; using it, one can determine the degree of influence various factors have on an outcome such as total property value. However, it does not allow multiplicative and additive factors to be used in the same model, and it does not usually yield values for factors such as rooms or square feet of property that make intuitive sense. For the taxpayer who is not mathematically inclined, explanations couched in terms of multiple regression may seem a form of voodoo assessment. This is unfortunate, because the technique is extremely powerful, with applications in many fields involving multiple variables influencing a measurable outcome.

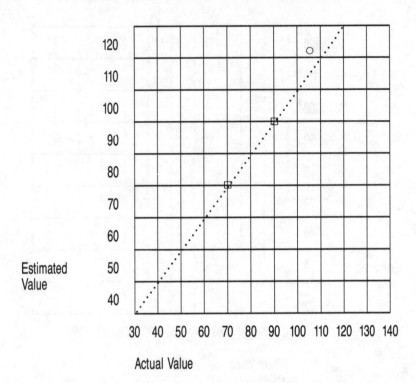

Actual Value

FIGURE 2: A NON-LINEAR RELATION AMONG THREE PARCELS

AUTOMATING BLIND MAN'S BLUFF

Partly because of this liability, however, the assessment profession has more recently been giving attention to a newer valuation technique known as "feedback," or the adaptive estimation procedure. Like multiple regression, it is an attempt to find a model, or equation, that will produce estimated values as close as possible to actual values, given a manageable number of variables and a much larger number of transactions in which price of sale is available. Here, however, the approach is to utilize the computer's ability to perform a great many repetitive calculations in rapid succession. Feedback is essentially a systematized trial and error procedure, in which the computer continually calculates property values, compares them with actual values, adjusts the valuation model in light of the comparison, uses that revised model in the next computation, and so forth.

The model builder starts off by selecting those factors he believes to be

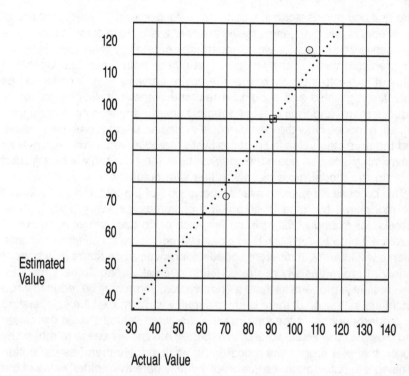

FIGURE 3: LINE REPRESENTING APPROXIMATE LINEAR RELATION
AMONG THREE PARCELS

salient. That is, he assumes that certain factors, such as number of rooms, total property area, frontage, exterior condition, and the like, play a role in determining value. From these he creates an equation representing the relation between total value and the value of the individual factors. In doing so, he assigns more or less arbitrary initial coefficient values to the terms in his equation. Some of the factors can be preliminarily assigned a dollar value. Others are assigned a weight, according to their value in the assessor's database, and this weight determines how strongly they affect the initial estimate. If the factor value is high (for example, if the building is in good condition), a high weight may be assigned which enhances the total property value; conversely, if the value is low, a low weight may be assigned to scale it back. This model is described in more detail in the next section.

The initial weights and dollar values assigned (called coefficients) are tentative, since the user does not know for sure how much a square foot of land or a bedroom is worth in a particular neighborhood. Therefore the valuation model is one that "learns by experience." It is used to compute the value of a series of parcels for which recent sales data are available. Suppose the predicted value of the first parcel is higher than the actual, observed value. It is fair to infer, then, that the assigned weights and dollar values were too high also and should be reduced somewhat. So the computer reduces them, and thus creates a slightly altered equation constituting the valuation model. Now the next parcel is evaluated using this revised model, and the predicted value is compared with the observed value. Again it will not match exactly, so again the coefficients in the equation will be adjusted to bring the model more closely in line with actuality.

This process is repeated over a succession of parcels. Not all factors in the model will be used in computing estimates for every parcel (some parcels, for example, will have no fireplace or no second story), so not all factors will be adjusted each time a parcel is considered. Therefore, the coefficients will change at different speeds. Moreover, since some may appear mainly in properties where the equation overvalues, and others may appear mainly in properties where it undervalues, some may be reduced while others are increased. If there is any rationality to the market forces operating on property prices, in the long run the predicted values should get closer and closer to the actual values. When they essentially cease to move any closer, the user judges the model to be finalized. He then has the option of using it in subsequent estimates of value, where the "actual" value of the property may not be known.

Figure 4 shows schematically the operation of the feedback process on the computer. The valuation model is applied to each parcel in turn, yielding an estimated value. This value is compared with the observed value from actual sales data, and the coefficients in the model are adjusted in a way that would yield a closer estimate. The next parcel is then evaluated using this revised model, again the result is compared with the observed value, and again the coefficients are adjusted. This process continues until all parcels in a specified range have been treated (i.e., for one complete iteration), whereupon the same parcels are then considered in reverse for the next iteration, and so forth.

It is easy to see why a computer would be virtually essential to perform the numerous repetitive calculations that must be done before an acceptable valuation model is achieved. Because the model changes with the consideration of each parcel, the computer is in effect "learning" from experience, with the results of each computation fed back recursively into the system. Computers can readily be programmed to do these tasks, but the most useful programs are those that let the user specify any starting model he chooses.

Parcel (By Date of Sale)

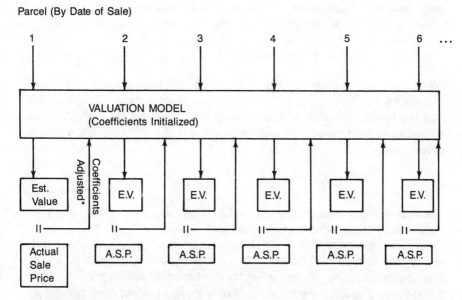

*Damping factor prevents "complete" adjustment in each case, thus slowing oscillation from one parcel pass-through to the next.

FIGURE 4: MODEL OF THE FEEDBACK COEFFICIENT
DETERMINATION PROCESS

A SIMPLE FORMULA MADE COMPLICATED

On a first encounter, such a generic program seems more perplexing than a multiple regression problem: unlike regression, the feedback method will not identify which factors—out of all possible ones—most influence the dependent variable. It is up to the user to make an educated guess, on the basis of his experience, about the likely candidates. Of course, the more factors one includes, the better the chance of finding some that make the difference; but also, the longer a microcomputer will take to process them. From the beginning, knowledge and intuition are useful in narrowing the field.

Intuition can also be useful in assigning initial coefficient values. In order to set up the feedback process, the model builder needs to know in detail how the equation for estimated value is composed. In the "bare bones" form of this equation, estimated property value is treated as comprised of building value plus land value, just as in the primitive model discussed earlier:

$$EV = B + L \tag{1}$$

Both of these values are computed by multiplying quantifiable features of each type (e.g., number of rooms, number of square feet) times a dollar value, or coefficient, denoted in the following equation by "A":

$$EV = f_B A_B + f_L A_L \tag{2}$$

Since there are usually several land and several building factors relevant to a determination of value, each is multiplied by a coefficient (dollar value), and the results are summed to arrive at a composite building value and a composite land value. The estimated value of the property is the total of these values.

$$EV = \Sigma f_B A_B + \Sigma f_L A_L \tag{3}$$

These building and land factors to which dollar values can be attached are called *quantitative* factors in the feedback system.

As assessors recognize, however, there are other considerations that affect value, such as the condition of the property, the neighborhood it is in, and its age and style. These factors may enhance or detract from the basic dollar value. Feedback takes account of them by creating coefficients based on them which can be multiplied by the elements in equation 3. Thus if a building is on balance of less than average quality, its value may be multiplied by a *qualitative* coefficient of somewhat less than 1 (say, .93), while if a land parcel is superior to the average because of excellent landscaping or a good view, its value may be multiplied by a qualitative coefficient greater than 1 (say, 1.07). The equation now looks like this:

$$EV = Q_B \Sigma f_B A_B = Q_L \Sigma f_L A_L \tag{4}$$

Once again, there may be several qualitative coefficients of each type; if so, they are multiplied together to produce a composite product for building and another for land. The "pi" in the following equation denotes this product.

$$EV = \pi Q_B \Sigma f_B A_B + \pi Q_L \Sigma f_L A_L \tag{5}$$

When an attribute is to be processed as qualitative and a manageable number of discrete values can be anticipated, it is possible to specify the particular coefficient values that the computer is to set into the equation in response to each attribute value. Thus five factors (or factor levels) indicating a range of exterior quality from poor to superior could be assigned respectively coefficient values of .8, .9, 1, 1.1, and 1.2. It is also possible to hold the coefficient for "typical" quality steady at a value of 1, regardless of what adjustments feedback would ordinarily produce, and let coefficients for neighboring levels vary around it; this is a technique recommended by one of feedback's developers, Robert Carbone.

But what should be done for attributes with a continuous range of values that one wants to play a qualitative role in the feedback equation? If we are dealing with, say, age of building, which may have hundreds of possible values in our database, do we have to specify in advance the coefficient for every possible year? Or do we turn a smooth curve into a series of steps by grouping the data into ten-year intervals and assigning a coefficient to each group?

The answer varies depending on the software used. Some versions do not permit automatic assignment of coefficients to continuous variables, so one of the just-stated options must be chosen. Others incorporate an algorithm that computes a qualitative coefficient from any number within a specified range that enters the model from the database. The nature of this algorithm varies with the developer. It may or may not produce coefficients that move systematically on either side of 1 in response to the incoming value. It may require the user to specify certain parameters, some less intuitively understandable than others. It is likely to be a little cumbersome to set up, but it will pay for itself later by shortening the machine time required to produce an acceptable model.

Assuming that our computer model has the ability to assign coefficient values to continuous attributes, we incorporate an M, or *multiplicative* coefficient, into the feedback valuation model in the following way:

$$EV = \pi Q_B M_B \Sigma f_B A_B + \pi Q_L M_L \Sigma f_L A_L \qquad (6)$$

(In fact, qualitative and multiplicative coefficients are mathematically identical. They are represented separately here only for the sake of clarity.)

Finally, the valuation model takes account of the fact that some factors appear to affect both land and building value. Neighborhood grade might be an example of such a factor. Both qualitative and multiplicative *general* factors, operating on the entire equation, are thus provided for, and the final form of the equation becomes:

$$EV = \pi Q_G M_G [\pi Q_B M_B \Sigma f_B A_B + \pi Q_L M_L \Sigma f_L A_L] \qquad (7)$$

This is the form of the feedback equation used by the Lincoln Institute in its SOLIR microcomputer valuation system. SOLIR feedback is referred to now and then in the remainder of this chapter, because it is a readily available version of the process that users can obtain to investigate for themselves.

In summary, there are eight types of factors that the feedback user needs to know about in order to incorporate them in his model:

> General Qualitative
> General Multiplicative
> Building Qualitative
> Building Multiplicative
> Building Quantitative
> Land Qualitative
> Land Multiplicative
> Land Quantitative

In building a model, one usually starts with the quantitative factors—those characteristics of land or building that can be given a dollar value and that thus will have a direct bearing on the estimated value of the parcel. Then the model is "qualified" using the qualitative and multiplicative terms that enhance or degrade the value of land and building. Finally, the model builder adds those features that affect the value of both land and building at once, such as quality of view or distance from a school.

As an assessor considers the initial values for the coefficients, he or she may be concerned that some coefficients might travel so far, during the feedback iterations on the computer, that they would no longer have plausible values. Suppose, for instance, the qualitative term of aluminum siding proved to treble the value of a house, according to the feedback-derived model. Or suppose a square foot of land in a modest neighborhood proved worth fifteen dollars, so that in effect almost the entire value of a parcel came from its land rather than the building upon it. While such results might be mathematically possible, they are not plausible. The model builder can prevent these extreme examples from occurring, with the Lincoln Institute's SOLIR feedback model, by stipulating hard and soft lower and upper limits on the movement of the coefficients.

Hard limits are those that absolutely cannot be overstepped by a coefficient value. Soft limits are those beyond which travel becomes increasingly more difficult, but not impossible. Coefficients constrained between those limits will tend to remain in the central area where they have the greatest intuitive plausibility. As long as enough coefficients are free to move over a wide enough range, the mathematical integrity of the feedback model will not be compromised, and its explanatory power will be maintained. It is worth adding, however, that in a well constructed model, coefficients usually do not move beyond all plausible bounds. In fact, it is often unnecessary to impose any limits on coefficient movement, unless one wishes to restrict a given value artificially to make a point. An assessor might decree, for example, that the qualitative value of a frame exterior shall be 1.0 exactly, regardless of values that might be assumed by factor levels representing composition siding (on the one hand) or stone (on the other).

To use feedback effectively, it is necessary to know one further detail about the operation of the model. Figure 4 implies that each time a parcel is considered, the model "learns" something from that parcel without "forgetting" what was learned before. That is, the successive parcels have a cumulative effect in "training" the model by progressively modifying its coefficients. The correction factor—the amount by which the model coefficients are changed each time a parcel is considered—is based on the difference between the computed value of a parcel, using the current version of the model, and the actual value derived from recorded sales data. But if that difference were the sole determinant of the correction, then the model would be too "gullible"; like a simple-minded town gossip it would adjust its story to reflect each new source completely, with no regard for information gained from previous encounters.

What is needed is a damping factor—a number indicating the percentage of information contributed by each new parcel or, conversely, the amount of information retained from all previous parcels while correcting in light of each new input. Typically, a user would set the damping factor, which is built into the feedback algorithm, at around 0.1, indicating that ten percent of the information governing each correction would be contributed by the parcel currently being considered.

THE MODEL IN ACTION

With these concepts we can set up a feedback model to examine a series of sales recorded in our database, using our knowledge of neighborhood characteristics and local market dynamics to choose the most likely factors and to set their starting values appropriately. If possible we will use sold parcels that represent all the types of housing and neighborhood to be found in our database. If the properties are heterogeneous, then it is a good idea to include in the model factors accounting for the differences (such as average family income, distance from the city center, or average age of structures); otherwise, there will be too much unexplained variance among the parcels, and the mean error rate of estimation will remain high.

If not enough data exist to distinguish high and low selling properties, then it is better to focus coefficient determination on a single, more or less homogeneous neighborhood, and create separate models for each such area, one at a time.

Figure 5 illustrates the first stage in the construction of a model designed for a set of attribute and sales data on a group of parcels in a small community. Note that many of the columns in the table are blank; they will be

SOLIR   IF QUALITAT   Model Mult. HARD SOFT   # of ..INCOMING DATA VALUES..   **COEF.LIMITS**

FB#(Act)Fac#	Srce	LoLim HiLim	Type	ParA Lower Lower	Case	MinVal	Mean	COV	Coef-Prior	@	%Diff.	Min	# Up
NAME	Proc	LITERAL	DampF	ParB Upper Upper		MaxVal	.Std.Dev.	COV	Coef-Now	L	%Range	Max.	Down
1	27		Ncat	Lquan	1000 5000	0	0	0	0	0		0	0	0
TOTAL ACRES			Cont	.1000	15000 14000		0	0	0	10000	L	0.00	0	0
2	31		Ncat	Bquan	0	0	0	0	0	0		0	0	0
BATH			Cont	.1000	0		0	0	0	2000	H	0.00	0	0
3	32		Ncat	Bquan	0	0	0	0	0	0		0	0	0
SFLA			Cont	.1000	0		0	0	0	15	H	0.00	0	0
4	19		Ncat	Bmult	0 0	0	0	0	0	0		0	0	0
EXTER COND			Cont	.1000	3 0		0	0	0	1	H	0.00	0	0
5	9		Ncat	Bmult	1940 0	0	0	0	0	0		0	0	0
YEAR BUILT			Cont	.1000	20 0		0	0	0	.5	H	0.00	0	0
6	34		Ncat	Bquan	0	0	0	0	0	0		0	0	0
PORCH SF			Cont	.1000	0		0	0	0	5	H	0.00	0	0
*7	35		Ncat	Bquan	0	0	0	0	0	0		0	0	0
PATIO SF			Cont	.1000	0		0	0	0	5	H	0.00	0	0

FIGURE 5: STARTING VALUES FOR A SIMPLE FEEDBACK MODEL

filled in after a coefficient determination run has taken place and the incoming factor values for the parcels in question can be analyzed, along with the fluctuations in coefficient values. The table does specify the type of factor classification for purposes of the feedback model; that is, whether each factor is quantitative, qualitative, or multiplicative and whether it applies to building, land, or both (general). The table also indicates the value of the damping factor, for each factor, and the initial coefficient value.

Setting the coefficient's starting value requires some "art" on the part of the model builder. In contradistinction to multiple regression, which can survey the range of potential factors and identify which ones combine, and in what order, to influence the dependent variable, the feedback model will never consider a factor until the user puts it into the table. Furthermore, while it is theoretically possible to set all coefficient values equal to some arbitrary value (say, 1 or 100), and let the adaptive processes do their work, in practice this procedure is inefficient for two reasons. First, it will probably require longer computer running time to reach a point where the mean absolute percent error of estimation is acceptably small. On a microcomputer, such processing time can be quite significant, even for modest numbers of parcels.

Second, there is no guarantee that the coefficients finally arrived at will make intuitive sense. Mathematically, it makes no difference if a parcel is valued by counting the number of broom closets in the house and multiplying the result by $30,000, so long as the estimated sales price comes reasonably close to recorded sales figures, where these exist. Given no guidance in the setting of initial coefficients, feedback might come up with just such a model, and it might prove to be a good predictor of value. But it would be hard to defend or justify the model to a taxpayer; so, in general, users of the process prefer to set initial values of quantitative factors somewhere near a figure that might be reasonable in a cost model. Model builders who do this find that during coefficient determination the variation in coefficient value, while it might be significant, usually is not so great as to produce absurd-appearing figures at the end.

SOME PERFORMANCE MEASURES

What results can we expect with feedback, and how well does it work in field settings? To achieve convergence—that is, a condition in which the average absolute error does not change appreciably from one iteration to another—anywhere from half a dozen to twenty or more iterations are often necessary. How long these iterations take will depend on the size of the model (the number of factors), the number of parcels being considered, the type of program (i.e., the language in which it is written, and whether it is

interpreted or compiled), and the size and power of the computer being used. A coefficient determination process that took all night, using the
Lincoln Institute's SOLIR program running in interpreted BASIC on a Radio
Shack Model II microcomputer, can be completed in less than an hour on
the IBM PC/AT using a compiled version of the same program. A similar
run with the same size database and the same number of iterations might
be completed in only a few minutes on a minicomputer. Clearly, the available
hardware and software have important implications for the practicality of
feedback as a tool in city and town assessors' offices.

Figure 6 shows how the coefficient values converge over a series of iterations. The vertical axis is the mean absolute percent error of estimation,
figured within each feedback iteration for all sold parcels in the coefficient
determination run. The horizontal axis represents the number of iterations.
The data, comprising properties in a small community in upstate New York,
are typical, in terms of completeness and variance, of the kinds of data encountered in many field settings, and the behavior of the feedback process
is also typical. From an initially high error rate (on the first iteration), there
is a rapid drop to a level below 20 percent. Thereafter the curve begins to
level off, and to fluctuate about an asymptotic line. As the iterations proceed, the fluctuations gradually become less. They also become more nearly
equal in each direction. That is, their second-order differences—i.e., the difference between each peak or valley and the previous peak or valley—
approach zero. (These are graphed in Figure 7.) When they are satisfactori-
ly close to zero, we say the process has converged, and the resulting coefficients may be used in the feedback equation to determine the value of
other, similar properties.

While no precise definition of convergence has been offered, we observe
a further interesting phenomenon at this point: coefficients are now revised
downward about as often as they are revised upward. Previously, an upward or a downward trend would predominate in any one iteration (with the
directions tending to alternate from one iteration to the next). Now a state
of balance is reached in which virtually every property causing an upward
adjustment of coefficients is matched by a countervailing property causing
a downward adjustment. In such equilibrium, fluctuations will continue, but
they will not result in a net lowering of the mean absolute percent error.

The particular model shown here converges at an error level of around
15 percent, which would be too high for satisfactory performance in most
field settings. Model builders need to have ways of examining the sources
of error in an attempt to improve model functioning. The SOLIR feedback
package provides an analytic module that can serve as a useful first step.
It offers, among other tools, the means of constructing a histogram showing the parcels that fall into each of several levels of error. This aids the
user in visualizing the distribution of parcels among error levels, as well

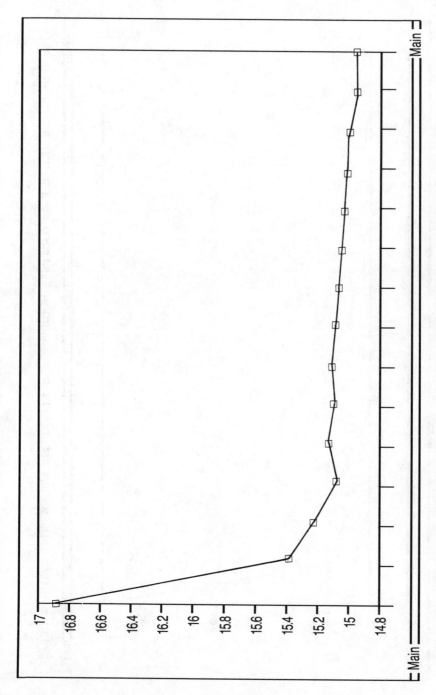

FIGURE 6: MEAN ABSOLUTE PERCENT ERROR OF ESTIMATION (VERTICAL AXIS) GRAPHED AGAINST ITERATIONS

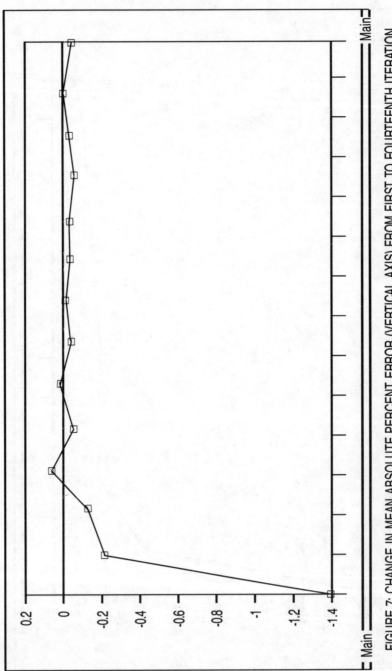

FIGURE 7: CHANGE IN MEAN ABSOLUTE PERCENT ERROR (VERTICAL AXIS) FROM FIRST TO FOURTEENTH ITERATION

as in identifying those parcels in which the estimated value was farthest from the actual value.

The analytic module also produces a scatter diagram in which actual value is plotted against estimated value for each parcel, and each parcel number is printed at the appropriate point on the graph (Figure 8). Outliers can be readily spotted on such a graph, and the model builder can then examine the data to discover, if possible, what additional factors, not included in the original model, might account for the disparity.

Sometimes the answer can be simple and immensely helpful. In the case of the data illustrated above, for example, we discovered that some of the parcels in question were vacation properties, seasonally occupied, and tended to obey quite different pricing rules. When appropriate factors, representing this status, were included in the model as general qualitative terms, the error rates dropped significantly.

At other times the source of the problem can be complex. Inflation produces particular difficulties for the model builder. Moderate rates of inflation, over short periods of time, can be accommodated within the feedback process itself, simply by alternating forward and backward iterations (in order of date of sale), so that tendencies for values to increase with time (and thus for the coefficients to reflect the higher dollar amounts in effect at the end of a period) are counterbalanced by re-exposing the model to earlier sales reflecting presumably lower unit costs.

However, in periods of rampant inflation, the problem is not simply one of spreading error evenly but of fixing a reference point for unit values. Otherwise it can happen that a property will sell for $80,000 on July 1 and a year later an identical property (or even the same one) will sell for $160,000. What is the feedback model to do? The coefficients that produced a correct estimate of value the first time will produce a 100 percent error rate a year later. There is no way, if this trend is typical over a short period in a given neighborhood, that an acceptably low error rate can be achieved.

Instead the model builder must create an artificial or proxy variable representing the effect of inflation on costs, and make this variable one factor of each parcel being considered in the coefficient determination run. Clearly the variable will be based on the elapsed time from some reference point—the base date. It may be exponential rather than linear, if such a function best fits the curve in average property sales over the period in question. But it may also take other matters into account. It is arguable that not all properties react to inflation in the same way. Larger, more expensive properties may inflate more slowly. Properties in neighborhoods undergoing social change may inflate more rapidly. Typical properties, with regularly shaped lots and houses of average size and age, may inflate most rapidly of all, as middle class families hasten to buy so that the inflationary curve will work for rather than against them.

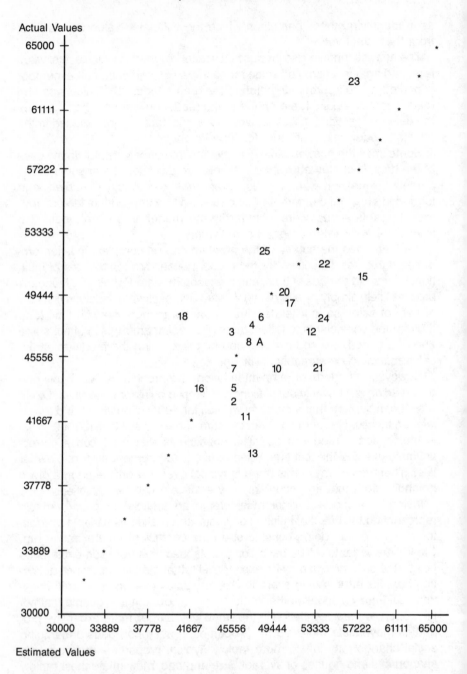

FIGURE 8: SCATTER DIAGRAM SHOWING PLACEMENT OF EACH
PARCEL ON A GRAPH OF ACTUAL VS. ESTIMATED VALUES

The model builder will probably want to cast his proxy variable in a form that will permit it to be used as a feedback general multiplicative or qualitative factor. That is, it will be a number somewhat more than 1, which can be multiplied by the entire value of the property estimated by the rest of the feedback equation. Depending on the database system being used, it can be relatively easy to create such a variable and set it into all affected records; the hard part is determining precisely the uneven and selective effects of inflation in the market one is studying. Once again, there is clear advantage in close familiarity with the neighborhoods being valued.

Everything said so far presumes that markets behave with sufficient rationality to allow mathematical models of pricing to be inferred from sales data with acceptable error rates. On occasion, however, particular properties will not obey the market forces, and when that happens, they can greatly disrupt a process like feedback that works by drawing from each sale some of the information on which the final model is based. Consider the large house that is "sold" to a charitable institution for "one dollar and other good and valuable consideration." If its sales price is entered in the property records as one dollar and it is allowed to become part of the data set on which the coefficient determination run takes place, it will play havoc with the estimation procedure. Even though it is only one property among many, its estimated value will inevitably differ from its actual value by a factor of several thousand percent. The resulting adjustment of the model coefficients, even if modulated by a conservative damping factor, will cause the model to misestimate all the other parcels in the data set rather badly.

Even with less extreme cases where market forces are not obeyed, a similarly disruptive effect can occur. It is thus in the assessor's interest to scrutinize the data before the coefficient determination run takes place, and remove from the database (or inactivate) any parcels that flagrantly violate the normal market process. If all such outliers cannot be identified in advance, the scatter diagram shown in Figure 8 will make any remaining ones obvious, and they can be removed before further runs take place.

CAN WE ESTIMATE A TREND?

Feedback is still a new methodology; all the returns on its effectiveness are not in. It has been used successfully in upstate New York; in Pinellas County, Florida; in Allegheny County, Pennsylvania; and at various other sites around the country. It has been applied mainly to owner-occupied residential properties, but there have been some attempts as well to adapt the model to apartments and to commercial properties. In many cases the pioneers of feedback made it work by programming the algorithm into a large computer. More recently, it has been run on microcomputers as well;

the Lincoln Institute's SOLIR version of feedback represents one of the first truly generic versions of the program, capable of being adapted to a wide range of model types according to the wishes of the user. In this form it is now being taught in modeling courses by the International Association of Assessing Officers.

The most recent versions of feedback to appear on the microcomputer have gone a long way to overcome the major objection to its use for CAMA in a production context, namely its slowness. A compiled or machine language version of the algorithm, running on a 16-bit microprocessor, is capable of sufficient speed to satisfy the needs of at least medium-sized cities.

How to construct the best feedback model is still a matter of art rather than science. Numerous questions remain to be answered. How can the model builder best assure himself that all relevant factors are included in the feedback equation? Is it necessary or advisable to conduct a multiple regression run before using feedback, to reveal which factors have the greatest effect on the dependent variable? What advantages, if any, accrue to the use of dynamic damping, whereby the program is allowed to change the damping factor depending on the degree of convergence currently being achieved by the model? How does a uniform feedback model process a series of different data sets, each definable in terms of its deviation from a normal distribution?

In April of 1985, the Lincoln Institute sponsored a colloquium on feedback attended by key researchers in the field. Their objective was to develop a research agenda to explore, over the next two or three years, the answers to these and related questions. It is certain that while this research goes on, more and more jurisdictions will begin using feedback, at least occasionally, as one method of valuation. If the quest is even partially successful, the users who are active in three or four years will know vastly more about the strengths and limitations of the method than do any of us who were involved in developing the early programs.

Chapter 9

COMPUTERS AND COMPARABLE SALES

Bruce Sauter

Value is an abstract concept of a property's worth different for each individual. When negotiations culminate in a sale price, this indicates that two individuals or parties have reached an agreement as to that particular property's value. Although sale prices may fluctuate around the true market values of property, a sufficient number of sales tends to indicate the consensus of both the buyers and sellers. Thus, through careful verification and analysis, a pattern between location, time, physical inventory characteristics and the typical market values emerges.

Market data is the best evidence of value because it represents the direct actions and reactions of buyers and sellers. However, an individual sale of the subject property cannot, by itself, constitute market value. Even arms-length transactions may be biased toward either the buyer or seller depending upon the degree of willingness and need by either party to buy or sell. Only when supported by other market evidence could a sale be considered evidence of market value. The comparable sales approach involves a realization that the indicated selling prices of individual sales transactions must be analyzed to properly evaluate what the typical market value of the property might be worth.

The advent of computer technology has led to several improvements in the assessor's ability to evaluate the market sales transactions more effectively. First, the use of computers allows the storage and nearly instantaneous retrieval of appraisal data. From floppy disk and hard disks

141

in microcomputers, to mainframes with gigabytes of memory, to the advent of optical and laser disc storage, technology has put us only at the threshold of modern storage capacities. Second, computers have the capability of handling repetitive calculations with great speed. Calculating the most comparable sales from numerous sales in a neighborhood based upon possibly fifty to one hundred data elements may take hours without computers, but only fractions of a second with computers. Finally, large quantities of data can be analyzed with the use of computers in ways never before possible. The routine use of distributional analysis, dispersion, regression, correlation, feedback and scatter diagrams makes objective evaluation of appraisal data possible.

STRATIFICATION

The first step in a market data approach involves analyzing the market of the comparables available. This stratification requires categorizing similar uses of property, size, neighborhood, location and other features. These groupings are critical to the direct sales comparison because the process limits the number of comparable sales available for sales analysis. When many sales are available, such techniques as multiple regression analysis, feedback, or base home approach can be used to develop a general aggregate model of the neighborhood. When limited numbers of sales are available or when refinement into a specialized stratification for a neighborhood is the desired goal, direct sales comparison becomes the optimal technique. Computers are used more efficiently than manual procedures when the comparison of many sales may involve twenty, fifty, or one hundred or more variables. This allows responsiveness in a way that was never before possible in a timely or cost-effective manner.

Stratification usually is the key to defining the most important indicator of value—location. Certain physical and economic elements can indicate a preliminary neighborhood profile. Since the most abundant property use by parcel volume often is residential, these profile indicators may include:

1. Groupings of similar property uses (sometimes but not always related to zoning restrictions).

2. Median net income levels of the residents.

3. General range of values of the residences (a corollary for many other factors).

4. Type of employment of the residents.

5. Natural or man-made boundaries.

6. Access to services (gas, electric, telephone, water, sewer, cable television).

7. Access to facilities (schools, churches, hospitals, shopping facilities, employment).

8. Predominant age and condition of housing.

ADJUSTMENT ANALYSIS

In market analysis, the stratification is the beginning of a search for homogeneity known as comparable selection. The next step would involve further analysis of the neighborhood to isolate non-typical properties known as "outliers". Computers can quickly isolate potential outliers with any of the following techniques:

1. Conforming or non-conforming screening edits.

2. Plots and graphs.

3. Correlation reports.

4. Dispersion reports.

5. Distributional data analysis reports.

Isolating these outliers is important so as not to distort the typical market value indications or value contributions associated with specific physical characteristics.

To take advantage of the computer capacity to repeat arithmetic calculations on data at great speed, the relationship between specific physical characteristics and the true market value as approximated by the individual transaction sale price must be defined in the form of an equation. If the market model equation is improperly defined, the results will not reflect the typical value contributions of the model components but rather the statistical coincidental relationships which reflect the defined data patterns. The use of a model formula which allows an interaction of additive and multiplicative terms or a hybrid model in which new variables are generated from combinations of existing variables to simulate such interactions are usually the most successful.

Even when model equations are defined properly to reflect the market actions and reactions, the possible interaction of closely correlated terms may cause problems. Although the aggregate effect on market value predictions using a model formula may be insignificant, the decomposition of the model would lead to a misrepresentation of the individual contributions of the colinear terms. Both the improper model definition and the colinearity problem may have a major effect on the comparable sales prediction process. If these problems could be eliminated, the subsequent use of the unit price contributions associated with each term would be the optimal adjustment to be made to sales prices to compensate for corresponding differences in inventories.

The analysis of value adjustments is critical to the process of direct sales comparison. Since no two properties are exactly identical, an adjustment must always be made for any differences in time, location and physical or economic factors with a corresponding compensation made to the indicated sale price. Sometimes the properties do not reflect all the characteristics evident in the other properties which comprise the neighborhood. In such cases, additional adjustments may be manually determined based upon appraisal judgment or adjustments can be assumed to be similar to those present in other comparable neighborhoods.

SELECTION OF COMPARABLES

Once value contributions are determined, the process of selection of the most comparable sales to an individual subject property begins. Properties in the comparable sales approach utilize the basic principle of substitution which states that no property has a value greater than that for which a similar property can be purchased within a reasonable time period that can meet the buyer's demands. Computers can be used to search similar property in two different ways. The first method is basically an iterative matching process. Sales inventories are compared with the subject inventory for one or more data characteristics. Only the sales which most nearly share the same physical attributes of the subject inventory's specified characteristics are considered comparable. Depending upon the number of sales available and the required level of similarity desired, the number of characteristics being matched may be adjusted to develop larger or smaller subsets of comparable sales.

The second method of comparable selection is more complex. This method involves assigning a weight or the equivalent of penalty points to the relative differences in characteristics. This is known as a dissimilarity index. A complex weighting system may involve many subtle weights sharing relativity importance to each other. Setting up a dissimilarity index requires decisions to be made which would provide answers to the following questions:

1. In the same hypothetical neighborhood, two sales exist, similar in certain ways to the subject property. One has the identical size

but is of a different building style, while the other is the same building style but a much different size. Which is more comparable?

2. If the size parameter is varied on a continuous basis, at what point does one sale become more comparable than the other? This decision reflects on the relative similarity.

Certain variables, such as neighborhood or building style, which seldom have an orderly linear relationship, are assigned a binary weight which is added to the dissimilarity index total whenever the subject and sale are different. Other variables, such as square feet of living area, age or sale date, are generally treated as continuous weights. Continuous weights are assigned proportionally to the absolute difference in each inventory item found between the subject property and the sale. If two sales were similar to the subject with the first being five years older and the second being ten years newer, the first would probably be considered the most comparable.

A form of the metric formula used in most selection weighting procedures is:

$$\sum_{j=1}^{k} [W_j | (X_{sj} - X_{ij}) |]^n$$

where j is the property attribute, k is the number of property attributes being weighted, W_j is the weight assigned to attribute j, X_{sj} is the value of the subject property's j^{th} attribute, i is the sale being compared, X_{ij} is the jth attribute of sale i and n is the exponent (if $n = 1$ this becomes the city block metric method, if $n = \frac{1}{2}$ this becomes the Euclidean metric, or distance, method).

While the use of regression coefficients as selection weights (W_j) does have the advantage of weighting attributes relative to their contribution to sale price, this may disproportionately distort the influence of colinear attributes. While creating a convenient starting point, the integration of binary weights for neighborhood or building style, which may not be among the model coefficients, is essential to the weighting scheme.

Most computers from micros to mainframes use a comparable selection routine which incorporates an iterative search routine. Many major mass appraisal firms and municipalities use a hybrid of both an iterative search on major influences, such as neighborhood and building style and the detailed discrimination of user-defined dissimilarity index weighting system. It is important to note that the relative ratios are more important than the actual weights used. If one system uses 1000 points for neighborhood, 200 points for building style and 2 points for SFLA and a second weighting system assigns 15,000 points to neighborhood, 3000 points to building style and 30 points for SFLA (all else being equal) it will always select identical comparables in the exact same order.

Further expansion on this concept has led to the use of the dissimilarity index to weight the average of the adjusted sale prices of the comparable sales selected and put more emphasis on the sales which are weighted, whose average tends to minimize the differences and thus the subjective adjustments made to the actual sales prices.

COMPARABLES REPORT

The main by-product of the computer-generated comparable sales estimate is the comparable sales report. This can clearly display the subject property and the most comparable sales selected, individual inventory items (for property identification, selections analysis, adjustment analysis, and value estimation), adjustments, selection weights, and value estimates. This report is useful for preliminary testing and evaluation, field review, public relations and even defense of values. Since this closely parallels the traditional manual reports, it is an excellent communication medium.

Many systems exist which may vary the number of comparables selected, how they are selected, how adjustments are made (user specified, regression, feedback, base home), how comparable reports are generated (online, batch, selectively upon request), whether individual adjustments are shown, how many comparable sales are shown on the comparables report, report formatting flexibility, potential use of cluster and discriminate function analysis, override and turnaround documents, use of index files for rapid comparable reselection, as well as the hardware, software and protocol required to operate the program.

ESTIMATION REFINEMENT

Value estimates are an expression of the most probable sale price as of a given point in time within a reasonable range of error. It is important to identify potential error generation and minimize the error in order to derive the best possible estimates. Assuming that all precautions have been taken to insure accurate data and independent adjustment coefficients, the comparable sales method allows more responsiveness to specific submarket influences and trends, as opposed to the central tendency of most market models. Secondly, the use of the weighted average of the most comparable sales tends to indicate the typical value derived from direct market transactions while minimizing any potential error evolving from the use of generalized model coefficients as adjustments.

Valid sales which may indicate outliers relative to normal market transactions may be screened through use of a dissimilarity index ratio or an estimate dispersion analysis. High variances in dissimiliarity ratios or estimates would indicate non-comparable sales (or a unique subject property).

The model estimate, the weighted average of the most comparable sales or any of the most comparable sales is a valid estimate of market value. The median estimate is usually as good an estimate as any other and it can be arguably supported by any of the others. The highest estimate and lowest estimate would tend to indicate a relative confidence parameter around the selected value estimate.

CONCLUSION

Computer usage through the comparable sales approach can shorten the calculation time, improve mathematical accuracy and increase equity of decision making for comparable selections and adjustment of sale prices, and create user-defined reports for field and office analysis, disclosure purposes and administrative analysis. In general, comparable sales with the use of computer assisted mass appraisal methods improves the efficiency, equity and cost-effectiveness over manual methods.

Chapter 10

THE USE OF COMPUTERS IN FEE APPRAISAL PRACTICE

Gene Dilmore

Appraising is a multi-discipline discipline. The fee appraiser utilizes elements of a number of other disciplines, including accounting, investment analysis, econometrics, architecture, land planning, statistical analysis, and demographics, among others.

The availability of the reasonably low-cost microcomputer has enabled the appraiser to adapt analytical procedures from this variety of disciplines which in the 1960s would not have been temporally or financially feasible. The major distinction between the utilization of the computer by the assessor and the fee appraiser is probably quantitative rather than qualitative: the fee appraiser is working with a much smaller database, and at a given time is usually focusing on the value of one specific property, possibly (but not necessarily) being able to apply more resources to the analysis of that particular property.

GETTING STARTED

The fee appraiser just entering the world of computerized information processing is confronted with a bewildering array of choices as to hardware and software. The best way to narrow the range of choices is to work backward from your objectives: Why do you want a computer? What do you want to do with it that you cannot do as well or cannot do at all manually? Then find out what kind of programs are available for these uses, and last, what kind of computer will run them.

One basic rule is that you should always buy more capacity than you can imagine ever needing, and, if practical, a computer capable of further upgrading. And do not succumb to the "first kid on the block" syndrome; you may well find that you have a beautiful machine with racing stripes and dual exhausts, for which no programs have been written. You may also find that the company folded right after selling your computer, leaving you with no support or maintenance.

My wisdom in this regard was acquired the hard way; i.e., I am a burnt child. The popularity of the IBM PC is due to the security of ownership of a widely accepted standard machine. It has nothing to do with the quality of the computer, which most computer users agree is considerably below the level of many other machines. But the user feels safe in assuming that IBM will not enter Chapter 11 in a year or so, as so many computer companies do. Moreover, the great majority of new programs are being written first for the IBM, then for the Macintosh, then for CP/M machines (possibly), and considerably later, if at all, for other makes.

Why do you want a computer?

Do you simply want to produce appraisal reports more efficiently, moving sections at will and loading in repeated sections? If so, all you really need—at first—is a good word processing program. You will most likely find, though, that new uses keep occurring to you as you go along. The major categories of uses may be classified as (1) word processing, (2) accounting, (3) database management, (4) investment analysis, (5) automated approaches to value, and (6) forecasting and statistical analysis.

Range of Applications

What can you do with a computer that you cannot do, or cannot afford to do, without one? To give you a feel for some of the possibilities, let's just look at a few examples of computer use as reflected in a few recent reports in my own office. The discussion to follow will be keyed to the exhibits.

Exhibit 1 shows a page from the market comparison approach in the appraisal of a small office building, with a portion of the explanation of the methodology. Since this explanation would be similar for a number of reports, a prototype market comparison chart section is produced with Wordstar (Sorcim) and simply "read in" to the current report. When the figures vary from the prototype market comparison section, they are just typed in right on top of the old numbers, with no need to spend time on tabulation and formatting.

In some cases, I start the report by loading in an outline report and expanding; in others, the property type is often similar enough to read in the most recent report of that type, and make changes directly to this complete report. Wordstar is probably the most widely used word processing program. It works well, and does most of the things the user needs it to do, except for indexing, outlining, and footnoting, for which supplementary programs have to be installed. As is the case with the majority of manuals in the software industry, the Wordstar manual is a model of noncommunication. Several individuals have written inexpensive paperbacks, however, which tell you what Micropro's manual fails miserably to convey. A good one is *INTRODUCTION TO WORDSTAR*, by Arthur Naiman, published by Sybex.

EXHIBIT 1 — WORD PROCESSING

In this step, the properties are assigned comparative quality points for the major property attributes. Points are in accordance with qualitative ratings, as follows:

Rating	Points
Excellent	26
Good	20
Average	15
Fair	13
Poor	10

The major categories of property attributes considered, and the relative weights assigned to each, were as follows:

Effective Age	10%
Space Quality (Construction, Design, Finish)	80%
Marketability (Accessibility, Linkages to Clients and Customers, Amenities)	10%
	100%

Each assignment of quality points is given its appropriate weight, and the weighted quality points totaled. For example, for Sale No. 1, a rating of Poor in regard to Age (10 points, x 10% weight); a rating of Average in regard to Space Quality (15 points, x 80% weight); and a rating of Good in regard to Marketability Factors (20 points, x 10% weight) gives a total of 15.00 quality points.

The report section shown is an application of the quality point rating method of applying the market comparison approach to probable price, first proposed by Dr. Richard U. Ratcliff, implemented and elaborated by Dr. James A. Graaskamp, with some modifications by me. In this technique, adjustments are first applied to the sales for the property attributes which are quantitative in nature, such as time of sale, size, and financing terms.

After the quantifiable adjustments are made, the appraiser then selects the major property attributes which are qualitative in nature, and assigns preliminary weights to each attribute. Next, each comparable sale is given a rating measured in points. In some cases, where the land component of the sales varies widely, as is often the case with suburban office buildings and restaurants, the land value is deducted, so that we then work with the price per square foot for improvements only. In other cases, particularly for apartment properties, land value is generally proportionate to the number of units, so there is no need to separate land and improvements, and we use price per square foot of improvements, including land value.

The example is taken from the report on a small, inexpensive office, in a neighborhood which reflects a quite weak market.

Exhibit 2 shows a later page from the market comparison analysis. The calculations were done with Supercalc2 (Sorcim), and the spreadsheet printed to disk rather the printer. Then the spreadsheet output was read into the appropriate section of the report as it was written with Wordstar. The spreadsheet most used on the IBM PC is 1-2-3 (Lotus).

This exhibit shows the analysis of sales of 4 small offices comparable with the subject property. The four sales were selected from a spreadsheet file which contained 18 small office sales, by quickly deleting the other 14 columns. Here, we first adjust for time of sale, then subtract land value from each sale to obtain the price per square foot of improvements. Then each property is assigned quality point ratings for the three major property attributes. Next, the weighted points are summed to give a total quality point rating for each comparable, and the price per square foot of improvements is divided by the rating, giving a combined variable of price per point per dollar per square foot. Then the mean and standard deviation are calculated.

Exhibit 3 shows the same page from Supercalc, showing the formulae that you actually have in it, rather than the output. You can see that the set of calculations for the first sale can be loaded in, and, with a keystroke or two, replicated all the way across to the last sale, so that they are really entered only once. The Time Adjustment for example, in Row 6, is automatically calculated for every sale. When you want to change the effective date and the rate of appreciation, you only enter the new date, and the new rate of time adjustment in the column for Sale No. 1, and copy it into all the other cells in this row.

EXHIBIT 2 — SPREADSHEET OUTPUT

Sale #	1	2	3	4
Date	82.33	82.33	82.5	82.92
Price	$105,000.00	$191,200.00	$101,750.00	$100,000.00
Adjustments:				
Time	1.0584	1.0584	1.055	1.0466
Size	1	1	1	1
Financing	1	1	1	1
Other	1	1	1	1
Adjusted Price	$111,132.00	$202,366.08	$107,346.25	$104,660.00
Less Land: SF	$10,000	18,000	7,000	7,050
	$4.00	$3.25	$4.00	$3.50
(Adjd for time) =	$42,336.00	$61,916.40	$29,540.00	$25,824.86
Improvements	$68,796.00	$140,449.68	$77,806.25	$78.835.15
NRA	1,996	4,100	2,500	2,650
Price Imps per SF	$34.47	$34.26	$31.12	$29.75
Effective Age Rating	10	15	15	15
x 10% Weight	1	1.5	1.5	1.5
Space Qual Rtg	15	15	13	13
x 80% Weight	12	12	10.4	10.4
Mktbility Rtg	20	13	15	13
x 10% Weight	2	1.3	1.5	1.3
Tot Quality Points	15	14.8	13.4	13.2
Price per Point/Pr SF	$2.30	$2.31	$2.32	$2.25
Mean				$2.30
Standard Deviation				.03
Coeff of Variation				.01

The spreadsheet programs, such as Supercalc, 1-2-3, Visicalc, and Multiplan, have made possible many more comprehensive analyses, and testing of alternatives, which would previously have taken more time than could possibly have been allotted to them. A change in one figure or formula is instantly reflected throughout the whole spreadsheet.

The present trend appears to be for more appraisers to type their own reports on the computer rather than dictate them. For those who may not already know how to touch-type, a suggestion: Why not get one of the inexpenive programs like Smartkey (FBN Software, distributed by Lifeboat Associates) which, along with utilities with which to save lengthy keyboard routines and put them into effect with a keystroke, also has the Dvorak keyboard in its files. Load it in and lo, your keyboard is the efficient Dvorak keyboard rather than the Qwerty, which was deliberately designed to slow down the typists. That way you can learn, from the beginning, to touch type much faster and with less energy, as the letters are distributed evenly between your hands.

EXHIBIT 3 — SPREADSHEET INPUT

	B	C	D	E
1				
2	Sale #	1	3	4
3	Date	82.33	82.5	82.92
4	Price	105000	101750	100000
5	Adjustments:			
6	Time	1+(85.25-C3)*.02	1+(85.25-D3)*.02	1+(85.25-E3)*.02
7	Size	1	1	1
8	Financing	1	1	1
9	Other	1	1	1
10	Adjusted Price	C4*C6*C7*C8*C9	D4*D6*D7*D8*D9	E4*E6*E7*E8*E9
11	Less Land: SF	10000	7000	7050
12	@	4	4	3.50
13	(Adjd for time) =	C6*C11*C12	D6*D11*D12	E6*E11*E12
14	Improvements	C10-C13	D10-D13	E10-E13
15	NRA	1996	2500	2650
16	Price Imps per SF	C14/C15	D14/D15	E14/E15
17	Effective Age Rating	10	15	15
18	x 10% weight	.1*C17	.1*D17	.1*E17
19	Space Qual Rtg	15	13	13
20	x 80% weight	.8*C19	.8*D19	.8*E19
21	Mktbility Rtg	20	15	13
22	x 10% weight	.10*C21	.10*D21	.10*E21
23	Tot Quality Points	C18+C20+C22	D18+D20+D22	E18+E20+E22
24	Price per Point/Pr SF	C16/C23	D16/D23	E16/E23
25	Mean			AVERAGE(C24:E24)
26	Standard Deviation			.03
27	Coeff of Variation			.01

Dedicated word processors (machines designed solely for the one purpose) may have a little advantage for high-volume production, but for most appraisers, a good word processing program accomplishes the same task, and leaves the computer usable for any other types of programs.

A good spelling checker greatly expedites the completion of a report. Even if you do not misspell any words, everybody makes typos; a program such as Word Plus (Oasis) spots them immediately, and corrects them. You can add any special or jargon words to your dictionary so that they will not be labelled as errors.

Exhibit 4 shows the final page of the market comparison section, where the subject property is assigned a rating, and land value added in for a total indication of most probable price, along with explicit expression of a confidence interval for the indication. Since the procedure is similar for the same classification of property, I simply typed the new numbers on top of the the old ones in the previous report that I had read into this file.

EXHIBIT 4 — PARTIAL "BOILER PLATE"

Most probable price for subject from this approach is indicated as follows: Effective Age is assigned a Poor rating of 10 points. Space Quality is assigned a Fair rating at 13 points, and Marketability Factors are assigned a Poor rating at 10 points, reflecting the weak market in the area. Therefore, 10 points x 10%, plus 13 points x 80%, plus 10 points x 10% = 12.40 points. Multiplying x $2.30 per square foot per point = $28.52 per sq. ft. x NRA of 2,950 sq. ft. = indicated value of improvements:

(R)	$84,000
Plus Land	$27,000
Probable Price Indication	$111,000

A standard deviation for subject is computed as follows: standard deviation of $0.03 x 12.40 points = $0.37 x 2,950 sq. ft. = a standard deviation for subject, in dollars, of plus or minus (R) $1,100.

Applying the standard deviation gives a 68% confidence interval of plus or minus one standard deviation, of:

$109,900 to $112,100, with most probable figure of $111,000

Exhibit 5 shows the output from a program which tests every possible combination of weights that could be applied to the ratings of the property attributes. The preliminary weights, 20% for Effective Age, 35% for Space Quality, and 45% for Marketability Factors, were those found appropriate for the parent spreadsheet template with 18 sales.

For this new, smaller sample, the weights were tested by the program, with a new set of weights being selected. For the four sales, there were 125 possible combinations, 19 of which totalled 100% and were therefore potential candidates for the optimal weighting combination. With 6 property attributes being considered, the number of possible combinations of weights is 15,625. We can easily see, then, that use of the computer enables us to utilize a powerful technique of market comparison (totally independent of any "income approach" figures), which would not be feasible otherwise.

In Exhibit 6, we see the output from a program which is used regularly in appraisals of vacant land. When we have adjusted our comparable land sales for every characteristic we can think of excepting size, we enter the "semi-adjusted" prices per acre or square foot, along with their sizes. The program then applies seven curves to the data, finding the one which is the best fit to the sales, defined as the curve which produces the smallest coefficient of variation.

In this instance, the original coefficient of variation of 37% is reduced to 12% by application of the "75% curve." (This means that a doubling in

EXHIBIT 5 — SELECTING WEIGHTS FOR ATTRIBUTES

**** 4 Small Offices ****
# ATTRIBUTES = 3
ATTRIBUTE NAMES, PRELIM WEIGHTS
   Effective Age   20
   Space Quality   35
   Marketability   45
OF OBSERVATIONS = 4
OBSERV. # 1 1732 Oxmoor PRICE 34.47
          Effective Age   10
          Space Quality   15
          Marketability   20
OBSERV. # 2 3500 Montgy Hwy PRICE 34.26
          Effective Age   15
          Space Quality   15
          Marketability   13
OBSERV. # 3 2717 S 19 P1 PRICE 31.12
          Effective Age   15
          Space Quality   13
          Marketability   15
OBSERV. # 4 2720 S 19 St PRICE 29.75
          Effective Age   15
          Space Quality   13
          Marketability   13
THE MATRIX:
  15 70 15
   5 60   5
  10 65 10
  20 75 20
  25 80 25

MEDIAN	=	2.29312
MEAN	=	2.28842
STANDARD DEVIATION	=	.0388686

WEIGHTS:

Effective Age	=	15
Space Quality	=	70
Marketability	=	15

FINAL RESULTS:

NUMBER OF COMBINATIONS	=	125
NUMBER OF COMBINATIONS ADDING TO 100%	=	19
MEDIAN	=	2.30643
MEAN	=	2.29726
STANDARD DEVIATION	=	.0307231

WEIGHTS:

Effective Age	=	10
Space Quality	=	80
Marketability	=	10

size of a tract would reduce its *unit* price to 75% of the price for the smaller tract.) In reducing the dispersion of the partially adjusted data, the size adjustment factors have accounted for *68%* of the remaining variation in the per acre prices.

This sort of technique, again, is not practical without automation of the numerous calculations.

EXHIBIT 6 — SIZE ADJUSTMENT FACTORS

ADJ FACTORS FOR	75%	77.5%	80%	82.5%	85%	87.5%	90%
# 1	0.74	0.77	0.79	0.82	0.84	0.87	0.90
# 2	0.91	0.92	0.93	0.94	0.95	0.96	0.96
# 3	1.05	1.05	1.04	1.04	1.03	1.02	1.02
# 4	1.82	1.70	1.59	1.49	1.40	1.32	1.24
# 5	1.25	1.22	1.19	1.16	1.13	1.11	1.09
# 6	0.98	0.99	0.99	0.99	0.99	0.99	0.99

MEAN OF PRICES = 27281.3
STANDARD DEVIATION OF PRICES = 10008.2
COEFFICIENT OF VARIATION = .366853

MEAN OF PRICES ADJ'D W/ 75% CURVE = 28100.3
STD DEV = 3235.4
COEFF OF VAR = .115138

MEAN OF PRICES ADJ'D W/ 77.5% CURVE = 27894.7
STD DEV = 3662.39
COEFF OF VAR = .131293

MEAN OF PRICES ADJ'D W/ 80% CURVE = 27725.6
STD DEV = 4277.9
COEFF OF VAR = .154294

MEAN OF PRICES ADJ'D W/ 82.5% CURVE = 27588.2
STD DEV = 4982.32
COEFF OF VAR = .180596

MEAN OF PRICES ADJ'D W/ 85% CURVE = 27480.9
STD DEV = 5709.68
COEFF OF VAR = .207769

MEAN OF PRICES ADJ'D W/ 87.5% CURVE = 27396.6
STD DEV = 6462.21
COEFF OF VAR = .235876

MEAN OF PRICES ADJ'D W/ 90% CURVE = 27336.4
STD DEV = 7199.27
COEFF OF VAR = .263358

Exhibit 6 (*continued*)

RECAP OF SIZES & PRICES

SALE#	SIZE	PRICE	FACTOR	ADJ PRICE
1	1.84	$45,245.00	0.74	$33,485.70
2	3.00	$29,792.00	0.91	$27,008.20
3	4.31	$27,132.00	1.05	$28,587.70
4	16.00	$16,050.00	1.82	$29,145.70
5	6.50	$21,266.00	1.25	$26,572.60
6	3.65	$24,203.00	0.98	$23,801.80
SUB	3.80			

Exhibit 7 is the output of a spreadsheet calculation which compares the net present worth of the costs to the client of (1) buying an existing office, (2) buying a lot and building a new office, and (3) continuing to rent their present location. All of the costs were calculated on a square foot basis, for fair comparison, with rents increasing at 5% annually, and all costs of occupancy discounted to present worth at 10%, the rate available to the client, a semi-public agency. This printout compared building or leasing with the terms of a particular offering, indicating that buying this property would be just a little less expensive than continuing to rent, but considerably cheaper than building.

As we located various properties fitting the client's criteria (preferred location in a certain part of town, 10,000 to 12,000 square feet, not too much partitioning, etc.), I loaded the previous template, gave it a new name to keep the property identities separated, and keyed in the specific terms of the new prospective property, replacing the numbers for the previously analyzed property. Thus, once the basic template was designed, the comparative analysis of each new property was only a matter of a few minutes.

EXHIBIT 7 — BUY/BUILD/LEASE

Buy/Build/Rt Analysis
RENT:

Year	0	1	2	3	4	5
Rent		9.31	9.78	10.26	10.78	11.32
Prsnt Wth		8.46	8.08	7.71	7.36	7.03
Tot PW						

BUY:	31
+ Renov	15
	46

Exhibit 7 (*continued*)

Down Pmt	11.5					
Debt Serv		5.00	5.00	5.00	5.00	5.00
Op Exp		3.50	3.78	4.08	4.41	4.76
Tot Exp	11.50	8.50	8.78	9.08	9.41	9.76
Prsnt Wth	11.50	7.73	7.25	6.82	6.43	6.06
Tot PW						
Less PW Rever						
Net PW						
BUILD:	64					
+ Renov						
	64					
Down Pmt	16					
Debt Serv		6.95	6.95	6.95	6.95	6.95
Op Exp		3.50	3.78	4.08	4.41	4.76
Tot Exp	16.00	10.45	10.73	11.04	11.36	11.72
Prsnt Wth	16.00	9.50	8.87	8.29	7.76	7.27

Buy/Build/Rt Analysis
RENT:

Year	6	7	8	9	10
Rent	11.88	12.48	13.10	13.76	14.44
Prsnt Wth	6.71	6.40	6.11	5.83	5.57
Tot PW					69.26

BUY:
+ Renov

Down Pmt					
Debt Serv	5.00	5.00	5.00	5.00	5.00
Op Exp	5.14	5.55	6.00	6.48	7.00
Tot Exp	10.14	10.55	11.00	11.48	12.00
Prsnt Wth	5.72	5.42	5.13	4.87	4.62
Tot PW					71.55
Less PW Rever	$46-6%-Mtge		79.29%	6.77	
	x PW Factr			.3855	2.61
Net PW					68.94

BUILD:
+ Renov

Down Pmt					
Debt Serv	6.95	6.95	6.95	6.95	6.95
Op Exp	5.14	5.55	6.00	6.48	7.00
Tot Exp	12.10	12.51	12.95	13.43	13.95
Prsnt Wth	6.83	6.42	6.04	5.70	5.38
Tot PW					88.07
Less PW Rever	$83.20-6%-Mtge		79.29%	27.46	
	x PW Factr			.3855	10.59
Net PW					77.48

Exhibit 8 shows a portion of the output from a stepwise multiple regression analysis program, testing the significance of the property attributes which appeared to be relevant, and obtaining a prediction of the monthly rent for a proposed apartment project. Step 2 in the regression was the optimum run, with the highest R^2, or adjusted coefficient of determination (the percentage of variation in the rents which is explained by the regression equation), and the smallest standard error.

In this printout, for each run, we have the critical t values for the standard levels of significance, so we can see immediately whether a variable's coefficient is significant at the level of significance we select. For example, in Step 2, size of the apartment (in square footage) is significant at the 5% level, but not at the 1% level, since its t value is in between the critical magnitudes for these two levels. The judgmental variable, quality rating, with a t value of 6.77, while a 1% significance level requires a t value of only 3.36, is obviously extremely significant.

This result points up a factor which becomes quite apparent after running a substantial number of regressions: Screening and testing all sorts of variables continually reinforces the fact that qualitative or judgmental ratings of property attributes are generally *at least* as significant as directly quantifiable or physically measurable attributes (size, age, number of baths, etc.). We can infer from this that appraisers should put more effort into rigorously logical methods of quantifying their qualitative judgments about a property, such as the quality point rating technique shown in Exhibits 2 and 3. This way, we have the best of both worlds, measurements where measurements are applicable (45,000 square feet of net rentable area, 17 years old), and "gut feelings" where they are appropriate ("Hmm...that solid wood paneling and high-priced carpet probably means that I should classify the quality of interior space as Good rather than Average...so, I'll rate it at 20 points instead of 15.").

Another feature of this application of regression analysis is that we can not only derive a prediction of possible rent levels for the apartments, but can make a probability statement as to the range of error, using the standard error of forecast, which is the proper measure for the probable error range of a prediction, rather than the standard error of estimate.

We can also learn, after trying a number of variables, that some of the property attributes that we at first thought were important, are probably not as significant as we had thought, so that we should concentrate our analysis on the really significant variables. For example, in this analysis, we tried 5 variables: Size, Number of Baths, Overall Quality of Space, Number of Amenities, and Location Rating. The regression indicated, however, that our best rent prediction could be made with only two variables—Size and Quality Rating.

EXHIBIT 8 — STEP 2 OF MULTIPLE REGRESSION ANALYSIS

STEP # 1 VARIABLE # 3 ENTERS
STANDARD ERROR OF ESTIMATE: 33.0459
COEFF OF VARIATION   : .118021
ADJ'D COEFF OF DETERMINATION (R^2):   .904501
COEFF OF ASSOCIATION (A STATISTIC):   .690971
DEGREES OF FREEDOM   : 9
F RATIO   : 95.7129
CONSTANT TERM   :-426.307

VARIABLE	COEFFICIENT	STD ERROR	t VALUE	BETA
3 QUAL	858.494	87.751	9.7833	.95606

CRITICAL t VAL @ .01 LEVEL OF SIGNIFICANCE = 3.2504
CRITICAL t VAL @ .05 LEVEL OF SIGNIFICANCE = 2.2628
CRITICAL t VAL @ .10 LEVEL OF SIGNIFICANCE = 1.8336
FOR SUBJECT: CONSTANT -426.307
VARIABLE # 3 QUAL .8 X 858.494 = 686.796
PREDICTED RENT = 260.489
STD ERROR OF FORECAST = 34.5729
COEFF OF VARIATION = .132723
90% CONFIDENCE INTERVAL = 197 — 323.881 MOST PROBABLE 260.489
80% CONFIDENCE INTERVAL = 213 — 308.311 MOST PROBABLE 260.489
****
STEP # 2 VARIABLE # 1 ENTERS
STANDARD ERROR OF ESTIMATE: 25.2046
COEFF OF VARIATION   :   .0900164
ADJ'D COEFF OF DETERMINATION (R^2):   .944445
COEFF OF ASSOCIATION (A STATISTIC):   .764299
DEGREES OF FREEDOM : 8
F RATIO   : 86.0009
CONSTANT TERM   :-404.641

VARIABLE	COEFFICIENT	STD ERROR	t VALUE	BETA
1 SIZE	.145936	.0533915	2.73332	.298034
3 QUAL	663.164	97.9101	6.7732	.738531

CRITICAL t VAL @ .01 LEVEL OF SIGNIFICANCE = 3.3559
CRITICAL t VAL @ .05 LEVEL OF SIGNIFICANCE = 2.3066
CRITICAL t VAL @ .10 LEVEL OF SIGNIFICANCE = 1.8600
FOR SUBJECT: CONSTANT -404.641
VARIABLE # 1 SIZE 918 X .145936 = 133.969
VARIABLE # 3 QUAL .8 X 663.164 = 530.531
PREDICTED RENT = 259.86
STD ERROR OF FORECAST = 26.3997
COEFF OF VARIATION = .101592
90% CONFIDENCE INTERVAL = 211 — 308.964 MOST PROBABLE 259.86
80% CONFIDENCE INTERVAL = 223 — 296.741 MOST PROBABLE 259.86
****
STEP # 3 VARIABLE # 2 ENTERS
STANDARD ERROR OF ESTIMATE: 25.6518
COEFF OF VARIATION : .0916137
ADJ'D COEFF OF DETERMINATION (R^2): .942456
COEFF OF ASSOCIATION (A STATISTIC): .760116

Exhibit 9 is the printout of a portion of a program designed to test the internal consistency of an appraisal's final results, whether it is your own appraisal, or someone else's which you are reviewing.

The first part shows the input data in regard to final value estimate, net income, and so on. Using this input, we derive the subsequent measures which are *implied* by the conclusions, based on the final value estimate. In this instance, taken from the review of a recent actual appraisal, we see that the valuation has implied a negative equity dividend, lower than acceptable debt service coverage, and a breakeven point which says the property would have to show better than 100% occupancy.

Testing the stated parameters of the cost approach against the final value estimate, we find that the proposed project has appreciated before it is even built. The appraiser, in his after-tax cash flow projection, did not state

---

EXHIBIT 9 — ANALYSIS OF INTERNAL CONSISTENCY
ANALYSIS OF CONSISTENCY IN FIRST YEAR RATIOS:

WITH VALUE CONCLUSION OF	$940,000
GROSS POTENTIAL RENTAL OF	$136,320
NET OP INC OF	$85,068
MTGE OF	$705,000
INTEREST RATE OF	0.1450
MTGE TERM OF	30 YRS
PMTS PER YR OF	12
AND OP EXP OF	$45,800

GAM =	6.90
OAR =	0.0905
EQUITY DIVIDEND =	-.2737
DEBT SERVICE COVERAGE =	.821139
BREAKEVEN RATIO =	1.0959
EQUITY PAYBACK PERIOD =	%-12.68

WITH TYPICAL D/S COVERAGE OF 1.2
LENDER'S SAFE OVERALL RATE = 0.1323
(LOAN RATIO * CONSTANT * COVERAGE)

WITH THESE STATED COST APPROACH PARAMETERS:	
FINAL VALUE:	$940,000
LAND VALUE:	$64,000
REPLACEMENT COST NEW	$847,290
Implied APPRECIATION is	3.39%

WITH:	
OCCUPANCY RATE	0.9600
EXPENSE RATIO	0.3500
GROSS INCOME GROWTH RATE	0.1000
EXPENSE GROWTH RATE	0.0600
PROJECTION PERIOD	10

IMPLIED NET INCOME GROWTH RATE: 0.1175

an assumption as to the rate of growth of the net rental, but did state his projections of growth of gross income and of expense. From the inputted factors, we can derive the implied growth in net income which, in this instance, is 12%. If he had *known* that he was implying this rate of growth in net income, the appraiser might have revised some of his assumptions.

These figures, of course, do not *necessarily* mean that the conclusions of the appraisal are incorrect; they are merely guidelines reflecting the level of internal consistency in the report, and only serve as caution flags, so that we know to check this portion of the report a little more closely.

In Exhibit 10, the first section shows the input to a cash-flow program. Since the output down through the internal rate of return calculation is routine, the next section shows only the portion of output subsequent to the internal rate of return figures.

Nine of the columns give ratio analyses, which are primarily used as tests of the consistency of the assumptions in regard to the various measures entered into the program. If we see a sudden jump in one or more of these ratios, or if one of them has unacceptable results (breakeven ratio of 110%, payback of total investment in 3 years, debt service coverage of 50%, etc.), we know to go back and examine our original assumptions.

The columns after "Payback of Equity, After-Tax Basis" include modified internal rates of return, with reinvestment assumptions, Financial Management Rate of Return, and Net Present Value. The third from last column is Annualized Net Present Value, or the amount by which the cash flow could be reduced each year, and still produce the desired rate of return (11.21%).

Dividing these figures by the equity gives the next column, the Risk Absorption ratio, which gives a measure of risk in comparison with either a second investment, or the subject property with alternative assumptions. The final column is the Profitability Index, the present worth of the cash flows and reversion, divided by the equity investment.

EXHIBIT 10—CASH FLOW

OFFICE BLDG - DR SAMUEL

INPUT DATA SUMMARY
MORTGAGE INFORMATION FOR LOAN 1

INITIAL MORTGAGE	$750,000
MORTGAGE INTEREST RATE	13.5%
MORTGAGE TERM	25 YEARS
MORTGAGE CONSTANT	13.9877%
PERIODIC PAYMENT	8742.33
ANNUAL PAYMENT	$104,908

Exhibit 10 (continued)

TOTAL DEPRECIABLE ASSETS	$747,500
LAND	$202,500
TOTAL INVESTMENT	$950,000
TOTAL DEBT	$750,000
INITIAL EQUITY	$200,000
ORDINARY INCOME TAX RATE	50%
CAPITAL GAINS TAX RATE	20%
SAFE RATE FOR MOD IRR	9.21%
REINVEST RATE FOR MOD IRR	9.21%
MARKET REINV RATE FOR FMRR	11.21%
MINIMUM REINV AMT FOR FMRR	$150,000
DISCOUNT RATE FOR NPV	11.21%

DEPRECIATION INFORMATION FOR ASSET 1

AMOUNT DEPRECIABLE	$747,500
DEPRECIABLE LIFE	18 YEARS

DEPRECIATION METHOD....STRAIGHT LINE

NON-RECURRING 1ST YR EXP 0
COMMISSION RATE ON RESALE 6%
VACANCY RATE 5%
GROWTH RATES (% COMPOUNDED ANNUALLY)
PROPERTY VALUE: CURRENT NOI @ 10%
POTENTIAL GROSS INCOME 5
OPERATING EXPENSES 6

	POTENTIAL GROSS INCOME	VACANCY ALLOWANCE	MISC INCOME	OPERATING EXPENSES
1	131,544	6,577	0	23,448
2	138,121	6,906	0	24,855
3	145,027	7,251	0	26,346
4	152,279	7,614	0	27,927
5	159,892	7,995	0	29,603
6	167,887	8,394	0	31,379
7	176,281	8,814	0	33,261
8	185,095	9,255	0	35,257
9	194,350	9,718	0	37,373
10	204,068	10,203	0	39,615
11	214,271	10,714	0	41,992
12	224,984	11,249	0	44,511
13	236,234	11,812	0	47,182
14	248,045	12,402	0	50,013
15	260,447	13,022	0	53,014

YEAR	OAR	EQ DIV	COV	BRKEVN	EXP RATIO	GIM	PYBKTOT
1	10.69%	-1.69%	96.77%	97.58%	18.76%	8.76	8.81%
2	11.20%	0.73%	101.38%	93.95%	18.94%	8.34	18.04%
3	11.73%	3.26%	106.22%	90.50%	19.12%	7.95	27.71%

Exhibit 10 (*continued*)

4	12.29%	5.91%	111.28%	87.23%	19.30%	7.57	37.83%
5	12.87%	8.69%	116.57%	84.13%	19.49%	7.21	48.45%
6	13.49%	11.60%	122.12%	81.18%	19.67%	6.86	59.56%
7	14.13%	14.65%	127.93%	78.38%	19.86%	6.54	71.21%
8	14.80%	17.84%	134.01%	75.73%	20.05%	6.23	83.41%
9	15.50%	21.18%	140.37%	73.21%	20.24%	5.93	96.18%
10	16.24%	24.67%	147.03%	70.82%	20.43%	5.65	109.57%
11	17.01%	28.33%	154.01%	68.56%	20.63%	5.38	123.59%
12	17.81%	32.16%	161.31%	66.41%	20.83%	5.12	138.27%
13	18.66%	36.17%	168.95%	64.38%	21.02%	4.88	153.65%
14	19.54%	40.36%	176.95%	62.46%	21.22%	4.65	169.75%
15	20.46%	44.75%	185.32%	60.63%	21.43%	4.43	186.62%

YEAR	PYBK EQBT	PYBKEQAT	MOD IRR	MOD W/REIN	FMRR
1	-1.69%	8.56%	8.06%	8.07%	8.07%
2	-0.97%	18.19%	16.35%	16.09%	16.09%
3	2.29%	28.93%	18.76%	18.10%	18.10%
4	8.21%	40.82%	19.68%	18.65%	18.65%
5	16.90%	53.88%	20.04%	18.70%	18.70%
6	28.50%	68.16%	20.15%	18.53%	18.53%
7	43.15%	83.69%	20.12%	18.27%	18.58%
8	60.99%	100.50%	20.04%	17.97%	18.31%
9	82.17%	118.62%	19.92%	17.66%	18.03%
10	106.84%	138.08%	19.77%	17.35%	17.75%
11	135.17%	158.90%	19.62%	17.05%	17.48%
12	167.32%	181.10%	19.48%	16.77%	17.22%
13	203.49%	204.69%	19.32%	16.50%	16.97%
14	243.85%	229.68%	19.17%	16.24%	16.73%
15	288.60%	256.06%	19.04%	15.99%	16.51%

YEAR	NPV	ANN NPV	RA	PI
1	-5,655	-6,288	-3.144%	97.17%
2	18,206	10,661	5.330%	109.10%
3	40,329	16,564	8.282%	120.16%
4	60,812	19,689	9.845%	130.41%
5	79,745	21,691	10.845%	139.87%
6	97,220	23,120	11.560%	148.61%
7	113,323	24,212	12.106%	156.66%
8	128,138	25,087	12.543%	164.07%
9	141,743	25,808	12.904%	170.87%
10	154,215	26,417	13.209%	177.11%
11	165,627	26,938	13.469%	182.81%
12	176,046	27,388	13.694%	188.02%
13	185,537	27,778	13.889%	192.77%
14	194,161	28,118	14.059%	197.08%
15	201,976	28,414	14.207%	200.99%

Exhibit 11 is the output of a program that partitions the internal rate of return reflected by the cash-flow analysis in Exhibit 10. This analysis assumes a ten-year holding period. The first section shows the portion of return contributed by each of the seven components. For this property, it is significant that 25% of the return is generated by projected tax shelter of other income (Component No. 7).

In the lower section, we assign acceptable rates to each component. Return of the original equity appears fairly certain, so a rate a little below the base rate of 19.81% is assigned. Equity growth from appreciation in value, we judge to be a bit riskier, so we assign a rate of 20%.

The particular client, at the end of our projected 10-year holding period, may well not be in sufficiently high an income bracket to benefit from tax shelter of other income, so this component of return, constituting 25% of the total internal rate of return, is assigned a rate of 23%. The resulting weighted internal rate of return, giving individual attention to each of the seven components of the income stream, is 20%. The next step, of course, involves simply re-running the cash-flow analysis to obtain the price indicated by an internal rate of return of 20%.

Exhibit 12 shows an automated and probabilistic version of James A. Graaskamp's well-known Backdoor Approach. If you follow the program lines from 1600 on, we are saying that the justified investment in this property is equal to: (Line 1600) Net rentable area x Rent Rate, x Occupancy Rate, minus operating expenses; (Line 1601) divided by Debt Service Coverage Ratio; (Line 1602) divided by Annual Constant; (Line 1603) plus (equity ratio x net income) divided by desired equity return.

The earlier lines say that we are assigning Low, Most Likely, and High estimates for the four key variables: Potential Gross Rent at $9, $10, and $11, respectively; Vacancy Rate at 3%, 5%, and 10%; Operating Expenses at $3, $3.46, and $4; and Annual Constant based on likely terms obtainable at .135340, .139877, and .149222. The data are entered as pairs: midpoint, and implied standard deviation. We are also assuming (Line 50) an 80% correlation between Gross Potential Rental and Operating Expenses.

The program then constructs 100 random combinations within these specified limits, for 100 possible outcomes, printing out a frequency distribution, with a mean justified investment of $1,141,720.

This was a program run for my own satisfaction, and not included in the appraisal report. You will find that many programs are useful in this manner. For example, I may run half a dozen regressions, just to screen for significant variables (property attributes), and one of the Monte Carlo programs to test the boundaries of probable price under my preliminary assumptions, without mentioning any of them in the appraisal report.

You will also find that many useful programs have a surprisingly low

EXHIBIT 11 - COMPONENT CAPITALIZATION

THIS PROGRAM PARTITIONS THE INTERNAL RATE OF RETURN AND THE EQUITY
INVESTMENT INTO THEIR 7 COMPONENTS:
1. Return of original equity investment.
2. Growth of equity from amortization.
3. Growth of equity from value appreciation.
4. Value of cash flows at 1st year level.
5. Growth (decline) of cash flow stream.
6. Tax shelter of subject's cash flow.
7. Tax shelter of external income.

For subject, the return is partitioned as follows:

Component	Equity -$	Eqty -%	IRR
1. Return orig eq	$32,927	0.1646	0.0325
2. Eqty grwth frm amort	$12,618	0.0631	0.0125
3. Eq grwth (decl) frm appr	$52,173	0.2609	0.0516
4. Csh flw 1st yr lvl	-$7,160	-.0358	-.0071
5. Grwth (decl) of csh flw	$35,075	0.1754	0.0347
6. Tax shltr of sub csh flw	$24,509	0.1225	0.0242
7. Tax shltr of other inc	$50,256	0.2513	0.0497
	$200,397	1.0020	0.1981

The individual IRR's assigned to the components reflect rates adjusted upward for risk.
The final weighted IRR is a risk-adjusted internal rate of return.

Component	% of IRR/Equity	IRR	Weighted IRR
1. Return orig eq	0.1646	0.1800	0.0296
2. Eqty grwth from amort	0.0631	0.1850	0.0117
3. Eq grwth (decl) frm appr/dep	0.2609	0.2000	0.0522
4. Csh flw 1st yr lvl	-.0358	0.1981	-.0071
5. Grwth (decl) of csh flw	0.1754	0.2000	0.0351
6. Tax shltr of sub csh flw	0.1225	0.1800	0.0221
7. Tax shltr of other inc	0.2513	0.2300	0.0578
			0.2013

cost—just the time to key them in. A number of computer magazines
regularly print program listings which you are free to copy and use; that's
why they were published. Some books, too, include useful programs. The
Monte Carlo program used for Exhibit 12, for example, is one of several
in *PROBABILISTIC MODELS*, Volume Four of the Mathematics for Management Series, by Springer, Herlihy, Mall and Beggs (Richard D. Irwin, Inc.).

EXHIBIT 12 - JUSTIFIED INVESTMENT MONTE CARLO APPROACH

SAMPLE MEAN = 1,141,720
STD DEVIATION = 54,269
SMALLEST VALUE = 1,026,220
LARGEST VALUE = 1,279,220
FREQUENCY DISTRIBUTION

FROM	TO	FREQ	PCT	CUM PCT
0	227,994	0	0	0
227,994	455,988	0	0	0
455,988	683,982	0	0	0
683,982	911,976	0	0	0
911,976	1,139,970	51	51	51
1,139,970	1,367,960	49	49	100
1,367,960	1,595,960	0	0	100
1,595,960	1,823,950	0	0	100
1,823,950	2,051,950	0	0	100
2,051,950	2,279,940	0	0	100

10 DATA 10,.33,.05,.0117,3.46,.17,.139877,.0023
49 DATA 0,0
50 DATA 1,3,.8
89 DATA 0,0,0

1600 LET V1 = 20780 * X(1)*(1-X(2))- 20780 * X(3): REM = NOI
1601 LET V2 = V1/1.2: REM = AVAIL FOR DEBT SERVICE
1602 LET V3 = V2/X(4): REM = MTGE
1603 LET V4 = V3 + (.25*V1/.08): REM = JUSTIFIED INVESTMENT
1604 LET Y = V4

Exhibit 13 shows one of the many useful forecasting tools. Adaptive filtering is a technique applicable to time series which do not show a seasonal element. It, in effect, keeps using its previous errors to revise the current estimate. I use it, for example, to project a current estimate of population in between the times when new data become available.

The exhibit shows forecasted and actual figures for the population of Jefferson County, Alabama, with figures projected for 5 years. In actual practice, I normally use this technique for a one-year projection.

In Exhibit 14, we are attempting to project single-family residential building permits in Huntsville, Alabama. Despite its exotic name, Holt's technique is often the best forecasting tool for some sets of data. The analyst enters one smoothing constant to reduce randomness, and a second smoothing constant for trend. Initial values for level data and for trend are also entered. Note that here, the technique must cope with a bad year, 1981, when permits dropped 50%. Nevertheless, by 1984 the program has closed in on the actual data. The resulting forecasted figures are consistent with those derived by other approaches to the problem.

EXHIBIT 13 — POPULATION PROJECTION WITH ADAPTIVE FILTERING

TIME PERIOD	ACTUAL VALUE	FORECASTED VALUE	FORECASTING ERROR	PERCENTAGE ERROR
1972	638600			
1973	646900			
1974	645900	646790	-890.125	-.137812
1975	646700	650463	-3762.63	-.581819
1976	650600	650362	237.938	.036572
1977	657000	652727	4273	.650381
1978	658200	657909	290.563	.044145
1979	662600	661733	866.875	.130829
1980	672900	664551	8349.13	1.24077
1981	675500	671947	3552.69	.525935
1982	674000	678438	-4437.5	-.658383
1983	675000	678991	-3990.81	-.591232
1984		678739		
1985		681124		
1986		684205		
1987		686955		
1988		689889		

MEAN SQUARE ERROR (MSE) = 1.26707E + 07
MEAN ABSOLUTE DEVIATION (MAD) = 2554.27

EXHIBIT 14 — BUILDING PERMIT PROJECTION WITH HOLT'S TWO-PARAMETER SMOOTHING

TIME PERIOD	ACTUAL VALUE	FORECASTED VALUE	FORECASTING ERROR	PERCENTAGE ERROR
1976	637			
1977	752	711.005	40.995	5.45146
1978	764	751.062	12.9377	1.69342
1979	517	789.749	-272.749	-52.7561
1980	794	813.469	-19.4695	-2.45208
1981	340	849.805	-509.805	-149.943
1982	720	860.350	-140.35	-19.493
1983	1015	889.016	125.984	12.4122
1984	942	931.314	10.6858	1.13437
1985		967.874		
1986		1003.90		
1987		1039.93		
l988		1075.95		
1989		1111.98		

MEAN SQUARE ERROR (MSE) = 41356.1
MEAN ABSOLUTE DEVIATION (MAD) = 125.886

Exhibit 15 shows a forecast of employment in Huntsville, Alabama. Total employment and manufacturing employment are shown separately. Then a 5-year forecast is made for total employment, using double exponential smoothing to reduce the noise in the data. This technique is often appropriate when the data display a strong positive or negative trend.

This program is one in a package called SmartForecasts, by Smart Software. Some other good statistical and forecasting packages useful to the appraiser include: The Statistician, by Quant Systems, Forecast Plus, by Walonick Associates, and S.P.S., by Southeast Technical Associates. Your best bet in selecting software is to first decide just what you want to accomplish with a computer. If you do not intend to be doing any forecasting or statistical analysis, for example, but, say, only financial analyses, then you do not necessarily need programs such as those used for Exhibits 13, 14, and 15.

EXHIBIT 15 — EMPLOYMENT PROJECTION WITH DOUBLE
EXPONENTIAL SMOOTHING

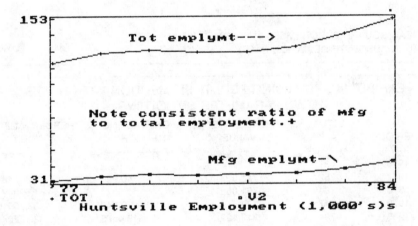

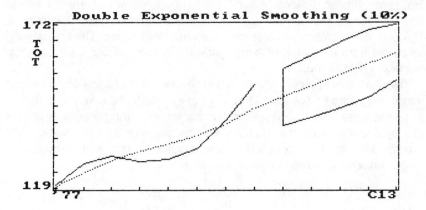

Forecasts of V1 TOT using DOUBLE EXPONENTIAL SMOOTHING with weight = 10%.
Based on 8 cases: C1 '77 to C8 '84.

Approximate 90% Forecast Interval

Time Period	Lower Limit	FORECAST	Upper Limit
C9	139.189	148.309	157.430
C10	141.913	151.888	161.863
C11	144.825	155.467	166.109
C12	148.073	159.046	170.020
C13	153.524	162.625	171.727

GETTING UNDERWAY

I should think that the first indispensable programs that you would want to acquire would include a good word processing program, such as Wordstar, XY Write II Plus, Multimate, or Freestyle, and a good spreadsheet program, such as Lotus 1-2-3 or Supercalc. Once you become accustomed to solving problems with a spreadsheet program, you will find more and more problems that require no other programs for their solution.

Visit your local computer stores and buy several of the computer magazines, such as Byte, Microcomputing, PC World, Creative Computing, Infoworld, Computer Shopper, and Personal Computing, for a few months, and you will develop an idea of the array of hardware and software available. Some of the reviews of computers and new programs tell you things about them that the manuals do not mention.

Two good compilations of information on software are: (1) "Real Estate

Applications Software Directory," compiled by the Texas Real Estate Research Center, College of Agriculture, Texas A & M University, College Station, Texas 77843, and (2) "An Annotated Directory of Statistical & Related Microcomputer Software for Socioeconomic Data Analysis," available from the Dept. of Agricultural Economics, MSU, East Lansing, Michigan 48824-1039.

The examples of output shown in this chapter are just a few of the several score programs I have found useful in my own practice. You should find out what other local appraisers are using, remembering that most people are loyal to the hardware and software that they are currently using. Also browse around in the computer stores and in the computer magazines, to get an idea of what is available.

CONCLUDING EXHORTATION

A few rules of thumb: Buy hardware from a source which can service it. When ordering software, call; do not write. And ask whether the program is on the shelf and ready to ship. You would be surprised how many software vendors run advertisements to bring in the money to finance *writing* the program. You might even be surprised to learn how many phones have already been disconnected by the time the ad appears. Pay by credit card, not a check, unless you do not mind the two-week wait for your check to clear.

Take advantage of the considerably lower prices of the discount houses for software, unless you are really concerned about technical support. But do not count too heavily on customer support from most (not all) of the original sources. If you plan to do some of your own programming, be skeptical, if not downright cynical, about the rave reviews of all sorts of miscellaneous languages in the periodicals; introducing a new language every six months increases advertising revenues. May I suggest 'True BASIC' (distributed by Addison-Wesley)?

And remember the basic rule: Buy machines and programs that are already popular. You can bet that the first few users helped in the debugging, resulting in later versions. In other words, with hardware, be the third kid on the block, and with software, always buy Version III.

Chapter 11

DATA COLLECTION AND DATA ADMINISTRATION

T. Robert Kitchen

The purpose of this chapter is to provide information and guidelines in the collection of data for the purpose of real property valuation with the assistance of a computerized mass appraisal system. This chapter discusses the tasks that need to be reviewed in order to properly plan for and execute a data collection project.

When I am asked what the three most important aspects of computer assisted valuation are, I quickly reply, "people, software and data."

The data collection phase of a mass appraisal project will consume the most time and be the largest single cost component. Failures in the data collection phase will put the entire project in jeopardy. Most of the time, the data failures are the result of personnel problems and/or shortcomings in the software. People, software and data must work in unison in order to accomplish a successful project.

GENERATING INFORMATION

I think we would all agree that the purpose of collecting data is for providing information. Many times, the terms data and information are used interchangeably, but they are different.

Sound information can only be generated from the correct manipulation and analysis of quality data. Manipulation of non-quality data will only

173

produce misinformation and cause extensive public relations and confidence problems.

Quality data collection and data administration cannot be compromised. Quality means accurate and current. The information generated will not just be for the appraiser, but will also be for non-technical people such as local officials and the public. Therefore, proper manipulation of data for generating information must also be reported intelligently.

DATA SOURCES

Data for computer assisted valuation can come in both existing forms and from new collections. Maps, assessment rolls, sales, building permits, and property record cards are but a few of the potential existing sources of data. Before you use any of these data sources, be sure of their quality. Generally, existing property characteristics that have not been computerized have not been adequately maintained and are out of date.

You will find that most property characteristics will have to be collected by visiting the property and recording the data on forms designed for data collection.

IN-HOUSE OR HIRE A CONTRACTOR

Regardless of who does the original data collection, you will be responsible for the continued maintenance. This chapter does not address the merits of doing the original collection *in-house* or by a *contractor*. The chapter does lead you through all the major steps describing the work to be performed. After you have finished this chapter, I think you will find yourself in a better position of being able to answer the question, "In-House or Contractor?"

PLANNING YOUR DATA COLLECTION

If you have spent time doing careful planning and have looked at all aspects of what is involved with data collection, your project will have a greater chance for success.

Every jurisdiction is different, but you can learn from those who have completed a data collection project. Therefore, the first element in planning would be to contact jurisdictions who are similar to yours and discuss their data collection project. At this stage you also might want to elicit outside assistance in preparing a plan with recommendations.

The next few segments of this chapter will address project components that need to be reviewed during planning. In your own project you will have to review each task and establish your own plan. The important part of planning is to address all these tasks before a project starts because they are all interrelated and must mesh together.

DATA CHARACTERISTICS AND SOFTWARE

Your first review of data characteristics and software should be done together. Many good data management software packages exist and you should not reinvent programs—purchase one that will fit your needs and run on your hardware. Some software is very rigid and does not allow you to tailor data characteristics and the coding of each element. You are advised to stay away from rigid software. The best software to obtain is one that allows for some flexibility by incorporating in tables those elements you want to have available. Newer software now gaining popularity, especially at the microcomputer level, is completely generic and lets you establish your own data elements and edit criteria.

There are no fixed rules as to which data elements you should collect and maintain. You will find that the data you will need to collect and maintain can be categorized as follows:

— *parcel identification and location*: map identification, street address, school district and other important geographic references
— *control and auditing information:* collector's ID, date collected, source of collection, interior inspection code and, where necessary, estimated data code
— *site and neighborhood characteristics*: property classification, type of neighborhood, traffic, utility services, etc.
— *sales data*: most recent sales date and price plus a valid sale indicator
— *land information*: parcel size and, for agricultural property, a breakdown of the land areas into land value groups
— *main improvements*: exterior and interior components such as building size, age, condition, style, number of rooms, number of baths, etc.
— *other improvements*: such as garage, swimming pool, barn, etc.

Existing data, valuation software and appraisal approaches to be used will also dictate which data elements you will require.

A pilot project using the software and various data elements is one way to narrow down the elements you need. It is better and safer to collect too much rather than too little. It is relatively easy to drop data you do not need later, but it is expensive to go back to each property to collect additional data you may have missed. A pilot project can assist in balancing between too much and too little.

EXISTING DATA

If you have existing data on manually-maintained forms or property record cards and you have confidence in that data, then, by all means, utilize it in your project.

One way to save time and money when good data exists is to take the existing data and enter into the computer all the characteristics according to the new coding standards being established for the data elements.

After that phase has been done, all data should be edited for accuracy and reasonableness. Next, verify the data by visiting each property and add new elements that need to be collected.

Following this you would proceed with property owner review as discussed later in this chapter.

FORMS AND MANUALS

Different forms will have to be designed for the major types of properties: residential, farm, commercial. Portions of the forms will be similar and other sections will be quite different. The commercial form will generally be the most complex due to the variety of commercial properties. Usually, these different forms are easily identified by different colors.

Forms design must consider field use, office control and the ease of entry into the computer. The draft forms should be reviewed by each of these groups for comments and suggestions before being finalized.

The items to be field-collected should be established by the categories listed in the data characteristics and software section of this chapter. Within each category, the elements should facilitate orderly recording by arrangement in an acceptable order for the field data collector.

The codes on the forms to be entered into the computer need to be clearly identified without a data entry operator having to make decisions. Usually, each data element has a description plus a code. Both need to be easily identified. Many times the descriptions are in bold print and the space for codes to be recorded are organized in a column. An example of this might look like the following:

___STYLE (RR raised ranch, CL colonial, R ranch, CC cape cod)
___ROOMS
__CONDITION (1 = poor, 2 = good, 3 = excellent)
_____YEAR BUILT

This form should also have room for including a sketch of the property, a place to write notes, and a place for the signature of the property owner. The signature is to verify that a data collector visited the property, not to verify the accuracy of the collection.

Good forms design enables easier training for field, office and data entry personnel, provides for accurate and consistent field recording, allows for simple and orderly office calculations and reviews, and allows for conversion to computer form in an accurate and rapid method.

Manuals should be prepared at the same time that forms are designed as both have to be a major part of data collection training. The form and data element descriptions are part of the manual. Pictures, illustrations and examples should be used whenever possible. In addition to the manual, a one-page reference guide should be prepared for quick reference in the field for special instructions and codes that might be required that have not been incorporated on the form.

FIELD INSPECTIONS

One of the important considerations of data collection involves the control of forms between the office and the field. Manageable groups of properties, say 200 forms, should be provided to a field supervisor and that person is responsible for returning all of the batch back to the office. The batch should have some geographical reference, such as one route, a neighborhood, a map section, etc. This makes control easier.

Each data collector and supervisor should have visible identification badges and local law enforcement personnel should be aware that data collectors are in specific parts of a jurisdiction. Where security dictates, data collectors should go in teams of two.

Each data collector should visit a set number of properties from the batch and also be responsible for call-backs. If, after two visits, no one is available, the characteristics should be estimated and so noted on the form.

Field supervisors should be randomly reviewing completed work. At the beginning, for new data collectors, the supervisor may spend a few days working with each person and checking work carefully. Gradually, the amount of spot checking can be reduced or, if work is not accurate, additional training or release from the project may be necessary. Also, in some projects, the supervisors are responsible for the coding of site and neighborhood subjective characteristics. This provides a greater degree of consistency for such elements. Each field crew normally consists of one supervisor and four to six data collectors.

One important key to accurate field data collection is close supervision. Another important consideration is that the field work needs to be put in computer form as quickly as possible. This will provide for timely computer edits and can point out data collection problems and/or inconsistencies.

DATA ENTRY

Sometimes the planning and preparation for data entry is set aside with an attitude of "We can worry about how to get it into the computer later on—no problem." That type of posture usually leads to a problem and creates project difficulties.

The ability to get your data into the computer system accurately and timely should be a major objective during data collection planning.

There are basically four different methods of data entry. Your existing resources, location of equipment and the development time you want to spend up front will, in part, determine the best approach for your project. I now want to share with you the four methods.

1. Batch Data Entry

This involves keying the data from the forms and building the data file by batches. Equipment used today allows for the editing of data as it is being keyed. Control reports are established when the main data file is updated with each batch. Many times, the batch data entry process requires the most time because of other workload demands being put on the data entry staff and the recycling of corrections.

2. On-Line Data Entry

This is similar to the batch process. The major difference is that the data file is dynamically updated. Editing at the terminal is mandatory for this type of entry. Both the initial entry and all subsequent maintenance can be performed using the same terminal screen designs. A major consideration in using an on-line approach for the initial entry would be the volume of forms coming in from the field and the demand you will be putting on both the human and machine resources. In some situations the on-line process will result in files being updated quicker than with batch, but if there is competition for terminals and machine time, the responsiveness of an on-line approach may not be timely during the initial program. One compromise used successfully in many projects is to do the voluminous entry for the initial data collection by batch and all subsequent maintenance on-line.

3. Portable Computers

If your data is being collected in an area located away from the main computer system, the use of handheld or portable devices should be investigated. In one of our applications in New York State, we have been using 50 handheld computers for entering the field data from the forms and transmitting this data over telephone lines to our computer system. By using these devices, we have accomplished two objectives: field data has a higher degree of reliability, and the data is reaching our main computer system much quicker. Accuracy has improved because of the extensive edit checks that have been included in the portable device and the field person is doing his own correcting at the point of collection. Timing has improved because the field person is always transmitting data at least weekly. Previously, the movement of forms back to the office and batching for centralized data entry could take as much as two months before a file was correctly updated. The use of handheld devices requires front-end planning, software development, testing and training. In our experience, the field people have accepted this process and like being more in control of their product.

4. Optical Scanning

In some areas of the United States, data collection projects have successfully utilized a mark sense type of optical scanning form. The coding of each element is accomplished by using a pencil to darken the appropriate coded node for each element, similar to exam scoring systems. Like the portable terminal, the process requires significant front-end planning and testing. More than any other process, the forms design is the critical path. The use of a mark sense form puts more emphasis on what the form must look like for acceptable machine use rather than for the convenience of the field data collector. Mark sensing is a very accurate and rapid method of getting data into the computer. This process eliminates the need for a human to key the data. While the field collection and recording may be a little slower, the rapid conversion to computer form provides for an accurate and timely process.

All data entry approaches need to be well thought-out, should be capable of edits at the time of entry, and allow for computerized data that is timely for your project. Once data is in the computerized system, more extensive editing should take place to check for logical and reasonable relationships between data items. While a 10-room house and 1,000 square foot area may each be within acceptable ranges, the relationship between these items at an average of 100 square feet per room may not be logical. Data entry would normally allow both items to reach the computer and more extensive computer editing should "kick-out" this illogical relationship for further review.

COMPUTERIZED EDITS

I touched upon the need to have the computer system capable of more extensive inter-data element comparisons. The editing capabilities should be closely reviewed when you are selecting the software system. Edits should not be predetermined and hard-coded in the computer programs. The edits and relationships between data items should be defined by the user at execution time. All of these inter-field edits should result in producing warning reports and should not remove data items from the file. Some systems allow for a series of "flags" to reside on a record in the file whereby the flag can be set to accept valid data relationships that are outside the edit range. In that way you can establish reasonable edit tests and not worry about the unique properties with valid data outside of the edit ranges.

PROPERTY OWNER REVIEW

An additional method of reviewing data as to accuracy is to have the property owner review certain data items that have been collected.

This can best be accomplished by mailing owners a list of the major quantitative data items collected. Instructions should accompany the data inventory list. I would not recommend that subjective data items be included on the inventory list. Trying to explain the differences in subjective responses can add confusion to the inventory mailer. Stick with items like number of rooms, number of baths, year built, and building size. These can easily be explained to the owner and the owner can check for accuracy.

When you have complex commercial properties, the mailing to the owner should not be a list of data items, but an invitation for the owner to make an appointment to visit the office to review the collected data.

Property owners should be invited to return their data mailer to the office and/or call the office with comments. Some comments may require that an appointment be made to visit the property and recollect the data or make corrections. This is especially true if the original data was estimated.

It has been my experience that making the data visible to the property owners can be a very positive public relations move and can bring credibility to the project and increase the confidence in the project. The review of the data before a value is established also makes later valuation reviews easier. It takes away the argument at assessment reviews that, "The data is all wrong!"

This visibility of the data and the project should be high on your "to do" list during data collection planning.

The software system you choose should have the ability to include the date the data was mailed to the owner. Also, as a follow-up, if corrections are made as a result of the owner review, a corrected mailer should be sent to the owner.

The property owner review process can "backfire" if the data shown to the owner does not contain corrections suggested by the owner and if you do not have a follow up procedure.

SALES VERIFICATION

Properties are going to sell and it is important to be able to capture the inventory at the time the property sold and establish a file of just valid sales. The process of building a sales file must begin at the start of your project with the most recent sale of the property, within a couple of years.

The layout and design of the sales file should be identical to the "all property file." The sales file can be accumulated over time and can contain multiple sales for the same property. Periodically, the sales file can be purged of older sales that are no longer required. Normally, about three years of sales are maintained in the file.

The best way to verify a sale is to make an appointment to visit the new owner. At that time, the selling price and data inventory can be validated. Upon returning to the office, the "all property file" can be updated and the sale can be transferred to the sales file. If the sale is not valid, update the inventory file, put an invalid sale code in the file and do not move the data to the sales file.

CONTINUED MAINTENANCE

It almost goes without saying, "maintenance of your data is a continuous process required to protect your original investment."

The basic trick in maintenance is *do not get behind*. You will never catch up.

The techniques required in establishing the initial data file should also be used to maintain the data. As new properties are built, the same forms used for original collection should be used to collect the new property characteristics.

There are many different events signaling that maintenance may be required:

- building permits
- demolition
- new construction
- fires
- sales of properties

Each jurisdiction has different procedures that signify an event has taken place and each event must have a maintenance procedure.

About every five years, it is advisable to send to each property owner a list of the major inventory items as previously described in the property owner review section.

ANSWERS TO QUESTIONS YOU'VE ALWAYS WANTED TO ASK!!

Should I take pictures of the property?

Yes. This is a worthwhile investment. With today's technology, you should seriously investigate having your pictures established on an interactive laser video disc. A video disc, such as the disc produced in the City of Rochester, can be used for multiple purposes. It is a very important tool in public relations. A video disc can be a cost effective process for your CAMA project.

Should I look for software that can accept the sketch so that the sketch can be maintained on the computer?

Sketch vectoring consumes more time during the initial program, requires additional data entry and demands a closure in order to work. Many software packages offer sketch vectoring as an option.

If you want to maintain sketches in the computer, make sure you thoroughly test the software before beginning your project. Older properties with many corners and juts will require careful inputting of vectors. Newer houses that are simply rectangular in shape require less effort. Personally, I think it is an expensive overhead that does not pay for itself.

How many properties can a data collector do in one day?

Where properties are close to each other, such as in a city or a subdivision, about 20 properties per day is a good target.

In rural areas where there are more farms and where more travel time between properties is required, the target may be closer to 12-15.

The procedures you develop and amount of data you collect will also determine the average number of properties per day.

If no one is at home, when should the data collector return for the second visit?

Early evening and weekends are the best times to schedule "call-backs." If no one is at home on the second visit, the data characteristics should be carefully estimated.

I realize there is a lot of work involved in data collection. What is really the most economical method—an in-house or a contractor project?

If you really understand the work and have experienced staff that can be used full time as supervisors for data collectors, an in-house project can be considered. However, I would observe that this is probably a rare occurrence and, therefore, I would recommend that an experienced firm be hired for most projects.

Experience in handling a data collection project is a major factor in making sure mistakes are not made. Mistakes can be very costly.

Should data collection be done over a short span of time or spread out?

Time is money. The shorter the period, the better. Shorter times also allow you to establish the maintenance program more quickly. Manpower availability and seasonal weather conditions will dictate data collection elapsed time.

SUMMARY

Enough said! By now I hope you have an appreciation of the major tasks that must be considered for a successful data collection project including continued maintenance.

At the beginning of this chapter, I indicated I felt very strongly about three important aspects of computer assisted valuation. In closing, let me reiterate these three factors:

People
Software
Data

Data collection is a challenge and must be done correctly the first time through. When not accomplished correctly during the initial project, more time, more money and expanded public relations are necessary. Usually, failures during data collection stop the project. Spending time at the beginning in planning and understanding what you are about to do can get your project off on the right foot so that you do not have to worry about redoing data collection a second time.

I hope this chapter does at least one thing for you and that is leave you with the impression that the focal point of a mass appraisal project is data collection!

Chapter 12

INTEGRATION OF LMS AND CAV DATA SYSTEMS

Richard Almy

The use of land-related information is so ingrained in the human experience that it is sometimes difficult to appreciate how valuable systematically collected and readily accessible land data can be. However, land data systems—whether rudimentary or sophisticated — have always been an integral part of the land title recordation and property taxation functions of government and, more recently, have become a part of the land use planning function as well. When computers capable of efficiently storing and processing masses of land data became available to larger units of government in the late 1960s, forward-looking officials recognized the potential value of multipurpose, computerized data systems. This chapter is about the integration of two types of land data systems: those used in property tax administration, especially in computer assisted valuation (CAV), and those used in land management (LMS).[1] The rationale for integrating systems and the obstacles that must be overcome will be discussed. Strategies for achieving successful integrations and places to look for guidance will be suggested.

---

1. In this chapter, neither CAV nor LMS systems will be defined precisely, although more precise definitions would be important in other contexts; see Angus C. Hamilton and Ian P. Williamson, "A Critique of the FIG Definition of Land Information System," a paper presented at an international symposium on land information systems, "The Decision Maker and Land Information Systems," 15-19 October 1984 in Edmonton, Alberta, sponsored by Commission 3 of the Federation Internationale des Geometres.

RATIONALE FOR INTEGRATION

Proponents of industry computer assisted valuation and land management systems envisage realizing one or more of the following benefits:

— *The connection of current deficiencies in data.* Development of an integrated CAV and LMS system would necessitate a general review of data needs and might provide an opportunity to collect additional data.

— *Improved access to existing data.* In an integrated system, data that formerly resided in another agency's system could be readily accessible.

— *The avoidance or reduction of duplicate efforts in collecting and maintaining data.* An integrated system would minimize the need to conduct parallel primary data collection efforts or would minimize the need to transfer data from one system to another, as well as reduce the uncertainties in maintaining parallel data files (e.g., knowing whether each update was performed in both files, knowing which file, if either, was correct in the case of a discrepancy in the data, etc.).

— *Obtaining the "critical mass" needed to be able to purchase a modern system.* Although computer systems have become more affordable, agencies in smaller units of government may find it difficult to cost-justify the purchase of a modern system alone, whereas two or more agencies could.

— *The more effective performance of governmental functions.* The use of sophisticated models to produce more accurate valuations has been detailed in other chapters of this book. Further improvements in valuation accuracy might be attained if the macroeconomic and demographic data used in land use planning applications were successfully incorporated in valuation models. Land management decision-making similarly might be improved if planners had access to the land use and land value data contained in assessment records.

In summary, integrated systems are seen as a means by which the economic and social costs of outmoded cadastral systems can be reduced.

OBSTACLES TO INTEGRATION

In view of the potential property of integrated CAV and LMS systems, it may come as a surprise that until very recently there have been comparatively few examples of successfully integrated systems. The reasons for this situation are numerous, and some of the more important reasons are mentioned here in hopes that problems encountered in the past will be avoided in the future. The obstacles to successful integration fall in two main areas: (1) technological and system design problems and (2) institutional and managerial problems, although problems in one area may contribute to problems in the other.[2]

Technological and System Design Problems

A variety of technological and system design problems have been encountered in the development of integrated CAV and LMS systems. While there have been many causes of the problems, a lack of technical expertise on the part of the design and an incomplete analysis of system needs seem to be frequent causes.

These kinds of failings have resulted in two broad types of problems with computer technology: (1) mismatches between information processing requirements, on the one hand, and the capabilities of computer hardware and software, on the other, and (2) failures to take advantage of new technologies. Examples of the former type of problem include insufficient information storage capacity and telecommunications and database management systems that cannot adequately handle file creation and maintenance, report generation, graphic display, and polygon retrieval commands in terms of volume of work or response time. These problems often are the result of making hardware and software acquisition decisions before requirements are fully determined. The latter type of problem is exacerbated by rapid changes in computer technology that can make both hardware and software obsolete. Hardware costs, expressed in terms of data processing abilities, have been declining, while the costs of developing programs and software have been increasing. Many minicomputers, for example, have online processing capabilities that equal or exceed the capabilities of large computers a few years ago. Some microcomputers rival minicomputers. The general effect of these developments, however, has been to make computers more accessible and easier to use and to make system designs and computer programs easier to document. Systems that fail to take advantage of these developments tend to be less acceptable to their users and, therefore, less successful. The challenge

---

2. Some of the material in this section is drawn from Richard R. Almy, "The Joint Development and Use of Property Information," *Assessors Journal* 14 (June 1979): 73-92.

is to choose from the available software and hardware alternatives the optimum in terms of capabilities and affordability at the time the system is to be implemented.

Turning to design problems, a common problem with early attempts to develop integrated systems was a failure on the part of system designers to recognize fully that the objectives of the various users were in some ways incompatible. The Forsyth County (North Carolina) Land Records Information System (FCLRIS) provides an example of unrecognized incompatible objectives.[3] The agencies that participated in the development of FCLRIS included the county offices of the register of deeds, planning and zoning, building inspection, environmental affairs, tax collection, and assessment, as well as the special assessments agency for the city of Winston-Salem. The system was designed to treat each parcel as a separate file in which all available information on a given parcel was to be stored. The system was designed to enable users to obtain information on specific parcels randomly by means of online computer terminals. Since the county register of deeds played a leadership role in the development of the system, the system was better designed to meet the objectives involved in conveyancing and other activities concerned with information about individual parcels. As originally designed, however, the system could not provide the same level of service to planners and others who had a need for analyses based on aggregated data; such needs could be satisfied only by batch processing when there were no online demands on the system.

Unrealistic objectives have been another frequently encountered design and management problem. In the most extreme form of this problem, computers have been viewed by the uninitiated as capable of instantly providing information in a form that satisfies any user's immediate needs, and all one has to do is plug in the computer. While experienced government officials are less sanguine about the omnipotence of computers and the speed with which systems can be designed and implemented, it is easy to underestimate the time required to design and implement the system, the cost involved, or the technology needed. There also is always a lengthy learning process during which system designers and users come to appreciate each other's requirements. These time requirements may conflict with institutional requirements, which will be discussed later.

Data requirements also have presented design problems. At the most basic level, decisions must be made about the data that will be collected and maintained. There has been a tendency to collect more information

3. It should not be inferred from being mentioned here that the problems encountered in the development of FCLRIS were unusually severe or that the FCLRIS was a failure. Rather, FCLRIS is one of the few systems whose problems are described with candor in the literature.

than will be used or can be maintained. Also how data elements are described and coded is crucial. Different users often view the same general property characteristics in markedly different ways. For example, an assessor may find that describing the "condition" of a building as poor, average, or good is satisfactory, while a building or housing official may want much more detailed information on the condition of plumbing facilities, electrical service, the roof, or other building components. Similar differences occur in defining and counting rooms.

The absence of up-to-date property ownership maps can delay the implementation of a comprehensive property information system, since the accuracy of the legal descriptions of parcels cannot be verified without recourse to surveys and maps. Moreover, all acceptable parcel identification systems, most means of determining geographic coordinates, are dependent upon up-to-date property ownership maps.

The keys by which data are retrieved can also cause problems. At the parcel level, address, parcel identifier (parcel identification number), and owner's name are the usual alternatives, and various users have different preferences (geographic coordinates are an emerging means of assessing data). Each key can pose problems. Address, for example, may not be a unique means of identification: several streets may have the same name, a single street may have several names, there may be more than one spelling of a name, street numbers may be assigned inconsistently, or a single property may have more than one address. Some parcels may not have an address. Parcel identifiers usually originate in the assessor's office. Sometimes there is not a standard system for assigning parcel identifiers, and sometimes not all identifiers are unique. Names pose obvious problems as well: several persons may have the same name, and one person may own several properties. In summary, information retrieval problems can arise if the ways in which parcels are identified are not standardized and if there is no unique way of identifying each parcel.

Different users also have different expectations with respect to information about geographic location and the accuracy of legal descriptions. Surveyors, for example, would prefer to have each parcel described as accurately as possible. Engineers trying to locate underground utilities have similar needs. As far as property owners themselves are concerned, the required accuracy of legal descriptions is more a function of land value and intensity of land use, particularly where buildings and other land improvements cover the entire site. For example, most owners of, say, a thousand-acre tract of mountain land worth less than $100 per acre would not require a precise decription of their property. However, land worth more than $100 per square foot in the central business district of a city needs to be described very accurately. Information about the relative location of parcels can be quite generalized for most valuation and land management purposes, but may need to be more precisely known relative to such things as zoning and flood plain boundaries.

An additional problem is that some uses of property information involve information of a historical nature, while most other uses involve current information. Conveyancing is the most common example of a need for historical information. Assessors also use historical information in the analysis of sales prices. Including historical information in a system has obvious implications for record length, the size of files, or both, and for information storage and retrieval technologies.

Once decisions have been made about the information to be gathered, collected, and maintained, it is necessary to specify how to process this information. It is seldom satisfactory to rely completely on existing information and even existing information-gathering methods, and the task of collecting and maintaining the data in property information files is often of a greater magnitude than anticipated. Data coding manuals have to be written and tested, data collection forms must be designed, data collectors must be recruited and trained, and data edit procedures must be devised. In addition, the means of converting data into machine-readable form must be determined.

The design of integrated systems involves numerous other technicalities beyond the scope of this chapter. However, there are three additional points that deserve mention here to generate reports on an ad hoc basis. Aggregated data are used to develop profiles and to make analyses. They are also used to develop status reports. The property characteristics by which users will want to aggregate data will change from time to time and will change according to the needs of a particular user. Property owners, for example, most often will want information only on their own properties. An appraiser in an assessor's office, however, may need information on all the properties in a single neighborhood, while his or her supervisor may want descriptive statistics for several neighborhoods. The assessor or other local elected official may want a jurisdiction-wide status report. Similarly, officials concerned with land management may want descriptive data on all dilapidated structures, on property values in a school district, or on the condition of properties in a redevelopment area. Problems arise when it is necessary to make elaborate modifications in programs so that data may be aggregated in a new way, when the time required to obtain aggregated data is unreasonable, or when it is not practical to prepare a report that meets the needs of a user.

The second point is the handling of output from the system. Choices need to be made with respect to output media (e.g., paper, video display, or micrographics). Users of early batch processing systems often felt swamped with reams of output.

The third and final point involves ensuring that data in the system are accurate and secure. In addition to routine data edits that are designed to make sure that only accurate information enters the system, care needs to be taken to safeguard against information being entered, deleted, or altered without authorization. In addition, confidential information in the system should be accessible only to authorized personnel.

Institutional and Managerial Problems

Arguably, institutional and managerial problems in the development of an integrated CAV and LMS system are more difficult to solve than technological and system design problems. Most institutional and managerial problems stem from governmental organizational structures in which the officials or agencies responsible for property assessment, land management, and the like are independent of each other. In the absence of an organization with authority over those functions that is fully committed to the project, one of the interested officials or agencies must accept a leadership role. Usually the lead organization is the one with the greatest self-interest in the project in terms of either the benefits to be received by it or the professional gratification of its head in being a leader in adopting new technologies or solving a common problem. Even where a project coordinator is appointed from above, one organization may dominate. Whatever the situation, the leader or chief sponsor may suffer from a limited perspective that prevents him or her from appreciating the interests and needs of the other partners. When "junior" partners perceive that the system has a design bias or is operated in a way that accords their need relatively low-priority, or when they feel they are being asked to contribute more than they receive in return, friction and resentment result. The situation is exacerbated when one or more of the partners was reluctant in the first place.

There can be several reasons for reluctance. An official may believe that he or she does not have sufficient legislative authority to embark upon a data integration effort, no matter how valuable the effort might be to government as a whole or to society in general. A lack of budgetary authorization is a similar concern. Concerns about a loss of control over data integrity or over access to computing resources, also breed reluctance. So do professional jealousies and concerns about losing political power.

Legislation and regulations can hamper the development of integrated systems if they contain detailed requirements that perpetuate outmoded ways of performing governmental functions.

The terms of office of elected officials, which usually range between two and four years, also represent potential institutional problems. In some instances, there may be undue pressure to complete an integration project within a term of office. At a minimum, there is a need for a quick payoff. In other instances, a newly elected official may not attach as much significance to an integration project as his or her predecessor and may let the project die on the vine.

Turning to problems of a more managerial nature, there may be difficulties in selecting and working with consultants. Not infrequently, consultants also suffer from a limited perspective or area of expertise. Few consultants or contractors, even if they possess competence in systems development and computer technology, also have sufficient mastery of the many fields (e.g., assessing, deed recordation, fiscal management, land use planning, code enforcement, public health, fire fighting, and police protection) that may be partners in a joint effort but are united only by an interest in information about land parcels or events that took place on specific parcels. The failure of system designers to master all relevant governmental functions, of course, affects in-house system development activities as well. When this happens, inappropriate solutions are sometimes developed; at other times, consultants are regarded as expensive mimics of their clients.

The method by which consultants and contractors are selected can cause problems. Too often contracts are awarded strictly on the basis of lowest bid without sufficient regard for the qualifications of the contractor or the reasonableness of the proposal. Other times contracts are awarded on the basis of a "buy local" policy or a similar political reason. In each of these situations, it is possible that neither the best contractor nor the best proposal is selected.

The general area of project planning and control may also present problems, especially for government officials without project management experience. There may be problems in determining what capabilities are wanted from the system (and what limitations are acceptable) in developing a schedule for implementing the system, in monitoring progress, and in controlling the design and implementation effort.

Communication breakdowns are also frequently encountered, and, as problems and conflicts are encountered, the tendency for communications to fail becomes greater, thereby aggravating the original problem. Breakdown may occur "horizontally" among user agencies or "vertically" between project leaders and users, between contractors and clients, or between the system design and programming staff and users.

Inadequate documentation represents a communication problem of a different sort. If a system is not well documented, it may be as costly to modify as it was to develop — a serious disadvantage when system design mistakes are discovered or when the system must be modified to accommodate changing conditions.

A final type of management problem is retaining key personnel long enough to ensure that a system is running smoothly. While changes in project leaders and system designers are especially disruptive, changes in programmers can cause major delays and can incur additional costs if programs are not well documented. Contractors must also support the systems they develop for a reasonable period of time and train the operating staff.

In any management (or other) problem, the support of top management for the project is crucial. Without this support, soluble problems can become insoluble. Departmental friction and rivalries become more disruptive.

STRATEGIES FOR INTEGRATION

In essence, a basic strategy for successful integration of a CAV and an LMS system is to anticipate all of the problems that might arise. Initially, consideration should be given to: (1) a preliminary survey of users to determine the extent to which the integration of systems is desired; (2) a consideration of how the integration effort might best be organized and managed; and (3) the establishment of realistic objectives, given likely institutional, resource, and technical constraints.

The preliminary survey of user needs should attempt to determine which offices or agencies use land data and the specific functions in which those data are used. The survey should result in a general understanding of land data needs and particularly the degree or commonness in data needs. Matters that might be investigated include: (1) the spatial unit or units of interest (e.g., ownership parcel, tax parcel, block, census tract, governmental unit, cell in a coordinate grid, etc.); (2) the time periods of interest (e.g., the present, some specific time in the past, a historical record, a projection, etc.); (3) the scope of coverage of the items of interest (i.e., is the user interested only in data for a few specific items or events or for all such items or events?); (4) the specific things that are of interest (e.g., measurements and descriptions of physical characteristics of properties, events such as fire, transactions such as sales of property, or some combination of things); (5) the degree of data aggregation that is required; (6) if measurements are of interest, the degree of precision of the measurements; (7) keys or linkages (e.g., parcel identifiers, addresses, names, geographic coordinates, etc.); (8) the degree of accessibility that is required (i.e., is data usually required instantly, the next day, once a year, etc.?). If there is not a substantial degree of commonness in data needs, an integrated system may not be feasible. Of course, data systems can be modular, with common needs handled by an integrated system and specialized needs handled by dedicated systems.

The consideration of how an integration effort might best be organized and managed must take into account the governmental organizational structure of the offices or agencies interested in an integrated data system and the legal framework upon which that structure is based. Ideally, the structure will permit the creation of a body to operate the system on behalf of the various users. If all the users are part of a larger agency or of a general-purpose government, there usually will be no substantial organizational barriers. There will, however, be a choice as to the degree of centralization of the data system. In other words, the managing agency might be responsible for the maintenance of *all* data in the system or a "model" or decentralized structure might be developed in which each agency in the system is responsible for maintaining only specific data elements.

If the existing government structure presents organizational problems, a determination must be made as to whether it is politically feasible to amend that structure or whether some alternative strategy should be attempted. Among the possible alternative strategies, two seem most common. One strategy is to form an informal consortium, with leadership delegated to one of the members. Such consortiums tend to be fragile organizations, since financial support can be withdrawn at any time and since leadership depends on the consent of the governed. The second strategy is for one of the parties to assume the role of an entrepreneur, taking on the responsibility for developing and maintaining a system that will meet the needs of other users, and thereby hoping to obtain financial and other assistance from potential users. Such an approach is also subject to the vagaries of either the system sponsor or the clients.

If it appears that an integrated CAV and LMS system is both technically and politically feasible, the next step is to define specific objectives and to begin a formal system design, development, and implementation process that will result in the achievement of those objectives. One lesson is clear: the objectives should be realistic (i.e., attainable), since perception of the success of, and continued support for, an integrated system depends on objectives being attained. The best strategy, therefore, appears to develop the system in an incremental or modular fashion so that there are clearly identifiable results at critical points (e.g., at the time future authorizations are being considered, at the time of elections, or at the time of transitions in governments).

The chances of success of an integration effort are largely dependent on the quality of project management. Careful attention must be given to each step along the way (e.g., design, development, and implementation).[4]

---

4. Some of the material in this section is drawn from National Research Council, panel on a Multipurpose Cadastre, *Procedures and Standards for a Multipurpose Cadastre* (Washington, D.C.: National Academy Press, 1983), pp. 93-97.

Effective project planning is crucial. The plan identifies needs that the system is to meet, the steps to be taken in implementing the system, resource requirements, and timing considerations. The plan also serves as a project control tool and is used to measure progress. Necessarily, the plan should be in writing.

A major part of the planning effort is scheduling. Scheduling involves dividing the overall process into discrete tasks and subtasks, noting which tasks can begin only after other tasks have been completed and which tasks can be performed simultaneously; estimating realistic production rates and available resource levels, particularly personnel, for each task; and depicting time and resource requirements for each task on a Gantt chart or some other form of bar chart. A refined schedule should be made during the system development phase as soon as major features of the system are decided. More sophisticated project planning and management techniques, such as critical-path management/program evaluation and review techniques (CPM/PERT), should be used if the project is large and well analyzed.

As previously mentioned, the functions and responsibilities of the agencies that will be using the system must be carefully analyzed to determine the scope of the various applications and, therefore, the capabilities required of the system. System analysis should identify the resources required in system design, system implementation, and system maintenance. The analysis should identify data requirements and should coordinate data element definition and related requirements of the various users. An estimate of the benefits and costs associated with each application will help determine priorities among the various possible applications. Consideration also should be given to whether the infrastructure (e.g., geodetic reference framework, base maps, and cadastral overlay) of a modern land data system is in place.

System analysis begins with interviews with key individuals in user agencies and groups. The purpose of these interviews is to determine functional responsibilities, information needs, analytical and decision-making processes, and sources, availability and condition of existing data. An interview guide or an interview form should be prepared to ensure that all relevant lines of inquiry are followed with each interviewer. Copies of procedural manuals, forms, and reports that are used, processed, or prepared should be carefully reviewed. A helpful intermediate step in the analysis of information flow is to create two matrices, one showing data elements and their sources. The interview notes and the matrices are then used to prepare an accurate description of information processing by the entities involved.

The system analysis is used as the basis for system design activities or for developing the technical specifications for a request for proposals

(RFP) for developing software under a contract. The first step in designing the system is to develop a rough concept of what the system is to be. Brainstorming sessions involving key users and technical personnel can be helpful in the conceptualization process. After decisions on the general system features are made, the design effort turns to more detailed concerns.

The system itself should be decomposed into tasks. A narrative description of each task should be prepared. The narrative would indicate whether a particular task or subtask is to be performed by human or by computer. For each computer task, a program solution should be prepared to guide the programmers. A data dictionary also should be prepared.

There are a number of useful programming techniques that are oriented toward the human side of computer use and that offer a number of benefits. The database is defined early, before programs are written to retrieve information. This helps to avoid problems that sometimes arise when different parts of a program are written by different programmers at different times—parts that later have to be meshed together. System and program documentation is written as the system design and program structure are developed. Documentation is, therefore, more complete, accurate, and useful. The documentation also is organized in hierarchical levels, usually by function, making it easier to locate specific components of the program structure. Program code is easily intelligible to other programmers, and programs are easier to modify. The techniques also necessitate regular communications among users, system develoment personnel, and data processing operations personnel. Taken together, these programming techniques can increase the confidence of both programmers and users in the programs and, therefore, in the system.

System development activities occur concurrently with system design activities. An early decision is whether the system is to be developed internally or acquired from some external source. No general recommendation can be made as to which alternative is preferable. On the one hand, complete reliance on internal development may result in system design personnel redeveloping existing systems while ensuring that the system meets the specific needs of the locale in question. On the other hand, systems developed elsewhere are seldom, if ever, completely transferable and, if they were, there appears to be an inherent contradiction in designing systems that are at once integrated and transferable. Of course, system transfers can occur at several levels, ranging from system concepts down to specific program code, and system components usually can be transferred more easily than entire systems. A related question is whether to use external technical assistance in the system development process. Actual experience with the use of consultants is mixed. Consultants can be a source of expertise not available locally and can also augment the system development work-force on a temporary basis. Much depends on the client's ability to clearly define the scope of work, the standards of performance, and the respective responsibilities of the client and the contractor, as well as the client's ability to evaluate proposals objectively. In addition, the client must have the capability of managing the contract and monitoring the contractor's performance.

With respect to project management in general, several observations and recommendations can be made. First, the project planning and management techniques and the programming technique mentioned earlier can be of assistance in system development. The steady flow of products resulting from such techniques makes monitoring the project easier. Moreover, parts of the system can be tested incrementally, in contrast to a massive testing effort at the end of the development phase. The techniques also give managers, system design personnel, and users a clear picture of the system as it evolves, thereby making it easier to spot errors and omissions and to suggest modifications and improvements.

System implementation activities revolve around making sure that the system performs the way in which it was designed. The information that the system receives must be converted into a form that the system can use. The chief recommendations that can be made in this regard are (1) to use existing data, if practical, since data collection is very time-consuming and costly, and (2) to take all feasible steps to ensure that only accurate data are stored in the system.

User orientation is a major activity during the system implementation phase. User manuals are prepared, and orientation and training sessions are held.

PLACES TO LOOK FOR GUIDANCE

A search for sources of information and guidance should include published works, scientific and professional organizations dedicated to improving land data systems, and individuals and agencies that have participated directly in an integration effort.

Published Works

The literature on integrating CAV and LMS systems is extensive, but not well controlled. However, a number of excellent bibliographies have been published in addition to the bibliography appended to this book. These include:

Alberta. Land-Related Information Systems Coordination Project. *A Con-*

solidated Bibliography on Land-Related Systems. Edmonton: Alberta Treasury, Bureau of Statistics, 1981.

Alberta Energy and Natural Resources. Bureau of Surveying and Mapping. Land-Related Information Services Group. *A Consolidated Bibliography on Land-Related Information Systems.* Edmonton: Alberta Energy and Natural Resources. Annual, beginning in 1984. On microfilm.

Clatanoff, Robert M. *Computer Assisted Appraisal and Assessment Systems: An Annotated Bibliography Supplement I.* Bibliographic Series. Chicago: International Association of Assessing Officers, 1983.

Denne, Robert C. *Computer Assisted Appraisal and Assessment Systems: An Annotated Bibliography.* Bibliographic Series. Chicago: International Association of Assessing Officers, 1977.

Lincoln Institute of Land Policy. *Computer Assisted Mass Appraisal/Assessment Ratio Bibliography.* Monograph 77-4. Cambridge, Mass.: Lincoln Institute of Land Policy, 1977.

McLaughlin, John D. *A Selected Annotated Bibliography on the Cadastre.* IRS Working Paper No. 2C. Madison: University of Wisconsin-Madison, Institute for Environmental Studies, 1976.

Moyer, D. David, Comp. *Land Information Systems: An Annotated Bibliography.* Falls Church, VA: North American Institute for Modernization of Land Data Systems; distrib. by American Congress on Surveying and Mapping.

While most of the literature is in the form of conference proceedings and journal articles, a few larger works deserve mention:

Auerbach Publishers, Inc. *Computers in Local Government: Finance and Administration.* Pennsauken, NJ: Auerbach Publishers, 1980. Looseleaf.

Auerbach Publishers, Inc. *Computers in Local Government: Urban and Regional Planning.* Pennsauken, NJ: Auerbach Publishers, 1980. Looseleaf.

Lincoln Institute of Land Policy. *National Survey of Opinion on the Attributes of a Successful Land Data System, Part I: Ratings of Attributes of Systems.* Lincoln Institute Monograph 82-4. Cambridge, Mass.: Lincoln Institute of Land Policy, 1982.

Lincoln Institute of Land Policy. *National Survey of Ratings of the Attributes of a Successful Land Data System, Part II: Profiles of 75 Operating Systems.* Lincoln Institute Monograph 84-3. Cambridge, Mass: Lincoln Institute of Land Policy, 1984.

National Research Council, Panel on a Multipurpose Cadastre. *Procedures and Standards for a Multipurpose Cadastre.* Washington, D.C.: National Academy Press, 1983. Contains a bibliography.

Of the available conference proceedings, the following three are among the most recent:

Federation Internationale des Geometres. Commission 2. *The Decision Maker and Land Information Systems.* Proceedings of an international symposium on land information systems, 15-19 October 1984, Edmonton, Alberta. Photocopied.

Leick, Alfred, editor. *Land Information at the Local Level: Proceedings of the International Symposium on Land Information at the Local Level, 9-12 August 1982 at the University of Maine at Orono.* Orono: University of Maine at Orono, Department of Surveying Engineering, 1983.

Neimann, Bernard J., Jr., editor. *Seminar on the Multipurpose Cadastre: Modernizing Land Information Systems in North America.* IES Report 123. Madison: University of Wisconsin-Madison, 1984.

A journal of particular interest is *Computers, Environment and Urban Systems* published by Pergamon Press (quarterly).

Organizations

A large number of educational, scientific, and professional organizations have an interest in integrated land data systems. Among them are the following (an asterisk(*) designates that the organization is affiliated with the Institute for Land Information):

American Congress of Surveying and Mapping*
210 Little Falls Street
Falls Church, VA 22046-4392

Both ACSM's journal, *Surveying and Mapping*, and conference proceedings contain useful information.

Federation Internationale des Geometres

Institute for Land Information (formerly the North American Institute for Modernization of Land Data Systems—and later the Institute for Modernization of Land Data Systems (MOLDS) 440 1st Street, N.W., Washington, D.C. 20001

ILI is an organization in which about thirty associations, national-level government agencies, and other organizations participate. It fosters cooperation among its member organizations and cosponsors conferences. In addition to the previously mentioned bibliography, MOLDS has published the proceedings of conferences held in 1975 and 1978.

International Association of Assessing Officers*
1313 East 60th Street
Chicago, Illinois 60637-9990

IAAO is dedicated to improving the administration of the property tax, and computer assisted appraisal and assessment systems has long been an area of interest to the Association. It has a special interest group, the Computer Assisted Appraisal Section, which publishes a quarterly newsletter, *CAAS News*.

International Geographical Union

Lincoln Institute of Land Policy*
26 Trowbridge Street
Cambridge, Massachusetts 02138

In addition to the series of courses on computer assisted valuation, LILP has published the results of research and conducted education in the areas of CAV and LMS systems.

National Association of State Information Systems
(Affiliated with the Council of State Governments,*)
P. O. Box 11910, Lexington, Kentucky 54078

NASIS publishes an annual survey of computer applications by state governments.

Urban and Regional Information Systems Association*
1340 Old Chain Bridge Road, Suite 300
McLean, Virginia 22101

Individuals and Agencies

Integrated CAV and LMS systems have been developed in a number of countries, and the number of experienced individuals and agencies is growing rapidly. Unfortunately, it is virtually impossible to develop a directory of all the individuals and agencies to whom one might turn to for guidelines. In addition to scanning the names of authors and the names of agencies and systems in the literature, at least one fairly current directory has been published:

International Geographical Union. Commission on Geographical Data Sensing and Processing. *Directory of Individuals in the Field of Geographical Data Handling.* Ottawa: Government of Canada, Environment Canada, Lands Directorate, 1981.

There are certain patterns in the development of integrated CAV and LMS systems. Some European countries (e.g., Austria, Denmark, the Netherlands, and Sweden) have developed national systems. In the Federal Republic of Germany, systems tend to be developed on a state-wide basis (e.g., Berlin, Pheinland-Pfalz, Hessen, Nordorhein-Westfallen, and Niedersachen, Hanburg and Saarland). The development of land data systems in Australia and Canada also tends to be on a statewide basis. In Australia, systems have been developed or are under development in a number of states, including New South Wales (the Automated Land Titles System), South Australia (the Land Ownership and Tenure System), Victoria (the LANDATA project), and Western Australia (the Western Australia Land Information System). The Canadian provinces in which systems are under development include Alberta and the Maritime Province (the Land Registration and Information Service). In the United States, local governments (e.g., counties and municipalities) are largely responsible for the development of integrated land data systems. This makes it very difficult to monitor progress, since about 60 percent of over 13,000 local assessment jurisdictions have automated some portion of their records.

Chapter 13

BASIC ECONOMICS OF COMPUTER ASSISTED VALUATION

Bruce F. Nagel

INTRODUCTION

The use of the computer to assist appraisers/assessors in performing calculations relating to the development of appraised values is a well established fact. What is not so well established is the relationship of computer assisted valuation to the cost of maintaining equitable assessment rolls that form the foundation of local government financing. The fee appraisal community, along with the insurance and real estate industries, have been using the computer for several years to perform appraisal calculations for individual properties. In addition, the private sector has been developing shared databases, such as multiple listing services, to better serve the needs of the broker and appraiser. Local government, however, is faced with a different type of appraisal problem—the need to periodically appraise all of the real estate, and in some cases taxable personal property, within an assessing jurisdiction.

This chapter will review the history of Computer Assisted Mass Appraisal (CAMA) as it applies to the assessing community and discuss the basic economic impact that CAMA has with regard to assessment administration. The very nature of the dramatic technological change to the information processing aspects of our world may not lead to clear-cut cost benefit analysis of the impact of computers on assessment administration. This chapter will point out, however, that the future of the property tax and the

203

ability for local governments to continue as relatively self-supporting entities is dependent upon their ability to cost-effectively administer their revenue base.

CAMA HISTORY

The initial use of computers in the processing of property tax administration data can be traced to the initial availability of commercially priced data processing hardware. This event took place in the mid-1950s and took the form of using the computer to perform the repetitive tasks of printing assessment rolls, calculating taxes due for individual properties, printing tax bills and processing tax payments.

A newsletter written in 1967 by John D. Cole II, at that time a principal in a mass appraisal firm, reported that his company had been using computers since 1957 and had processed over three million property appraisals for local tax equalization purposes. Mr. Cole added several functions to the then traditional list of how computers can be used by local assessing jurisdictions:

1. The mass computation of individual appraisals.

2. A continuing statistical study to test the quality of assessments.

3. The annual reappraisal concept.

4. The data bank concept.

Mr. Cole also concluded that "Few single governmental departments have enough volume of work to justify a computer." It is interesting to note that the definition of the CAMA work that is the desired output of the computer has changed very little in almost 20 years, but the cost justification with regard to volume of work has changed dramatically.

Those comments written in 1967 coincide closely with the advent of second generation computers, most notably the IBM 360 series. Faster computers, with greater capacity, were beginning to change the way that computers could be used as an appraisal tool. Multi-variate statistical analysis was suddenly available to individuals with access to newer computers. Simple regression had long been an analytical tool for plotting property value relationships. Most appraisers manually performed the necessary calculations needed to arrive at average selling price per square foot of living area, lot frontage or acreage. Multiple regression analysis, however, enabled the appraiser to analyze the interrelationship of several descriptive features of a property with each other as well as with selling price. The early CAMA systems were strictly based on the cost approach. The cost approach was relatively easy to program and process, but suffered from the fact that it did not derive estimates of value directly from the market place. Multiple regression analysis (MRA), provided the appraiser with predictive capabilities along with statistical measures of accuracy of the predicted results. Pilot studies in the late 1960s in California, New York and elsewhere seemed to indicate that the era of fully computerized appraisal/assessment systems was at hand. Unfortunately, reality has a way of imposing itself on the transfer of a promising new technique into an operational environment. Again referring to Mr. Cole's 1967 newsletter, he observed the following: "If you supply accurate input information to the appropriate computer program, the machine will respond with mathematically correct answers. If the input information is not correct and accurate, neither will be the answers." To the statistician dealing with large numbers of observations, a certain error level does not damage the overall conclusions that are developed about the relationships of physical characteristics of properties and the selling prices. When these conclusions are then applied to an individual property that is described incorrectly, the results can be disastrous to the individual property owner. In a manual assessment system, the errors can be corrected with an eraser and an individual error on a sold property does not compound itself as a component of a procedure that produces valuation criteria for unsold properties. Initial production testing of MRA-based appraisal systems yielded the following results:

1. While accurate predictive models could be created for the "average" property, properties on either end of the spectrum were either undervalued or overvalued.

2. Frequent update intervals (say, annually or biennially) tended to change the value relationship of similarly described parcels. That is to say that this year parcel A would have a value greater than parcel B and next year parcel B would have a value greater than parcel A.

3. Data quality standards are much higher in a computerized environment, causing a much greater expenditure of time and money for data maintenance than in a manual environment. A manual error correction system need only concern itself with the change in assessed value. The computerized system requires that the base data used in the computation also be changed.

4. A major re-orientation of staff is needed to accommodate the changes in work flow that occur when the appraisal process is mechanized.

5. MRA models and equations are difficult to understand and often confound users, who expect a change in physical description of a property to have a certain effect on value only to find that MRA is trying to tell them that the opposite is true. The classic example of this manifestation, called multicolinearity, is the model that concludes that the addition of another bathroom to a house has a negative effect on the predicted value. The explanation, of course, is that the number of bathrooms is highly correlated with the square footage of living area and can cause the bathroom variable coefficient to be negative. This explanation does not normally satisfy the average taxpayer when it appears that an effective tax reduction strategy would be to add a bathroom or two to his or her house.

The early 1970s saw the introduction of third generation computers, such as the Burroughs B6700, that were immediately put to use to solve some of the problems discovered in the early CAMA production applications. The capacity of these new machines was such that more extensive editing of data was possible, performing logical checks of data interrelationships. A certain group of analysts in New York also looked at the possibility of using the computer to more closely emulate the analytical and intuitive processes followed by the appraiser during the appraisal process. The faster computers made it possible to search through large quantities of data to find comparable sales for each parcel being appraised. The feeling was that appraisers and taxpayers could relate to similar parcels that had sold recently more easily than to complicated equations or arbitrary cost tables that may or may not provide the best answer for an individual property. The comparable sales technique, along with more understandable methods of sales analysis, greatly facilitated the acceptability of CAMA techniques by the assessing community.

All of the techniques that were developed during the period from 1970 to 1976, while moving towards systems that were easier to use, required the biggest and fastest computers available. The support network included operations personnel with significant and expensive skills needed to operate the systems. Better equity, accurate and understandable appraisals and relatively error-free databases were possible for those jurisdictions with access to the relatively expensive type of computer resource required to operate CAMA systems with the appropriate features.

The minicomputer, in 1975, followed in a matter of just a few years by the microcomputer, changed forever the dependence of the computer user on large expensive mainframe computers to supply the kinds of computing power needed to do a proper CAMA system. The availability of powerful computing machines that were inexpensive enough to allow the assessment department to acquire a computer that could be totally dedicated to that department's processing needs is still being digested by the potential users of this expanded processing capability.

THE BASIC ECONOMIC IMPACT OF CAMA

The major impact of CAMA techniques on the cost of assessment administration has never been the cost of computer hardware. Even when hardware costs were measured in millions rather than thousands of dollars, adequate computer time could be purchased at reasonable cost, when reasonability is measured relative to the cost of doing a reappraisal. Data available from a mass appraisal company indicates that the cost of the computer for processing data in a mass appraisal environment averages about 5 percent of the total project cost. Why then is the cost of a CAMA reappraisal about 25 percent higher than a comparable manual reappraisal project? The answer today is the same as it was in 1967: data quality and ease of use of the system.

A CAMA project puts the information that is gathered in the field under a magnifying glass, while data used in a manual system is looked at through a telescope. This intense scrutiny demands that rigorous quality control standards be applied to the data processing operations. The software that is used to process and analyze information has to not only perform rigorous checks of data, but also must perform these functions in a way that enables an average user to be able to easily interact with the system. People, not machines, have been the rising cost component in both the manual and computer assisted environments.

A good way to illustrate the changing relationship of the economics of computer assisted valuation is to take a look at two projects conducted in New York State that share similarities in CAMA systems used and the basic ground rules followed. One project was the Town of Islip, conducted during the period 1977-1978, and the other was the City of Rochester, conducted during the period 1982-1983. Both are also similar in size—90,000 parcels vs. 70,000 parcels, respectively. While there are dissimilarities with regard to parcel make-up and geographical area, they do represent one of the few instances where the basic procedures followed are the same even though five years separate the execution of the projects. The Islip project cost about $25 per parcel to execute, while the Rochester project cost about $35 per parcel. The difference in per parcel cost represents an increase of about 40 percent during a period of time that the average price increase of everything was over 60 percent. This would indicate that the computer assisted valuation component of the CAMA project decreased enough to partially offset the increase in labor and expenses associated with the other project components. This fact is also borne out by the changing relationship of the cost comparison of manual vs. CAMA projects. In the mid-1970s, a CAMA project was almost two-thirds as costly as a manual reassessment project. Today that gap has been narrowed to the point where only a 25 percent premium is paid to conduct a CAMA project rather than a manual project.

The revelation that computer costs have decreased during a period of high inflation is well known to those who follow the trends of the computer industry. The software to perform the calculations and the manipulation of data has also become less expensive and is easier to use. There is still resistance, however, to the notion that computers should make the assessor's office more productive and hence make property tax administration more cost-effective.

First, the assumption must be made that the manual procedures that will be replaced by the computer assisted methods represent an adequate system of property tax administration. From an appraisal standpoint, the author is familiar with only one state, Ohio, where manual appraisal techniques are routinely applied in such a way that assessments derived from those appraisals are relatively equitable. Ohio enforces periodic adjustments to assessments (triennial) and periodic reappraisals (sexennial) to meet certain measures of assessment accuracy. This frequent attention to assessment accuracy has meant that the cost of periodic reassessment has remained low ($6 to $10 per parcel) and, until recently, only the largest counties have attempted to use CAMA. There is an increasing trend in Ohio for other counties to follow the larger counties in implementing more sophisticated CAMA systems. This trend has been stimulated by the availability of hardware and software to do the job and the upward pressure on the price of the more traditional manual reappraisals.

In other parts of the country the tradition of frequent reappraisals to maintain equity is either very new or non-existent. This environment is normally where the figures are derived that indicate CAMA is an expensive proposition. The reason that CAMA would appear to be expensive in this context is that the first cycle of CAMA use must carry the burden of all the hardware, software and file building costs associated with implementing the system. As is mentioned earlier in this chapter, machine time costs represent about 5 percent of the total cost of a CAMA project. The software installation cost component may run as high as $100,000, depending upon the hardware to be used, the amount of on-site support that is required and the software options to be installed. Software costs could be as low as $10,000 for small jurisdictions that can utilize a microcomputer for project data processing needs. The major project cost component is the creation of an error-free database, a cost which can represent from 40 percent to 60 percent of the total project cost. Often it is a relatively inexpensive project component, such as data entry, that has a significant impact on the total project cost. Data entry or keypunching costs for a CAMA project today averages somewhere around $1 per parcel or about 3 percent to 5 percent of the total cost. An error-prone data entry operation can easily lead to data collection costs that are 50 percent higher than they should be, increasing the total project cost by as much as 30 percent.

The basic economics of computer assisted valuation must be analyzed in the context of what it is replacing. If it is replacing a well-staffed manual operation that has maintained adequate records and relatively current assessments, the cost impact can be related directly to the cost of hardware, software, data entry and staff training, all of which can be amortized over the future life of the system. If the system is being implemented from scratch in an environment that has been inadequate to perform the functions associated with property tax administration, the analysis should take into account the money being spent to correct past deficiencies. The money spent to implement CAMA must be looked at as an investment that will yield benefits for several years into the future.

Massachusetts provides an example where municipalities that have been able to absorb the initial higher cost of implementing a CAMA system are now benefiting from the system outputs. Proposition 2-1/2 severely limited the taxing power of most local governments to 2-1/2 percent of the total market value of taxable real property. In addition to the obvious need to maintain current assessments to protect the revenue base, motivation to maintain current assessments is supplied by the regulatory power of the Commonwealth's Department of Revenue. The regulatory pressure has resulted in a triennial need to perform a jurisdiction-wide reappraisal. Those assessing jurisdictions that were able to spend $30 to $40 per parcel to perform an initial CAMA project that resulted in an on-going system can now update assessments for a cost of $5 to $10 per parcel while non-CAMA jurisdictions are spending $20 to $30 per parcel to achieve comparable equity. More importantly, the ability to do an update frequently, consistently and equitably would literally be impossible for the larger jurisdictions without CAMA.

Through all of this discussion of the basic economics of computer assisted valuation, one needs to remember that increasing demands are being placed on local government funding resources and that these resources, most notably the local property tax, must stand up to ever-increasing pressure from local officials, courts and individual taxpayers. The late Michael O'Shea, the Deputy Executive Director of the New York State Board of Equalization and Assessment during the period that his agency was developing a standard CAMA system, answered complaints about CAMA project costs with the question "What price equity?" His basic assertion then is still true today: local governments cannot afford not to spend adequate resources to maintain accurate, defensible and equitable assessments.

History and current events point to Mr. O'Shea's wisdom and foresight. The basic economics of computer assisted valuation indicate that the dream of the early developers of CAMA systems will soon be realized— CAMA project costs will be no more than the cost to do the same project manually. Using a computer to perform many of the assessment functions related to property appraisal is already a fact in hundreds of assessing jurisdictions across the country. The microcomputer will make computer assisted valuation a fact in thousands of additional assessing offices. The computer terminal and associated appraisal software will become a standard part of the assessment office and the staff will look upon the use of this addition to the office environment as no more unusual than using the telephone or desk calculator.

Chapter 14

THE NEED FOR INTEGRATED CAV EDUCATION

Mathew E. MacIver and Michael Wheeler

INTRODUCTION

The continuing evolution of powerful, accessible computer technology is forcing a reexamination of virtually every element of valuation practice. Because of the computer, the administrative, statistical, and legal facets of professional valuation practice today are far different from what they were just a few years ago.

This rapid change has generated significant need for professional education, but until now this need has largely been met in an *ad hoc* manner. If, as predicted, interest in CAV will continue to accelerate, it is imperative that we define the precise educational need and identify what tasks are best suited for particular institutions.

A comprehensive view of CAV education includes not only technical training in the operation of hardware and software, but also instruction in the allied management, supervisory, and even clerical skills made necessary by the introduction of computer assisted methods. Furthermore, because these methods are based on a rapidly evolving technology, a broad assessment of CAV education must acknowledge the need for on-going curricular revision in response to innovation. Finally, it requires an examination of method as well as content: there are many opportunities for more imaginative and effective CAV instruction.

THE CURRENT EDUCATIONAL LANDSCAPE
The Lincoln Institute of Land Policy

The Lincoln Institute has been active in CAV education on several fronts. It has, for example, offered assessors and property tax officials a series of three intensive one-week courses in computer assisted mass appraisal. The introductory course stresses statistical techniques like multiple regression analysis and feedback for estimating values for commonly available property. A more advanced course focuses on the use of the microcomputer to develop sophisticated models using MRA and other techniques. The final course in the sequence is intended for tax officials who plan to implement the Lincoln Institute's SOLIR system or software like it. The overall purpose of the trilogy of courses is to enable such officials to institute and maintain a computer-based system at reasonable cost. In addition to the basic mass appraisal courses, the Lincoln Institute has also offered courses in the use of computers for the valuation of railroad, utility and other special properties.

These training courses for assessing personnel have been held at the Lincoln Institute's headquarters in Cambridge, Massachusetts, and at a variety of sites throughout the United States and abroad. They have included a heavy component of laboratory work; as is particularly true with computers, the best learning comes from experience. This emphasis, however, has been doubly constraining. Class size has been necessarily limited by the availability of equipment. Also, lab instruction is labor-intensive. As a result the Lincoln Institute has had to limit enrollment to eighteen a session.

The Lincoln Institute has also sponsored a variety of seminars and workshops to promote further CAV research and to disseminate the results of such work. It has, for example, offered advanced sessions in model building. It has also brought together researchers who are exploring the use of the feedback technique to estimate values. Participants in these sessions tend to be academicians and technicians with extensive experience and rather specialized interests.

In an effort to reach a wider audience, the Lincoln Institute convened the first World Congress on Computer Assisted Valuation in 1982 and has organized the second for 1985. Conferences of this scale promote the interchange of information that is important both for tax administrators who are considering the adoption of a computerized system and for those who manage existing systems but are open to further innovation. This is education of a broader and perhaps less formal sort, but it is essential that tax officials have the opportunity to learn from one another.

Other Academic Institutions

Few degree granting universities emphasize CAV research, let alone training, but some schools are becoming more involved in the application of computer technology in the related fields of land planning and real estate. Programs in city and regional planning, for example, use computer technology to teach statistical concepts and modeling techniques; principles of geographic data processing will likely be integrated in the near future.

Professor C. F. Sirmans, at Louisiana State University's Real Estate Department, adapts commercial spreadsheets to courses in investment appraisal and finance. At the University of Georgia, Professor William Shenkel supplements his real estate text with computer-based tutorials. Other computer uses there include an image bank for producing acetates and overlays and an extensive teleconferencing capacity. Professor Austin Jaffe of the University of Pennsylvania likewise uses generic programs in his real estate teaching and research.

The breadth and intensity of such activity is encouraging; it may ultimately enrich both the potential of CAV and our capacity to teach it. It is unrealistic, however, to rely on university-based programs to provide substantial CAV training at this point.

The International Association of Assessing Officers

The IAAO has a long history of serving its members with a curriculum of courses in the theory and practice of valuation. In recent years it has supplemented its basic offerings in land appraisal, valuation methods, and tax administration with several courses in computer assisted techniques.

Covering, as they do, many of the same topics, the IAAO courses in computer assisted assessment systems and model building bear considerable resemblance to the basic Lincoln Institute offerings, although the IAAO has developed extensive supplementary materials. Both the IAAO and the Lincoln Institute use SOLIR to demonstrate how generic CAV software can be applied in a variety of settings. The IAAO, of course, provides professional certification for those who successfully complete their programs. At present, however, it has not undertaken advanced workshops of the sort the Lincoln Institute has sponsored.

Other professional organizations are becoming active in the field, as well. The Society of Real Estate Appraisers has two courses involving computers: a one-day introductory session for microcomputers plus a course exploring methods of "after tax appraisal," using both spreadsheets and custom software. The American Institute of Real Estate Appraisers presently offers an extensive introduction to microcomputers and is developing new courses in valuation of income property and principles of syndication, both of which will use computer-based techniques. The Appraisal Institute of Canada sponsors a CAV users' group.

Other Sources of CAV Education

There are others engaged in CAV education, as well. Although their activities may not be as structured or as visible as those of the Lincoln Institute and the IAAO, they too have a considerable impact and should not be overlooked.

First, a number of jurisdictions, typically larger ones, have instituted their own in-house training programs. Often these are directed at introducing new personnel to systems that already are in place; the relatively high rate of turnover in the assessing profession means that the training function is never over. In some instances these programs have been set up by people who have been through the Lincoln Institute or IAAO training themselves, thus leveraging the efforts of these two organizations.

Second, there is an emerging cadre of CAV consultants who are available to help jurisdictions choose software and hardware, develop models, and implement systems. To some extent training is an inherent part of such consulting services, though such people are perhaps best used for specialized follow-up work after the assessing staff has been through a formal program.

Third, the large valuation firms do a considerable amount of training, albeit often in a limited context. Officials in their client communities need to know enough about CAV to coordinate their own data collection and analysis with that of the vendor. If a firm is providing extensive services, however, local officials will not have to be trained to do their own modeling. The need for this knowledge is not eliminated, of course; it is merely transferred from the public sector to the private. Companies which are doing an extensive amount of CAV thus must develop training programs for their own employees.

The Need for Coordination

CAV is a young field, yet it has already spawned a significant amount of educational activity. For the most part, the programs have responded to specific needs; to date there has been relatively little coordination of the various efforts. We are now at a point where we should assess where CAV education should be going and the responsibilities of various institutions in getting it there. Nonetheless, the rapid pace of developments in the area suggest some measure of modesty in formulating definitive answers.

Any inquiry about the future of CAV education must be informed by a careful look at its past. A detailed assessment is beyond the scope of this chapter, but it is possible at least to frame some questions. Successful planning rests on a better understanding of the following broad issues:

1. What is the CAV educational market; put simply, who has to know what?

2. Which institutions and organizations are best situated to meet that market, and in what particular ways?

3. What is the body of knowledge that must be taught?

4. What innovations in teaching techniques and materials will lighten the educational burden?

Definitive answers to these questions must await further investigation and discourse. What is beyond doubt, however, is the need to define the educational agenda more clearly. If those engaged in CAV education collaborate more actively, tasks that currently are overlooked will more likely be addressed, scarce resources more efficiently and effectively allocated, and there will be less duplication of effort.

THE CHANGING DEMAND FOR CAV EDUCATION

Market Assumptions

Any judgment about future CAV educational needs depends on assumptions about how quickly CAV will take hold and, more important, whether it will be performed predominantly by government employees or private contractors. These factors depend, in turn, on others. The recent development of the low-cost microcomputer has given smaller jurisdictions access to technology that not long ago was available only to states and the largest of cities. Software development for these new machines has necessarily been slower. Private firms engaged in the sale of assessing services have been working on new programs, but cities and towns that want to do their own valuation work may not have easy access to them. How commercial software developers will respond to the Lincoln Institute's example with SOLIR is not yet clear.

If private contractors come to dominate the assessing field, the need for local CAV education will be significantly lessened. Under this scenario, the contractors would do much of the training for their client jurisdictions. Whether this comes to pass, however, depends in part on whether there are economies of scale in CAV: will private companies be able to provide expert assessment services to mid-size and smaller jurisdictions more efficiently than local government agencies can? Alternatively, does the technology of CAV create a barrier of sorts that makes it seem easier in the short-run for a jurisdiction to rely on a contractor even though in time it might be cheaper to be self-sufficient? If there are such market forces, are they strong enough to overcome long traditions of autonomy in many communities? Will the private companies become more or less competitive? (If the former, local jurisdictions will have greater opportunity to buy only those services they desire.)

Given the paucity of hard information, it would be presumptuous to do more than speculate on these questions. It is hard, however, to imagine complete privatization of the CAV function. The present success of a number of jurisdictions in establishing their own stand-alone systems is likely to be an encouraging example to others. Working then from the assumption that some significant number of jurisdictions will be doing their own CAV, we need to identify more specifically who in local government needs what information and skills. A taxonomy of such need is prerequisite to any determination how it best might be filled.

Senior Managers

Different people in the valuation process have quite different responsibilities. At the top of the organizational hierarchy, senior managers must elect whether to convert to a CAV system and, if so, when and to which one. Such managers must know more about CAV in terms of system benefits and costs than the staff who actually will run it, but far less in terms of its technical operation.

Senior administrators often have only a partial understanding of the potential benefits of CAV methods. The advantages of streamlining administrative functions such as tax billing and accounting procedures may be clear, for example, but CAV technology can also help managers redefine their own working procedures. Advanced statistical packages can be used to achieve acceptable valuation results for a large proportion of a jurisdiction's property base far more cheaply than traditional techniques like the cost or comparable sales approaches. Their use may liberate scarce resources to deal with problem parcels or difficult classes of property that may not be as amenable to mass appraisal techniques. This principle of "management by exception" is a strategic policy that deserves broader attention in tax offices in both large and small local governments.

To make sensible decisions, senior managers need to have some sort of criteria by which they can compare competing options. Issues of system integrity and valuation quality require, if not technical skill, the capacity to assess technology. A tax administrator, mindful that valuations are inevitably controversial, must be able to defend not merely his or her specific assessments but more generally the choice of the system that generated them.

Senior managers, then, need education that will enable them to identify and choose among technical options in a way that will encourage public confidence. Most of this education is needed at the front end, before system selection and implementation, but managers of systems that are up and running need help keeping abreast of further innovation and its administrative implications.

Assessors

Local assessors constitute the largest and most conspicuous group of potential CAV students. Assessors create valuation models and apply them in initial valuation, revaluation, and assessment/sales ratio studies. These responsibilities suggest several discrete educational tracks.

First, there is a need to introduce valuation technicians to alternative modeling methods, such as multiple regression analysis. Although regression analysis has been employed rather successfully in larger cities, it is a new option to smaller jurisdictions. Generic microcomputer software packages, such as the Lincoln Institute's SOLIR package, now offer features that support these methodologies (as well as other more traditional techniques used in assessment practice such as the cost approach and comparables sales analysis). Regression analysis, however, represents a theoretical departure from the other assessment approaches and requires a strong familiarity with basic statistics and probability theory if it is to be used with confidence. Prior exposure to other valuation methods is of only marginal use in reducing the time needed to master even basic regression modeling and interpretation skills.

Second, technicians filling supervisory roles, particularly in model implementation, must master methods to evaluate the efficiency with which data are identified, collected, and otherwise manipulated in a computer environment. Experience with manually-based property record systems is, again, of limited relevance to a computer-based system. Tasks that are transferred to a machine environment do not carry the same cost implications as they did when performed manually, for example, and many new data handling routines can make older tasks obsolete. Electronic data transfer procedures, machine assisted data capture, and batch data editing functions represent a profound advance from the hand sorting of property record cards, but require far more technical sophistication.

These first two functions are generic, that is, an assessor could carry this experience from one jurisdiction to another. Assessors also have to know, moreover, how to operate the particular computer system that has been selected. These skills cannot be transferred to a new environment without some adjustment, though just as a typist who is conversant with one word processing program can more easily learn a second, so should an assessor be able to build upon experience with any given system. Software developers in other fields typically have been better at promising training and useful documentation for their products than in providing it. Whether that will be true with CAV software remains to be seen.

To the extent that software is user-apathetic (and sometimes downright hostile) and documentation is incomplete, the training burden is needlessly increased. By contrast, the provision of interactive help menus, computer tutorials, and good reference manuals simplifies the educational task, lessens the need for support, and thus greatly facilitates CAV implementation. Given the great number of assessors—likely more than 15,000 in the United States alone—even modest improvements in software friendliness will produce substantial educational benefits.

By contrast, the clerical staff who assist assessors with the voluminous and unglamorous chores of data entry and other related data processing tasks do not need comprehensive CAV training; their work can be transferred from a manual setting to a CAV environment with relatively little effort. Some training instruction is needed to ensure system integrity and security, but it can be conducted in-house by individual tax departments.

Data Processing Departments

Some jurisdictions that have already computerized other administrative procedures can use existing resources for their valuation tasks, but their data processing departments must be thoroughly familiar with the specialized needs of the valuation department. If existing systems already use batch processing methods for administrative functions, there may be little marginal effort required to automate tax billing procedures and related repetitive tasks. By contrast, analytical procedures may be more difficult to integrate. These processing requirements are best accomplished in an interactive fashion and so are often optimally distributed among many assessment technicians. System analysts must be given a clear understanding of the ways in which valuation activities are best performed in order to respond creatively with solutions that take advantage of existing system investments and newer options in generic software, distributed processing, and file transfer procedures.

As with education for senior managers, this sort of instruction should come at the front end, when a system is being chosen and implemented. Likely it can be handled internally without resort to formal training sessions. Access to experience (either through conferences or professional publications) in implementing systems elsewhere nonetheless should be useful.

The Magnitude of the Educational Market

If CAV education is thought of simply as training for assessors, their sheer numbers make the potential effort an enormous one. A broader definition—one that includes education for senior tax administrators, data processors, and the like—necessarily expands the task. In any event, organizations like the Lincoln Institute and the IAAO have served only a very small proportion of the potential market. It is important, however, to distinguish projected needs from current demand. In each of the last several years the Lincoln Institute has had between two hundred and three hundred enrollees in its various CAMA courses; because a fair proportion of people take more than one course, the actual number of individual students is less. Even so, the Lincoln Institute has essentially met existing demand. Given the novelty of the technology and the time required for people to become aware of its possibilities, the relatively modest demand should not be discouraging. The question is not whether CAV will become the norm but when it will. Some knowledgeable observers believe that we are on the verge of a massive transformation of assessment practice; with it will come a massive demand for CAV education in various forms. Whatever time remains before such an onslaught, educational providers would be wise to assess their particular strengths so that they can coordinate their efforts.

ALLOCATING EDUCATIONAL RESOURCES

The institutions and organizations that provide CAV education are largely autonomous; each has its own goals, resources, and constraints. No one entity can dictate the agendas of others, a fact for which we should be grateful. On the other hand, the very diversity of interests among the active educational entities suggests that there is (or should be) some natural specialization.

The Lincoln Institute of Land Policy

The Lincoln Institute has been active on a number of educational fronts, some of which have been described earlier. It undertook the creation of SOLIR in part to demonstrate that powerful valuation technology could be employed in a low-cost microcomputer environment. That proposition, doubted not long ago by some, has now been clearly and convincingly established. The Lincoln Institute also saw SOLIR as a teaching device and built training courses, again on a demonstration basis, around it. Finally, the Lincoln Institute saw the value of SOLIR (or other systems it might inspire) to countless jurisdictions in the United States and abroad. Recent work has been directed at making the program more user-friendly and allowing integration with other software packages. In the relatively near future, the Lincoln Institute plans to implement a distribution policy that will make SOLIR broadly available.

Given its experience with SOLIR and its academic orientation, the Lincoln Institute is particularly well situated to encourage further CAV research. Although others may assume more responsibility for the actual training of assessors, the Lincoln Institute may make a valuable contribution by promoting innovative teaching techniques, some of which are described below.

Because it is an academic institution, the Lincoln Institute also has the opportunity to serve as a neutral clearinghouse for CAV information through publication, conferences, and advanced seminars. Private companies must necessarily promote their own services and products. Local governments have limited resources for the dissemination of information. In theory, other academic institutions could fill this role, but in fact, the Lincoln Institute has played a dominant role. As more schools of planning and public administration include modern geoprocessing in their curricula, however, there will be still greater stimulus to research, at least on the land management side, and some of this may well have relevance to valuation.

The International Association of Assessing Officers

Professional organizations like the IAAO are best situated in some important respects to do regular CAV training for assessors. First, they have a comprehensive valuation curriculum into which courses on computer assisted valuation can easily be integrated; assessors who come to IAAO for one kind of training will undoubtedly get exposed to other opportunities. Second, while academic institutions like the Lincoln Institute can give CAV intellectual credibility, a professional group like the IAAO can legitimize its practical utility. Finally, with its close links to local governments, IAAO can provide training that responds to the needs of its constituents.

On the other hand, because a dues-supported professional organization is likely to be oriented more toward practice than to theory, the IAAO may not be able to support research to the extent that an academic institution can. Thus the interests of the Lincoln Institute and the IAAO appear to be entirely complementary.

Other Sources of CAV Education

Private valuation firms will provide CAV education as part of their services, but their training is necessarily tailored to the product they sell. It is unrealistic for a manager to look to such a firm for an objective assessment of the benefits and costs of CAV; likewise, any training for technicians will likely be quite limited in scope.

By contrast, the emergence of private CAV consultants holds great promise so long as such people are simply in the business of getting jurisdictions up and running on their own. Selling no long-term services and beholden to no particular software manufacturer, such consultants could give valuable advice to senior administrators; they could also design and offer training courses for their staffs. As with the IAAO, the work of such independent consultants would likely be enhanced with access to current research and new teaching materials from organizations like the Lincoln Institute.

As noted earlier, state and local tax officials can be both consumers and providers of CAV education. Even when local jurisdictions put on their own training programs, they will probably do so in collaboration with professional organizations or outside consultants. Once such a program is in place, it may be self-perpetuating. Again, of course, access to information on new CAV techniques and innovative teaching materials will enrich any program. Without such interchange, there is the danger that the wheel may be reinvented many times over.

Any jurisdiction's teaching and research priorities will be parochial; there is little local incentive to consider how local instructional programs might be useful elsewhere. The Lincoln Institute's plan to encourage the development of general teaching materials may counter this inefficiency to an extent, but if there is to be true coordination in municipally-conducted instruction, it will have to come from state governments. The state's need for more consistent and accessible local data (for more efficient equalization and revenue sharing) may one day require compatible computerization at the municipal level. That, in turn, would create a foundation for state-wide CAV training of local assessors. Unfortunately, current state regulations in some jurisdictions work the other way by creating bureaucratic barriers to innovation in tax administration.

EDUCATIONAL METHODS

No matter how the responsibility for CAV education is shared, teaching methods clearly can be improved. It is ironic that state-of-the-art technology is still often taught with the books and blackboards that have been with us for centuries. The formidable task of CAV education will be simplified significantly if we take intelligent advantage of the latest computer and video-assisted teaching technologies. It is important to remember, however, these methods are suited for some lessons but not for others.

Video and computer assisted instruction hold greatest promise in teaching basic CAV concepts to assessment technicians. Because this target population is potentially so large and the resources of CAV educators are limited, "stand alone" video modules should be used whenever possible. These modules could be supported with supplementary references or programmed teaching manuals to reinforce comprehension and aid recall. The content of these basic programs would be quite general, covering fundamental concepts in statistics, basic system design principles, and data management issues. Interactive video programs could handle somewhat more sophisticated material and would allow for self-paced learning. They are, however, fairly expensive to develop.

More detailed topics, such as system design or model building and interpretation, always require a significant amount of interaction between instructor and student in order to effectively establish in the student an intuitive "feel" for the proper avenues to explore given a large set of complicated technical options. Survey design, model calibration, and data communications are three areas that demand more than rote learning. Instructors can condense and transmit this experience most effectively in laboratory situations that allow the student to exercise judgment in a controlled environment. Watching the instructor respond more or less intuitively to unexpected results is often more valuable than the mastery of textbook material.

Some time in the future "expert systems" may be developed that will provide consultation and guidance in operational situations but also replace, in part, the human instructor in the experience-oriented environment of the teaching lab. In the shorter-term, it is possible to incorporate far more friendly software and thus reduce what has to be learned.

Realistically, high tech offers less promise for the general education of senior tax administrators. The information they need to select and implement a CAV system will not neatly fit on a computer diskette. (Even if it did, a tax administrator who needs to convince a superior to invest in a CAV system will be able to lobby far more effectively if he or she has personally talked with the experts and inspected sites where such systems are operating.) Conventional conferences and symposia clearly are not enough; however, there is plenty of room for imagination in demonstrating hardware and software.

CONCLUSION

The success of jurisdictions in implementing computer assisted valuation systems will depend less on the sophistication of the technology itself than on the sophistication with which such technology is acquired, managed, and operated. This sophistication in turn, is entirely a function of the availability of well conceived CAV education.

Chapter 15

POLITICAL AND ADMINISTRATIVE CONCERNS WITH COMPUTER ASSISTED VALUATION

Will Knedlik

Political decision-making in the United States has never been either a very exact science, nor an altogether uplifting art—or, at least, has not been since the U.S. Constitution was signed, sealed, and delivered. Government administration, which is more or less a contemporary art-science-of-necessity, also typically lacks both simple elegance and great intellectual rigor.

However, such general caveats are rather small potatoes compared with the almost innumerable political and administrative problems defining the context in which computer assisted valuation decisions actually occur in American government. Three examples will suffice to sketch necessary background.

During the last several decades, government has lost the confidence of many U.S. citizens. Further, the property tax is widely—and, almost, uniquely—unpopular. While concern has been clearly growing about the unequal treatment of similarly situated taxpayers and about the relatively high rates of the federal income tax experienced due to inflation-push on the middle class in recent years, the property tax has been unpopular for a much longer time and is likely to continue to be so. Finally, nearly every American adult has had some adverse experience involving computers used for record-keeping, bookkeeping, or billing purposes.

The specific CAV concerns discussed below, then, are appropriately considered in this real-world context in which government valuation activities

225

in general, and changes in valuation methods in particular, have been occurring for the last several decades. While many additional matters could be noted, the fact is that when politicians or administrators are reviewing decisions to initiate a change to incorporate CAV techniques, to continue such an effort from one budget period to the next (or to terminate it often substantially incomplete and over-budget), or to upgrade an existing CAV system, they do so in a path filled with numerous practical and difficult considerations.

NOTA BENE: THERE ARE TWO MAJOR POLITICAL AND ADMINISTRATIVE ARENAS—NOT ONE

This chapter will examine the political and administrative problems which have been experienced in a variety of state and local jurisdictions in two rather different arenas: *one*, the external arena involving government officials and the citizenry whose property is assessed, and *two*, the internal arena involving the professionals working in local and state governments in the assessment field before, during, and after adoption of CAV techniques. Further, since most of the existing literature focuses on the *external* political arena, this chapter will focus the majority of its attention on *internal* political concerns.

A book-length discussion of the issues involved would, of course, make further distinctions between statewide and local assessment jurisdictions, and would also discuss the internal politics of private appraisal and valuation companies, as well, with respect to the introduction of CAV methods and personnel. However, since the purpose of this book is introductory, these additional distinctions can merely be noted for the reader to consider if any such are of special interest in his or her professional life.

OFFICE POLITICS AND ADMINISTRATION

While much has been written about the external political and administrative problems faced by an assessing jurisdiction when instituting CAV operations, there has not been enough forthright attention focused on the sometimes deep and bitter divisions which have occurred in assessment offices over CAV methods and personnel, in a great many jurisdictions, throughout the world—and, unfortunately, which continue to occur between many offices' traditional "fee appraisers" and the new CAV personnel and operations.

The "fee appraiser" has traditionally held a place of substantial prestige and influence in government assessment offices. Many appraisers have reached such positions through considerable periods of service, serious professional study, and other genuine efforts on behalf of the jurisdiction and its assessment functions. Many appraisers are without college degrees (much less "advanced" degrees) largely because of changes which have occurred in society over the last several decades since their initial employment with a government agency. In fact, many senior appraisers with both ability and experience would not be *academically* qualified even to apply for the jobs which they currently hold if they were forced for some reason to apply for those jobs today.

Such fact patterns do *not* in and of themselves, of course, mean that such senior appraisal personnel are technically either qualified or unqualified for their jobs. In fact, there are many excellent people in assessment offices around the United States and elsewhere in the world, and there is, certainly, some deadwood. This is true in all agencies of government; all businesses of every type, large and small; and all other activities employing humans. Frankly, the virtual institutionalization of degree requirements into job descriptions in the United States is, upon examination, rather suspect. However, the point here is not to debate the merits of this difficult personnel issue but merely to point out a factual situation which may well contribute, *rightly or wrongly*, to the tensions actually often experienced to this day between traditional and CAV appraisal employees.

When the decision to undertake CAV techniques is made, a new breed of employee often enters established assessment office politics. This is not universal, of course, since existing personnel may well be utilized in new CAV capacities. However, quite often another personnel group is established, usually in a *separate* division within the office, in order to get the CAV system running. Such people are likely to be younger, with less formal assessment experience, but with considerably more formal academic training and other higher education—the alleged benefits of which they may well be quite prepared to expound, *at length*, particularly where they lack a hands-on appraisal background.

Thus, the interface between CAV and traditional appraisers would appear almost ideally suited for personnel conflict.

In visiting with many assessors and assessment office employees over the last decade, it has become apparent that potential problems involving a traditional appraisal division's prestige, prerogatives, and powers often are not adequately addressed in the planning undertaken for the CAV transition. Nor is this altogether inexcusable. As suggested above, public administration is not a precise or fully developed management science. Further, the monies available for the administration of an assessment office are seldom likely to overwhelm or otherwise put to final rest all of the legitimate needs of the office. However, budgets are often particularly tight during the transition from the traditional appraisal system toward an integration of CAV hardware, software, methods, personnel, and other related changes.

A number of other issues also arise which can create a bad relationship between traditional employees and the new "computer jockeys."

1. The expenses, time, and efforts involved in making the transition can often be—and, seemingly, almost always are—under-estimated.
2. Such miscalculations can crunch an agency's budget severely and over a rather long period of time.
3. The changeover often can and does involve additional burdens on existing employees, which such burdens are not adequately appreciated by those engineering the changes (at political and administrative levels), and which are often not adequately compensated (either in terms of recognition, payment in money, or reimbursement through compensatory time).
4. The benefits of CAV are often oversold or misunderstood. Many kinds of examples are possible here, but the fact is that CAV methods are much more likely to generate *better* assessment data (and, then, if and only if properly employed) than actually to reduce costs dramatically. Failing to focus on the real benefits, while alleging "phantom" benefits, often leads to political and administrative problems during CAV implementation.
5. Trade-offs exist between hiring outside consultants and hiring (or promoting) to new CAV positions from within the existing personnel system, but either case has many potentials for creating internal political and administrative headaches within the assessment office.

The list of examples could be multiplied many times over, but the point here is that many different and difficult types of problems are encountered in a CAV transition and are often faced with terribly inadequate planning for personnel or other impacts.

The message here is, above all else, that the person or persons deciding to implement a CAV system must:

(1) understand what a CAV system can and cannot do, and what is really involved in the effort, and, then,
(2) assuage the personnel and other problems as fully as possible through good planning, administrative, personnel, and other practices.

This will not eliminate all office politics, nor all administrative difficulties, but it will minimize them. Further, an agency forthrightly facing the difficult issues may well eliminate some of the worst potentials for deep-seated and, then, long-running turf battles between entrenched "fee appraisal" departments and newer CAV personnel, some of which unpleasant machinations have occurred in various assessment offices around the United States for over a decade now, with no indication that they are about to end.

INTERGOVERNMENTAL POLITICS

Another area which merits passing notice here is the pushing and shoving that necessarily go on in many jurisdictions between the legislative and executive branches on the one hand, and the assessment office on the other hand. The assessor's job or its equivalent is highly political, whether or not it is an elected or appointed position. Property tax issues, including valuation and most others, are much too controversial for this not to be the case in most state and local governments.

In such a context, the assessor will find that if there are unexpected problems or failures with the CAV transition, or with CAV methods thereafter, then he or she will receive all the blame by other branches of government. If there is real or perceived success, or any other potentially beneficial public relations opportunities, then he or she will be forced to share such political benefits. This goes with the territory generally, although there are almost innumerable permutations based on local political contexts.

However, keeping this in mind, the assessor should certainly consider with care before trying to "go it alone" in advocating or implementing a transition to CAV techniques since, if delays are encountered, if costs exceed reasonable expectations, or if any other adverse situation is faced, then he or she will likely be left twisting in the wind and very, very much alone (as well as, quite likely, splashed across the front pages of the local newspaper).

Further, the assessor who has not properly involved his or her legislative body and local government administrator in the CAV decision should keep in mind that the "computer" is also a very convenient *whipping-boy* for politicians and other local government administrators to blame for a host of issues—both relevant and largely unrelated. The most important instance probably is the tendency of policy makers to blame the assessor and CAV techniques for increases in property taxes which are, in fact, the results of political decisions largely unrelated to either the assessment office or CAV functions.

STILL MORE EXTERNAL POLITICS

While there are, of course, success stories in the institutionalization of CAV operations throughout the United States, the problems encountered to date offer an impressive catalog of the many ways in which to go wrong in introducing computer technology to the assessment function. While this section is necessarily somewhat anecdotal, it will illustrate several important areas in which political and administrative problems have arisen.

Since the early 1960s, most local California assessors have, with leadership from a strong, state-level Board of Equalization, dramatically upgraded the quality of assessments with the utilization of CAV techniques and able personnel. California assessors were, thus, successful in capturing the dramatic run-up in housing prices in the early 1970s—including unrealized capital gains. The voters of the state repaid their competence and efforts with Proposition 13.

Utah's Legislature, in 1969, enacted legislation to improve the quality and to increase the frequency of local property assessments. Considerable delays and cost overruns were experienced in introducing CAV methodologies; local assessors never came around to accepting them with much enthusiasm; and subsequent legislative sessions substantially weakened the effort. By the early 1980s, the legislation had been repealed.

However, in King County, Washington, a political maverick, Harley Hoppe, was elected County Assessor on a platform of outright opposition to computer assisted valuation in 1971, changed his mind virtually immediately upon obtaining office (if not before, as he was sometimes accused), and instituted a CAV operation that functioned rather well for the following decade. For this operation's efficiency, he obtained virtually no credit in a rather nasty election campaign in 1983, in which local newspapers and television stations pounded him very hard and in which he was badly defeated. However, CAV concerns were not a very major election issue in this rather unpleasant campaign, either. While the King County Assessor's Office continues to suffer some serious divisions between traditional "fee appraisers" and "computer jockeys" to this current day, the CAV operations technically continue to function rather well under the new County Assessor, Ruthe Ridder.

Needless to say, some leading CAV offices in the United States and abroad, such as that of Cuyahoga County, Ohio, were well led through the CAV transition from the beginning, have not suffered major political or administrative reverses, and continue to operate well to this day—long after the original leadership of George Voinovich in Cleveland has gone on to bigger and better things. But this important example also illustrates the importance of a strong and able leader, who was a good politician (in the best sense of that word), who was an able administrator, who realistically estimated the costs, and who put together a workable program over a reasonable length of time. Such a person of vision and administrative ability is relatively rare in government or anywhere else, and yet such are the components necessary to undertake a CAV project from the beginning to a successful conclusion.

RISKS AND REWARDS

At this point, the reader might well ask why any assessor, possessed of a fully sound mind, would want to undertake the risks and potentially adverse consequences of various kinds involved in introducing CAV methods. The answer is several-fold, but essentially the most important benefits are the ability to generate better value estimates, and thereby to do a better job of valuing real and personal property. Doing the job better may well involve better capturing the value of unrealized capital gains in an up-market—as was the case in California. But it is the job of the assessor to do so accurately, and to leave to policy makers the somewhat intractable issue of how to resolve the various political and policy problems created in such uncomfortable situations.

Furthermore, to improve the assessment function today, it is nearly essential to integrate state-of-the-art CAV techniques into the valuation activities of any competent assessment office. While doing the job better may sometimes be more controversial than merely using the assessment function to *fudge-over* policy and other government problems, the fact is that doing the job competently is what an assessor is elected or appointed to do.

The office of assessor is not a place for popularity contests; it is a place for professionals to do a job competently. Despite the many problems encountered, professionals all around the United States have been increasingly doing just that—through the introduction of CAV techniques and personnel, and through other equally difficult decisions.

Chapter 16

LEGAL CHALLENGES TO COMPUTER ASSISTED VALUATIONS

Will Knedlik

Legal adjudication is essentially *reaction*. The function of deciding cases pursuant to the common-law system is basically one of *responding* to those specific questions which are brought before the courts and other adjudicative tribunals by independent parties. Thus, those individual parties and government agencies which initiate and defend legal challenges of various kinds largely determine the questions which, in fact, ultimately will be decided—both in terms of selecting the substantive issues and, often of equal importance, in terms of procedurally framing those issues for decision.

Therefore, the adjudicative process is neither altogether rational, nor orderly. Critical issues can avoid attention for decades, while minutiae can dominate the process. In short, adjudication is much more a catch-as-catch-can activity in the common-law system (which is in place in the United States, the United Kingdom, and elsewhere in other Commonwealth countries) than is normally recognized either within or without the legal profession. But this is the real-world context in which computers and the law have largely met to date, and in which they will continue to interface in the future.

IF CHALLENGED, CAN COMPUTER ASSISTED VALUATION MODELING TECHNIQUES STAND UP IN COURT?

The most fundamental legal question regarding CAV modeling techniques is almost certainly whether they can, *if properly employed*, generate value estimates which can measure up to the minimum standards required by generally-accepted rules of evidence in order to be *eligible* to be considered by a judge, hearing officer, or other finder-of-fact. If CAV methods cannot meet this test, then they *cannot* be given any consideration if directly challenged.

After several decades of experience with CAV modeling techniques, the American legal system has apparently not yet squarely answered this most basic question—in a published judicial decision with authority as a precedent—although a handful of published decisions involving sales and assessment ratios and equalization rates have obliquely dealt with some of the issues inherent in CAV modeling problems. In fact, an early Arizona case, *State v. Rella Verde Apartments, Inc.*, 25 Ariz. App. 458, 544 P.2d 675 (1976), actually came close to confronting this central issue at several points in the decision, but finally finessed the issue and decided the case without squarely dealing with the admissibility of a CAV model.

Since the direct answer is not apparently available, it is therefore appropriate to formulate two additional questions:

1. Is CAV evidence *likely* to be accepted by U.S. courts, if and when the question is directly asked?

2. If so, under what circumstances?

In this case, the answer to the first and more critical question is most likely to be in the affirmative. In fact, there are important indications already from several fields of American law to support the admissibility of computer assisted modeling of various kinds—*if it is properly done.*

WHY THE VALIDITY OF CAV METHODS APPEARS TO BE UNDECIDED

As noted, courts generally decide only those questions that are brought before them. Thus, a key question at this point is why the validity of CAV techniques has not been specifically litigated (or, at least, challenged in non-judicial tax appeal proceedings), as appears to be the case.

Candor compels the admission that cases decided by both tax courts and boards of tax appeals are extremely difficult to research, since there is no systematic reporting system of the kind that is available in most other areas of American law. Thus, it is possible to engage in extensive legal research and still miss the odd case. However, the inability to find a case specifically on point regarding the validity of CAV techniques probably results, in this context, from the nature of the property tax appeals process as it functions throughout the United States.

Typically, a taxpayer challenges the assessed valuation placed on a particular parcel of property by an assessment office. This assessed valuation may have been generated with the aid of a computer in many jurisdictions, while in many other places it will not have been.

However, once the challenge is made and the battle lines are drawn, the evidence of value which computer assisted assessment offices typically advance in order to support the particular valuation under challenge is not the computer model which was used initially to value the property for tax purposes. Quite to the contrary, a battery of other tools is available to the assessment office, and are typically chosen; for example, a collection of particular comparable sales, a replacement cost table, or even a full-blown fee appraisal. In fact, a computer is also often going to be used to select the comparables, to generate the replacement cost table, or to assist the state-of-the-art fee appraiser. But in each instance, it is going to operate in the background and it is going to be essentially invisible, and so, when push comes to shove, the computer will not typically be the focus of the legal challenge.

Even those assessment offices which place the greatest reliance on computer assisted valuation do not appear anxious to answer an administrative or judicial challenge by a taxpayer to an assessed valuation by merely (1) putting its CAV model into evidence, (2) relying on such presumption of validity for its assessed valuation as legally exists in any given jurisdiction (which presumption of validity, incidentally, differs substantially from state to state), and (3) thereby forcing the challenger to test the assessment office's computer model—or, perhaps, the latter point might better be phrased in terms of *encouraging* the challenger to *test* the assessing office's computer model, the competence of its staff in using the model, and a host of other potentially related questions.

Given such a rather typical scenario, and given the general lack of expertise in the legal community in challenging property valuations, the party pressing for a lower valuation is not likely to attack an assessing jurisdiction's computer model, which typically has largely dropped out of the picture once the assessment was challenged and which usually has been replaced by a group of proffered "comparable sales" in the vast majority of simple cases, or by a "fee appraisal" of one sort or another in those cases of larger or more important valuation challenges.

A PREDICTION

Since predictions are risky in the adjudicative process, prudence would suggest that none should be made. Nonetheless, it seems likely that CAV methodologies will eventually be challenged by individuals or groups of taxpayers directly—or at least that the competence of some assessing agencies in using such techniques will be challenged. Further, as money becomes tighter for local governments during the next decade or so, it would appear likely that jurisdictions which rely on property tax revenues, but which are not responsible for assessment functions, such as schools or cities, might well find it appropriate to legally test the CAV models which are being utilized for assessment purposes in order, for example, to attempt to maximize total revenues or their jurisdiction's share of such revenues.

While such intergovernmental litigation would be quite different in many ways from run-of-the-mill property valuation appeals, fundamental computer assisted valuation questions might well play a central role in any such litigation if competently litigated. Also, while pushing far beyond several previous legal challenges to computer-generated assessment ratios, such intergovernmental litigation would naturally build on such earlier and unsuccessful legal challenges (to mere computerized arithmetical functions) even while redirecting their real attack onto the actual computer *models, sui generis.*

THE JUDICIAL TREND REGARDING COMPUTER ASSISTED MODELING IS GENERALLY TOWARD ACCEPTANCE IN SEVERAL FIELDS OF LAW

Frankly, litigation focusing on the most fundamental issue about computers and the law—namely, the basic admissibility of computer-generated-model evidence—also remains remarkably scant outside the field of valuation.

Questions regarding the use of computers for routine record-keeping, arithmetical, and other bookkeeping functions have been raised in many contexts, and rather clearly answered. The general direction is one of acceptance of such evidence by courts, although with caution and some misgivings, typically within authentication and "best evidence" rules, and within slightly expanded exceptions to ordinary prohibitions against "hearsay."

Judge Carlisle Roberts, Senior Judge of the Oregon Tax Court, nicely summed up the concerns and the general direction regarding the acceptance of such computer-records evidence in his presentation to the National Conference of State Tax Judges in March, 1983:

> In *Bronson v. Consolidated Edison Co.*, 350 F Supp 443, 444 (SD NY 1972), the court states: "The facts as set forth by plaintiff suggest an Orwellian nightmare of computer control which breaks down through mechanical and programmers' failures and errors." This is an unusually strong statement. Judges, properly, have accepted computer evidence with caution, recognizing the danger of error in all business record systems and noting that "(t)he computer is a marvelous device that can perform countless tasks at high speed and low cost, but it must be used with care. This is because it can also make errors at high speed." *Neal v. U.S.*, F Supp 678, 680 (D NJ 1975).

Such judicial acceptance is largely to be expected for at least two major reasons:

1. The general *prohibition* against "hearsay" has been largely swallowed by the numerous exceptions to the rule created by common-law courts over the last several centuries; and,

2. The need for society and its legal institutions to accommodate the overwhelming movement toward computerization of record-keeping functions by business, government, and individuals over the last several decades is essentially irresistible.

While such general acceptance of computerized records is important, it really has very little if anything to do with the much more difficult issue of the acceptability of computer assisted models as evidence — except, perhaps, in terms of indicating an increasing level of comfort by the courts with computer output generally.

The use of a computer model, however, is quite a different kettle of fish from the use of a computer for routine arithmetical, bookkeeping, or record-keeping functions, since the use of any computer assisted model actually falls within the realm of those evidentiary rules governing expert testimony. Thus, the computer model should be subject to the same requirements as any expert witness, including rigorous cross-examination, and therefore subject to the same probing of its "expertness," regarding education, skill, and experience, which underlies the admission of any "educated" opinion-evidence.

In short, the computer model, the programmer who designed it, and any persons who use it, should all be subject to rigorous examination in order for CAV techniques and practices to qualify for admission into evidence.

The leading case in the field is *Perma Research & Development Co. v.*

Singer Co., 542 F.2d 111 (2d Cir, 1976). This landmark case was written by a retired U.S. Supreme Court Justice, Tom Clark, sitting by designation in the Federal Court of Appeals, and it also contains a long, very strong, and intelligently argued dissent by Circuit Judge Ellsworth Van Graafeiland. Thus, it was decided by a vote of two-to-one, and was then appealed to the U.S. Supreme Court, where *certiorari* was denied at 429 U.S. 987 (1976).

In *Perma Research*, the Circuit Court decided that an unperfected anti-skid device was *perfectable*, basing its decision in substantial part on the testimony of expert witnesses who, in turn, had relied on the results of a computer simulation that suggested that it was in fact *perfectable*. Therefore, the Circuit Court sustained the large amount of damages awarded by the trial court because the Singer Company had not used its best efforts to *perfect* the *unperfected* device and, then, to market it after such unrealized perfection.

Judge Van Graafeiland's dissent focused on numerous evidentiary problems including those related to the need for allowing computer models to be fully examined by an opposing party. Also, he noted the importance of understanding what computer modeling is really all about (and how it differs from mere arithmetic):

> As courts are drawn willy-nilly into the magic world of computerization, it is of utmost importance that appropriate standards be set for the introduction of computerized evidence. Statements like those of the District [trial court] Judge that a computer is "but calculators [sic] with a giant 'memory' and the simulations the computer produces are but the solutions to mathematical equations in a 'logical' order" represent an overly-simplified approach to the problem of computerized proof which should not receive this Court's approval.

While his dissenting opinion did not prevail in this case, it has been noted in the legal literature and many of his concerns have been incorporated into legal thinking over the last decade. Basically, the court system has responded by requiring parties using computer-generated evidence to provide it to the opposing party, and to do so rather early in the process of litigation, so that it can be analyzed, tested, and challenged—as appropriate for all "expert-opinion" evidence. Thus, although Judge Van Graafeiland did not prevail in *Perma Research* in legally requiring such early and full disclosure, later cases have largely institutionalized his desire for such procedures. Given the nature of the evidence, this certainly appears appropriate.

Perma Research has been cited by judges in a substantial number of cases which have occurred since 1976, and it is generally recognized in legal literature as a pivotal decision regarding computer assisted modeling techniques. However, in recently reading all of the cases from both state and federal courts which have cited *Perma Research*, it became apparent that it has been generally relied upon for its decision on the damage question and on pretrial discovery issues. Few cases have actually relied directly on its decision on the fundamental admissibility of computer assisted models as evidence. Thus, while *Perma Research* is the leading case in the field, remains good law, and is, therefore, available for citation on the question of the admissibility of computer models, the fact is that this specific and critical question has seldom been pushed to the point of a written judicial decision since the Federal Appeals Court approved such models in *Perma Research* nearly a decade ago. Thus, in the law generally, the number of decisions directly regarding computer assisted modeling remains quite small.

However, a rather recent trial in a criminal matter in New York City also merits notice here—since Bronx Supreme Court Justice John Collins allowed into evidence a computer-generated graphic offered by the defense attorneys. The May, 1983 trial of Michael McHugh, reported on in the American Bar Association *Journal* in November, 1984, appears to be the first time that such a computer assisted reenactment of the physics of an automobile accident was admitted in a criminal trial. As such, it is also a noteworthy step in the march of computer assisted techniques toward general legal acceptability in the common-law system.

This case also nicely illustrates the fact that, eventually, as computer assisted simulations of various types become more common, the battles of expert witnesses will be expanded to new vistas. Legal commentary on this criminal trial has noted, for example, the substantial disadvantage which the prosecuting attorney faced by being without a computer expert to challenge the defense's computer simulation.

Counterexamples, however, are almost always available in the cases which characterize the common-law system. One relatively recent and potentially important one has to do with litigation regarding the Apex Rule in mining law —a rule which has figured prominently in mining litigation ever since the War of the Copper Kings in Montana. In *Silver Surprize, Inc. v. Sunshine Mining Co.*, 15 Wash App.2, 547 P.2d 1240 (1976), the Washington Court of Appeals determined that the only way in which Sunshine could show the continuity of a mineral vein was to follow its mineralization physically on its downward dip, and that *"speculative conjecture or even intelligent guess"* could not overcome the presumption that the neighboring claim-owner owns the ores found beneath the surface of its land, citing and italicizing *Heinze v. Boston & Montana Consolidated Copper and Silver Mining Co.*, 30 Mont. 484, 77 P.421 (1904). Given this strict and on-going legal requirement, which apparently precludes computer modeling in a field where sophisticated modeling has been relied on for years by mining companies, there is at least some basis for questioning whether computer assisted techniques will ever be *universally* accepted in American law.

POTENTIAL RISKS AND REWARDS OF SPECIFICALLY ASCERTAINING THE ADMISSIBILITY OF CAV TECHNIQUES

The situation regarding the format of typical property valuation appeals has delayed the direct legal testing of the admissibility of CAV techniques to date. Whether merely a result of happenstance or of conscious design, this delay has probably been in the best interests of the techniques, since CAV models have not had to bear the burden of making any totally "new law." However, with the likelihood being rather good that properly conducted CAV functions will be legally upheld, the question necessarily arises about whether it would be in the best interests of some or all parties, but particularly of assessment offices, to have the question directly and clearly determined by a court—with ideally, of course, a case in which the computer model is sound, in which the applicable computer programmers are clearly experts and would make good witnesses, and in which the personnel operating the system are also similarly well qualified.

A major risk, of course, is that even in the best of circumstances, a particular case can be lost at trial, with the additional risk that the right to use CAV techniques might, as a consequence, be adversely affected. However, given the fact that a test case could choose a particularly strong CAV application, the risk would seem much less in such an instance than it might well be if a less favorable application, in a less well qualified jurisdiction, were the first to be directly litigated.

The rewards of a successful test case might be several-fold; however, the most important benefit could well be to lessen the expense of handling appeals by eliminating the need for fee appraisals in most cases. Further, the burden placed on a party attempting to challenge an assessed valuation would be greatly increased since it would almost certainly require the challenger to retain computer expertise in order to attack the computer model actually used to value his or her property.

However, such potential benefits might well turn out to be more detrimental than beneficial in the long run, since such a state of affairs might well be unpopular with the public, might well vitiate the "safety value" function of property tax appeals in the political process, and might well also prove to be quite unpopular with appraisal professionals both inside and outside of assessment offices. As is more fully discussed in another chapter, the politics of CAV techniques within appraisal offices are not insignificant.

Thus, an increased reliance on CAV methods might well exacerbate an already deep division within the staffs of many assessment offices.

CONCLUSION

While the most basic question regarding the admissibility of CAV techniques has not been directly decided by the courts or other adjudicative tribunals, the general legal trend suggests that such CAV methods will be admissible if properly designed and utilized.

However, as the *Silver Surprize* case illustrates, it is quite possible that computer assisted techniques will be accepted for use in valuing a mine, even while the use of computer simulations to establish the mine's ore veins (under the federal mining act) will not be allowed. While perhaps ironic, such a scenario would certainly not be totally unexpected in a field as catch-as-catch-can as the common-law system. After all, the common law is not and does not claim to be an orderly computer science.

Chapter 17

ARTIFICIAL INTELLIGENCE AND BEYOND

E. Eugene Carter

Within a few pages, one cannot cover the area of artificial intelligence. Indeed, there is significant disagreement among leading writers in the area about just what it is. The list of publications under "Further Reading" will provide more information about the field to the interested reader.

Computers are now capable of far more sophisticated operation than in their earliest years. Two quotations from Nobel prize winner Herbert A. Simon are notable in this regard:

> "There are now in the world machines that think, that learn and that create. Moreover, their ability to do these things is going to increase rapidly until — in the visible future — the range of problems they can handle will be coextensive with the range to which the human mind has been applied."[1]

> "Within the very near future — much less than twenty-five years — we shall have the technical capability of substituting machines for any and all human functions in organizations. Within the same period, we shall have acquired an extensive and empirically tested theory of human cognitive processes and their interaction with human emotions, attitudes, and values."[2]

This chapter has benefited from the comments of Lutz Alt, Charlotte Boschan, Robert Hughes, Dennis Robinson, Rita Rodriguez, and Arlo Woolery.

1. Cited in Weizenbaum (1976), p. 138.
2. *Ibid.*, p. 245.

There is overstatement, perhaps, in these remarks. However, they give one a perspective on the designs of leading researchers in the area of advanced computer systems, which include artificial intelligence.

EXPERT SYSTEMS

Our interest is in the field of expert systems, as opposed to sophisticated robotics models. In any case, a correct generic term is really Advanced Computer Science. Researchers from the 1960s who worked in the areas of computer science, management science, and the like are often actively involved in this "new" field. What is new about it?

First, these scientists have a heightened sensitivity to cognition, and often a broader knowledge of linguistics and psychology. They are more sensitive to how people learn, how people react, and how people think. Thus, the first generation of information systems built on large mainframe computers is generally acknowledged by neutral observers to have been a failure, for reasons related to ideas discussed in Chapter 3. They did provide more accurate and complete information in a more timely manner. They failed because they ignored the need of managers for relevant information in a restricted quantity. Instead, the information systems buried managers in computer printout. Generally, there is increasing agreement that a general model of human problem-solving may not be as productive a research assumption as recognizing that expertise is very specific, and ought to be studied in a specific context. This field really began in the 1960s and was rather moribund in the early 1970s, in part because of the related over-promising of the management science researchers discussed earlier in this chapter.

There is an old tradition of using computers to find an optimal solution to some human problem, as noted earlier. Many of these optimization techniques should be transferred to the new field of expert systems. Further, there is a tradition of replicating human behavior, whether optimizing or not: trust officers, accounts receivable collection decisions, credit granting decisions, production engineers, chess players, and the like were modeled with varying degrees of effectiveness and accuracy in the 1960s. These models often relied not on optimizing models but on heuristics, rules of thumb or guidelines for finding an acceptable solution to a given problem.

Before discussing software and hardware innovations which have contributed mightily to this new field, let us think about what a typical expert system does.

One guideline is that the expert under study should have generally acknowledged expertise; i.e., the person should have some skill in some area which others recognize as talent. Second, the expertise should be capable of being applied to a setting, given the data, in five minutes to two hours. Under five minutes, it may be trivial; over two hours and the problem may be too complex to analyze with an expert system model today.

A *knowledge engineer* acts as a buffer between the computer programmer and the expert in some settings. This person extracts the expertise, typically after reading the general texts and articles in the field, talking with other experts, and the like. After interviewing the expert whose expertise is to be modeled, the engineer interprets the expertise to the computer programmer. The engineer clearly must have some knowledge of what information the programmer needs. Results are given, and the expert is debriefed after his or her review of the initial output. This process repeats, with the knowledge engineer attempting to gain greater insight into the subtle assumptions, perhaps the contradictions, and general conscious or semiconscious thought process used by the expert in reaching a conclusion.

The typical program involves a large series of steps, usually in the form of IF A/or B/and C/unless D, etc., THEN Z. These steps are coded in a knowledge base. The operator of this logic is a knowledge engine, and usually the base and the engine are kept separate. The engine might be used with other bases (i.e., in other areas of expertise) whereas the base might be repeatedly changed, altered, or just dropped.

At the simplest level, many of the templates sold commercially to work with a spreadsheet package such as VISICALC are expert systems. Consider capital budgeting. The template requires the user to enter such data as the level, frequency, and duration of cash flows; the cost of money; the tax rate; and so forth. The template, extracting from an expert's knowledge, decides how these factors interrelate and uses the microcomputer hardware and the spreadsheet software to produce decisions, or at least strong recommendations.

SOFTWARE

Often, the engines are commercially available in the form of *shells* which can be run on large mainframes, in a time-sharing environment, or even on large microcomputers such as the models from Zenith, Compaq, IBM, or Texas Instruments. These engines are often written in a specialized computer language such as LISP and PROLOG, which the Japanese have chosen for their highly-publicized Fifth Generation Computer. These languages facilitate working with words (as opposed to numeric variables), and structuring of statements such as indicated above. Further, the languages can permit altering the code by simply inserting the changes in a few statements. Inconsistencies are often readily highlighted by the language; otherwise, the change stands. Imagine, if you are familiar with a standard computer language such as ALGOL or FORTRAN, altering a program by simply throwing in a few statements anywhere you wish![3]

There are several examples of expert systems which are currently well-documented, although many of them obviously are far more complex than the specifications above suggest. These examples are in areas such as petroleum geology (where do we drill now and how do we react to various types of additional information?), medicine (infectious diseases, general diagnoses), computer installation and configuration, and the like.

The typical expert system (engine and base) needs to know when to break its own rules, since knowledge is typically incomplete, inaccurate, poorly specified, and contradictory. It needs to be flexible, and capable of being readily updated or revised. Ultimately, it should probably be transparent to the user. Finally, a good system should be capable of explaining *why* it is asking a question of a subsequent user at any point as well as *how* it reached a conclusion to some problem posed to it by a subsequent user.

One guideline is that the typical system takes five to ten years of effort of a single person. Some of the latest developments such as the shells should reduce this rate (and we certainly hope so with our own Lincoln Institute model!).

Today, software and hardware packages ranging from $200 to $200,000 are all called expert systems. Often, the lower priced systems essentially help a user structure a tree diagram. Tree diagrams start at point A with a decision to go to position B1 or B2, for example. In decision analysis, B1 and B2 may be probabilistic nodes (points), with a result from B1 of C1 with a probability of .3, C2 with a probability of .2, and C3 with a probability of .5. Notice the probabilities sum to 1. A similar range of outcomes D1 . . . DN extend from B2. Each of these C and D nodes, in turn, can be a decision point or a probabilistic outcome point. See Raiffa (1968) for additional reading.

One example of these packages is Expert Ease ($600). Critical variables are defined by the user who then indicates values for those variables and what his or her decision would be. The model can ask about unspecified options and can render a decision given the inputs. It cannot explain why it asks a question or how it reached a decision (other than presenting the

---

3. One of the earliest AI languages was R1, named by John McDermott at Carnegie-Mellon. He noted that three years before he had wanted to become an expert, "and now I are one."

entire tree diagram and a list of all the rules entered by the original expert). It cannot handle probabilistic information. A rule base involving the amount of money one has, whether the weather is sunny or raining, and whether one is alone or with someone suggesting different recreational activities is an example that is typical. Up to 40 variables can be handled by this model which plainly is not a toy.

This software interacts with an expert, bypassing the knowledge engineers used on the more sophisticated models. Other models involve clever means for the user to enter data. Sometimes pure graphics can be permitted, using a light pen, touch screen or other devices to indicate where on a line the outcome is in terms of cost, desirability, or whatever. Some expensive expert system shells permit a teaching mode, in which the user simply enters examples of what is a good decision given characteristics of variables (and the model may simply throw a sample trial at the user, asking for what the conclusion is).

At the inexpensive level, then, the most many "expert" systems provide is an able way to replicate a human in a situation by a combination of (1) speed and (2) enumeration of alternatives. The computer can process some types of information very rapidly, far faster than a human. By evaluating all alternatives, the computer expert can often match or beat the human. In other cases, patterns from a successful human approach can be embedded in the computer code, and the program seeks to match the situation it confronts with one stored in memory, responding as dictated. Neither alternative is impressive to me. As a non-computer expert I was doing things similar to this twenty-five years ago. I personally consider these models neither advanced nor expert, even though their availability on microcomputers is a fine achievement.

TIC-TAC-TOE

At the simplest level, consider tic-tac-toe (naughts-and-crosses), where the object is to get three of one's markers in a row in any direction. Any parent who has endured hours of the game with a child knows one can be sure to not lose if one goes first and often to win. Using speed and enumeration, a non-sophisticated expert system can simply take a position, A, take one or more opponent responses to which it in turn responds in different ways, followed by an opponent's range of responses, etc. It then evaluates position B in the same way. The choice of position A . . . I is then based on which move leaves the expert in the best position (i.e., one most likely to result in a win based on its own exhaustive enumeration of results which may follow from each position). However, since it can make foolish moves even starting with a dominant initial position, this *forward chaining* is not usually the complete way to play, certainly against a smart opponent. First, totally absurd responses, such as ignoring two markers in a row of either party by it or by an opponent can be eliminated on both sides from the enumeration. Second, to reduce search time, the program will at some point probably use *backward chaining* in each evaluation: given several winning positions, go to each of the positions one move before and see if one of these matches what the expert faces now. Furthermore, several *heuristics* may guide the computer play: seek two markers in a row, or seek two or more corners, etc. Each of these guides can help reduce the computer search time and may lead to a dominant move (i.e., one which cannot be defeated in any amount of time by the savviest of opponents, human or computer).

Perhaps all of the above replicates what the human does. In the better sense, though, what the real human expert does, I suspect, is simply *to know* there are right moves. How? Experience at play coupled with pattern recognition seem to me to be the best explanation. I know if I get two or three corners in the first two or three moves, I can win. I may not remember why, or may not be able to verbalize it, but initially I do not *need* to know why I seek those corners. So, too, could a programmed expert be given a series of patterned plays to mimic after one, two or more rounds. Even though there is a perfect algorithmic solution to tic-tac-toe, the expert may not be aware of it and indeed may not be subconsciously using it.

Here, the human expertise is more obvious to one who understands the program. There is less grinding calculation which overwhelms by sheer speed and exhaustive enumeration than there is pattern matching. Notice that the expert may not know why he or she does certain things in this scheme. Further notice that either approach would allow us to create an expert tic-tac-toe computer system.

CHESS

Many thoughtful researchers have studied chess over the years and have attempted to understand what makes a master chess player. Computer chess routines have been around for at least twenty-five years. In the last ten years, they have been routine products in airport gift shops and boutiques. They have increased in speed, variety of play and the like. At the most primitive level, most simple models replicate our tic-tac-toe model. They evaluate each of many possible moves, accepting one or more opponent responses to each possible move. They may cycle forward one or more future rounds of expert/opponent moves and do so in the slower play of a more advanced player. However, after many moves, the program evaluates the field in terms of what it controls versus the opponent. It also evaluates the number and desirability of pieces it still has versus its opponent. Plainly, some rules are embedded which are mechanical: a knight may move only in a 2-1 combination. Other moves may be strategic. Thus, some human skill is embedded.

However, Herbert Simon suggests there is a more fruitful approach to the problem, and the one program I know of which can play at the low master level is based on this other approach. First, Simon notes that experiments show that masters can describe or recall a chess board they are shown with a match in place more successfully than most others. Second, they do no better than non-masters in memorizing nonsense syllables or describing foolish chess board setups, eliminating the idea of superior intellect per se, photographic minds, or the like. Third, there is no record of anyone becoming a chess master in under ten years of regular full-time play, other than Bobby Fisher (nine years and some months). Fourth, Simon indicates he has been told that there are about 10 to the 120th power games possible in chess, far beyond the ability of any human or computer to remember under any conditions.

As a result, Simon suggests that grandmasters really spend the years encoding perhaps 50,000 game patterns, and regular play afterwards maintains that long-term memory. He suggests that relatively small human short-term memory then sees a pattern (or something close to one), and searches for hooks (cross indices or references) in long-term memory by which to retrieve one or more of those 50,000 embedded patterns. Play progresses, then, from guidance derived or encoded with the pattern selected. Even a grandmaster needs time to retrieve a pattern, however. That is why they can often successfully play multiple simultaneous games ending in at least a draw against talented oponents, but cannot typically compete successfully against another grandmaster in a rapid-response environment if the other master has far more time to play. Simon also suggests that ten years of encoding patterns may not be a bad way to describe the time it takes to become an expert in law, medicine, management, or other fields. Learning continues to take place, but other long-term memory becomes irretrievable. An alternative approach which gives the same conclusion is to suggest that if raw top-flight human physical and intellectual prowess is distributed throughout many professions, and expertise is always considered relative to others in the field, if ten years is the figure for chess masters, it probably also sets a standard elsewhere.[4]

EXPERT SYSTEMS – OVERVIEW

One can say that a Moline cab driver and the head of the National Aeronautics and Space Administration are both in the transportation

4. See Simon (1981).

business. While both may be talented, moral, and hard-working people, there is a vast difference in the problems they face. So, too, can one comment that simple packages which attempt to help people structure their thinking (such as Expert Ease) or to solve algorithmically defined problems (such as a tic-tac-toe "expert system") are not of the same kind as the chess model we discussed. At the higher end, General Learning Corporation's The Intelligent Machine Model (TIMM) and Texas Instrument's Personal Consultant are vastly more sophisticated products.

At the still more expensive level, special dedicated LISP processors from firms such as Symbolics and LISP Machine offer parallel processing, as opposed to the sequential processing common in virtually all computers today. They offer highly specialized software, internally or from other vendors, which tailors their machines to a specific problem at hand. As an example, part of the problem with Three Mile Island was that many alarms were sounded simultaneously in about 45 seconds, and even an alert, well-trained attendant could not know how to react. The problem was not lack of information but an abundance of information. What a good dedicated processor would do is simply have predefined operant responses to a wide range of signals from sensing devices. At the extreme, of course, such automatic reaction was the theme of many of the doomsday horrors of the 1960s, including "Dr. Strangelove."

In general, then, to a large degree expert systems are simply "smart" systems which turn the powerful computer hardware into an information appliance. The key is software which replicates or eclipses clever human decision-making, as my colleague Dennis Robinson has suggested. The computer has the raw power; the expert system turns it into a channelled, directed thrust. Put another way, a clever graduate or a bright untutored person, like a large computer memory base, often has a huge collection of facts. It is the collection of these facts into useful relationships (knowledge) and ultimately the derivation of greater insights (wisdom) that the sophisticated software makes possible.

What will happen? One researcher really asked for bright liberal arts graduates whom he could train at the graduate level, arguing that the typical undergraduate high-grade engineering student had all the sparkle, imagination, and playfulness knocked out of him or her. Society plainly will have ambivalent feelings about the expert. Most of us do not begrudge the power lawn mower versus our own efforts with a scythe, nor do we reject basic levers through automobiles instead of footpower. However, anything that eclipses our own intellectual quality can be disconcerting. One expert who was successfully modeled supposedly became so depressed that he left the field. On balance, one hopes that the clever computer scientist, who must now be sensitive to some psychology given the need for sensitivity to cognition in building expert systems, will also think about the user. Indeed, the very requirement for transparency shows some sensitivity to the problem. Simon's pattern encoding, recognition, and retrieval also seem to me to be the way in which expert systems dealing with interesting problems are likely to progress.

CAESAR

At the Lincoln Institute of Land Policy, several of us are involved in a project which we believe will deepen our knowledge of how a tax expert formulates recommendations to a legislative commission or a governor's assistant. We call the model CAESAR (Computer Assisted Expert System for the Analysis of Revenue). Plainly, we cannot model the expertise based on a two hour limit to this individual's contribution. On the other hand, we have made the decision to focus on how he looks at certain types of problems and to see how effectively we can replicate his behavior.

Our ultimate goal is to use this expert system for research in the programs which take place at the Lincoln Institute, in training of novice committee staff members, in discussion among judges and others who have to pass upon tax recommendations, and so forth. We expect to use the engine we develop and our own learning about the techniques of building expert systems with other areas dealing with land policy.

After some investigation involving a wide range of expert system shells and some specialized machines for which my colleague, Dennis Robinson, would have to build the engine, we have settled upon the Personal Consultant from Texas Instruments, a new product. This will run on a 512K TI machine with a 10 megabyte hard disk drive, which we have purchased.

Much of what our expert does is to assemble economic data on a state's tax/economic profile. These data permit judgments about the degree of progressivity, the adequacy of the tax base under various assumptions in meeting a need for revenue, and the growth possible in the tax base. When viewing the situation of fifty states, one may argue that every situation is unique—in which case the expertise is highly specialized (or perhaps non-existent). However, we feel that we can ask the user of the system we develop to enter some data (or accept some national standards regarding burden of taxation for particular types of taxes, grouped by income level of the citizens).

Essentially, we have embedded a national database, which contains information such as suggested above. We will ask a user to enter information which becomes a general information database—number of citizens/households in various income classification categories, estimated amounts of particular taxes exported and imported, and the revenue produced by each of the taxes currently in existence, for example. Finally, the user enters various constraints which become part of a constraint database, such as requirements about what taxes cannot be (or must be) increased or decreased by some amount.

We have then imbedded a number of rules in the expert system, which contain the heuristics our expert uses to determine what tax changes he would recommend in some situations. These rules include considerations of equity and progressivity, splits between business and individual tax burdens, and so forth.

CONCLUSION

We are only beginning our project. In any case, we are confident that we will not be undermining the consulting practice of our expert! Indeed, as we progress in our understanding of the expertise, we recognize the difficulties in generating even a simplified expert system in this area. On the other side of the issue, we are confident that our learning in this area, combined with our understanding about change and technology, means that this is one of the most fruitful areas for research. We believe the CAESAR model will offer insights into how our expert thinks as well as facilitate the training and development of many users of the system. I hope you will be inspired to follow our progress in this area in the coming months.

There is a great deal of hyperbole in the entire field of artificial intelligence. The software community is always trying to peddle a new product, and hardware producers happily ride the same bandwagon. University researchers usually believe in what they are doing, and proselytize, yet sometimes they miss the mark. For example, the opening remarks in this chapter appeared in 1958 and 1960, yet they seem to be timely prognostications in 1985.

One computer scientist, Joseph Weizenbaum, became disenchanted about what was done in the field of artificial intelligence. His 1976 remarks are pertinent today:

"There is . . . no project in computer science as such that is morally repugnant. . . .The projects. . .are not properly part of computer science. . . because they are for the most part not science at all. They are. . .clever aggregations of techniques aimed at getting something done. . . .Tinkers with techniques (gadget worshippers, Norbert Wiener called them) sometimes find it hard to resist the temptation to associate themselves with science and to siphon legitimacy from the reservoir it has accumulated. But not everyone who calls himself a singer has a voice.

"A theory, of course, itself is a conceptual framework. And so it determines what is and what is not to count as fact. The theories—or perhaps better said, the root metaphors—that have hypnotized the artificial intelligentsia, and large segments of the general public as well, have long ago determined that life is what is computable and only that. As Professor John McCarthy, head of Stanford University's Artificial Intelligence Laboratory, said, 'The only reason we have not yet succeeded in formalizing every aspect of the real world is that we have been lacking a sufficiently powerful logical calculus. I am currently working on that problem.' "[5]

There are arguments that computers will mimic biological processes, reproducing themselves and creating design insights beyond those of their original designers. Some of these processes already have been accomplished in the laboratory. Biochips can recreate part of themselves. We can place a billion bytes on the head of a pin using the newest laser technology which can draw a finer line than an electron beam. One leading scientist reportedly remarked years ago that in N years, we shall be lucky if the machines keep us around as pets.

I am very uncertain about how far the evolution of computers will go, nor how significant the machines will be in replacing humans throughout society. Apropos the field of robotics, any four-year-old still knows more about blocks than any computer. I am also wise enough not to believe anyone else's prognostications. As did some others, I believed thirty years ago that many pedestrian tasks would have humans replaced or supplemented by computers. I also felt that the machines would create features, options, and choices that never were available. Both judgments were accurate, though not always in the specific areas I forecast.

Part of the problem is that a human's reaction/insight/judgment is a function of all he is and was, biologically, emotionally, physically, experientially. One child deprived of affection becomes a musical genius and another a criminal. Why?

I think, then, that advanced systems probably will replace the less significant work of many people, leaving them with both drudgery and stimulation at two extremes. I do not think the truly great insights in music, science, or what have you will come from the machines 25 years from now, but they will have insights far beyond the above-average musician or scientist of today. The routine will more likely be done on the computer; the exceptional, by the human. On that routine/exceptional continuum, more and more will be considered routine, however.

We often criticize machines as we criticize the highly educated person: all brains and no street smarts. We ought to remember that many of the people with limited education still do not have much in the way of street smarts. Hence, accept the computers for what they will be able to do, rather than rejecting them for what they cannot do.

---

5. Weizenbaum (1976), pages 268 and 201.

FURTHER READING

Hormit, Elizabeth, "Exploring Expert Systems," *Business Computer Systems*, March, 1985, pp. 48-57.

Kinnucan, Paul, "Software Tools Speed Expert System Development," *High Technology*, March, 1985, pp. 16-21.

O'Shea, Tim and Marc Eisenstadt, *Artificial Intelligence: Tools, Techniques and Applications*, Harper and Row, New York, 1984.

Simon, Herbert A., *The Science of the Artificial*, second edition, MIT Press, Cambridge, Mass., 1981.

Weizenbaum, Joseph, *Computer Power and Human Reason: From Judgment to Calculation*, W. H. Freeman and Company, New York, 1976.

Winston, Patrick Henry, *Artificial Intelligence*, second edition, Addison-Wesley, Reading, Mass., 1984.

Winston, Patrick H. and Karen A. Pendergast, editors, *The AI Business*, MIT Press, Cambridge, Mass., 1984.

BIBLIOGRAPHY—GENERAL

Abbott, Walter F. "Use of Regression-Based Tax Assessments for Estimating the Current Fair Value of Existing Residential Dwelling Units." *Assessors Journal* 16 (June 1981): 89-108.

Alexander, Jay T. *The Use of Microcomputers in Assessment Administration.* Paper presented at the IAAO 50th International Conference on Assessment Administration, Hollywood, Florida, 1984.

Alkins, Arthur C. *Computers and Data Processing Today.* Homewood, IL: Dow-Jones-Irwin, 1983.

Almy, Richard. "Evolving Role of Property Assessment in Local Government." In *Land Information at the Local Level*, edited by Alfred Leick, pp. 73-79. Orono: University of Maine, Surveying Engineering, 1982.

Analyzing Assessment Equity. Chicago: IAAO, 1977.

Application of Computer Techniques to the Valuation of Income Producing Properties, An Overview. Ontario: Ministry of Revenue, Technical Research Section, 1975.

Barber, D.G. "Micro Computer Based Geographic Analysis." In *Practical Applications of Computers in Government*, edited by Rolf R. Schmitt and Harlan J. Smolin, pp. 118-125. McLean: Urban and Regional Information Systems Association, 1982.

Behrens, John O. "Assessors, Recorders, and Computers and Where They Now Stand." In *The Changing Role of Computers in Public Agencies*, edited by Rolf R. Schmitt and Harlan J. Smolin, pp. 208-222. McLean: Urban and Regional Information Systems Association, 1984.

Behrens, John O. "Census Bureau Contributions to a Land Parcel Identification System." *Assessors Journal* 15 (June 1980): 85-105.

Black, Ron. "Selecting the Correct Approach to Value in Mass Appraisal." *Assessment Digest* 5 (Jan/Feb 1983): 14-16.

Borst, Richard. "Computer Assisted Mass Appraisal—A New Growth Industry in the United States." In *Third International Symposium on the Property Tax*, Frankfurt, Germany, 1976, pp. 12-29. Chicago: IAAO in cooperation with Lincoln Institute of Land Policy, 1976.

Borst, Richard A. and Reinhard, Paul J. "The Role of the Data Mailer in Computer-Assisted Mass Appraisals." *Assessment Digest* 2 (March/April 1980): 8-15.

Borst, Richard A. "Use of Constrained Regression by Non-Statisticians." Paper presented at the World Congress on Computer Assisted Valuation, Lincoln Institute of Land Policy, Cambridge, Mass., August, 1982.*

British Computer Society. Developing Countries Specialist Group. *Use of Computers for National Development Transportation: An Annotated Bibliography.* New York: John Wiley, 1982.

Butler, Jay Q. and Henderson, Glenn V., Jr. "Computerized Exchange Evaluation Model." *Appraisal Journal* 45 (July 1977): 383-395.

Carbone, Robert; Ivory, Edward L.; Longini, Richard L. "Competition Used to Select Computer-Assisted Mass Appraisal System." *Assessors Journal* 15 (September 1980): 163-169.

Carbone, Robert. *The Design of an Automated Mass Appraisal System Using Feedback.* Pittsburgh: Carnegie-Mellon University, 1976.

Carbone, Robert and Longini, Richard L. "A Feedback Model for Automated Real Estate Assessment." *Management Science* 24 (November 1977): 241-248.

Carbone, Robert. "Notes on the Carbone-Longini Feedback Systems." Paper presented at Course 208: Feedback Computer Assisted Mass Appraisal, Lincoln Institute of Land Policy, Cambridge, Mass., April 1982.*

Chudleigh, Walter H. "Application of Correlation Matrix Analysis to Real Estate Appraisal." *Appraisal Journal* 47 (October 1979): 523-530.

Church, Albert M. *Statistics and Computers in the Appraisal Process* Chicago: IAAO, 1976.

Clatanoff, Robert M. *Computer-Assisted Appraisal and Assessment Systems: An Annotated Bibliography,* Supplement I. Chicago: IAAO, Research & Technical Services Dept., 1983.

Computer Applications in the Appraisal and Real Estate Analysis Process. Winnipeg: Appraisal Institute of Canada, n.d.

Compuer-Assisted Land Resources Planning. Chicago: American Planning Association, 1979.

Computer Assisted Mass Appraisal/Assessment Ratio Bibliography. Monograph #77-4. Cambridge: Lincoln Institute of Land Policy, 1977.

Cook, Charles C. *Computer Assisted Mass Appraisal.* Paper presented at the Third Annual Massachusetts Cherry Sheet Conference, Equalization Workshop, March 24, 1976.

Cook, Charles C. "Computerized Models for the Valuation of Commercial Property." In *Proceedings of the 6th International Symposium on the Property Tax*, May 3-9, 1982, London, pp. 118-138. Chicago: IAAO in cooperation with Lincoln Institute of Land Policy, 1983.

Cook, Charles C. *Considerations for New York City Revaluation Effort (Computer Assisted Mass Appraisal).* Paper, 1978.

Covington, Robert J., Jr. "Developing a Computerized System for Profiling Vacant Industrial Land." In *The Changing Role of Computers in Public Agencies*, edited by Rolf R. Schmitt and Harlan J. Smolin, pp. 334-342. McLean: Urban and Regional Information Systems Association, 1984.

Crunkleton, Jon R. "A Simplified Computer Assessment Model." *Assessment Digest* 4 (Nov./Dec. 1982): 14-16.

"Current Issues in the Development of Land Records Systems." *Computers, Environment and Urban Systems* 9 (1984) entire issue.

Davis, Joseph M. and New, Donald E. "Using Personal Computers to Analyze Real Estate Investment Decisions." *Real Estate Appraiser and Analyst* 45 (May-June 1975): 5-16.

Denne, Robert C. *Computer-Assisted Appraisal and Assessment Systems.* Bibliographic Series. Chicago: IAAO, 1977.

Dombal, Robert W. *Appraising Condominiums: Suggested Data Analysis Techniques.* Chicago: American Institute of Real Estate Appraisers, 1981.

Dum, Mary J. and Dum, Thomas E. "The Micro-computer in the Typical Appraisal Office." *Appraisal Journal* 49 (Jan. 1981): 126-135.

Eckert, Joseph K. and Epstein, Jeff. "The Use of Constrained Regression as an Update Methodology in Brookline, Massachusetts." Paper presented at the Colloquium on Stability of Annual Value Estimates as Related to Valuation Methodology, Lincoln Institute of Land Policy, Cambridge, Mass., May 1983.*

Eckert, Joseph K. "Using MRA to Deal with Missing Data and Land Value Determination." Paper presented at the World Congress on Computer Assisted Valuation, Lincoln Institute of Land Policy, Cambridge, Mass., August 1982.*

Eisen, Dennis. "Computer Connection." *Appraisal Journal* 50 (Jan. 1982): 127-134.

Elliott, Duncan and Cameron, James G. "An Overview of Computer Applications in the Appraisal Process." *Appraisal Institute Magazine* 24 (February 1980): 36-40.

Ernst, Gerald E. "A Multi-jurisdictional Approach to Computerized Assessments." In *International Property Assessment Administration 8, Proceedings of the 41st International Conference on Assessment Administration*, pp. 201-216. Chicago: IAAO, 1976.

Flanagan, Robert J. "The Minicomputer in the Real Estate and Appraisal Field." *Appraisal Institute Magazine* 26 (May 1982): 28-31.

Foden, Harry G. and Austin, James. "Trade Marks for Computer/Information Markets." *Urban Land* 43 (August 1984): 32-33.

Gadd, John L. "The Integration of Machinery and Equipment Appraisals Into the Real Estate Valuation Report." *Real Estate Appraiser and Analyst* 50 (Spring 1984): 5-7.

German, Jerome C. "How an MRA Model Can Contain More than Fifty Terms Successfully and Provide Consistent Decomposition of Value." Paper presented at the World Congress on Computer Assisted Valuation, Lincoln Institute of Land Policy, Cambridge, Mass., August 1982.*

Gilreath, Morgan. "Case Study: Appraisal Collection System Paces Citrus County Growth." *Assessment Digest* 5 (Jan/Feb 1983): 22-23.

Gipe, George W. *Mass Appraisal of Apartments with Comparable Sales.* Monograph #77-8. Cambridge: Lincoln Institute of Land Policy, 1977.

Glen, J.T. and Bailey, R.R. "A Computer-Assisted Appraisal System for Income-Producing Properties." *Aspects* (August 1977): 31-39.

Glen, John T. *A Progress Report on the Application of Computer Techniques to the Value of Income Producing Properties for Mass Appraisal.* Toronto: Ministry of Revenue, 1975.

Gloudemans, Robert. "The Base Home Approach to Explainability in Mass Appraisal." Paper presented at the Colloquium on the Stability of Annual Valuation Updates, Lincoln Institute of Land Policy, Cambridge, Mass., May 1983.*

Gloudemans, Robert J. "Simplifying MRA-Based Appraisal Models: The Base Home Approach." *Assessors Journal* 16 (December 1981): 155-166.

Griesemer, James R. *Microcomputers in Local Government.* Washington: International City Management Association, 1983.

Griffin, Gerald Jr. "Conventional Appraisal Techniques Can Be Computerized." *Appraisal Journal* 47 (April 1979): 253-262.

Haff, Courtney A. "Data Collection for Computer-Assisted Mass Appraisal: A Review of Alternatives for Multi-Family Properties." *Assessors Journal* 12 (June 1977): 105-120.

Haff, Courtney A. "Evaluation of Alternative Data Collection and Appraisal Procedures: New York City Research Issues." *Assessors Journal* 15

(December 1980): 181-190.

Haney, Kathleen. "A Computer Format for Timberland Grading and Valuation." *Assessors Journal* 9 (January 1975): 45-66.

Hayes, Edgar E. and Fauquier, John E. "Organizing the Cleveland Land Data System Around Micro Computers." In *Decision Support Systems for Policy and Management*, edited by Rolf R. Schmitt and Harlan J. Smolin, pp. 194-208. McLean: Urban and Regional Information Systems Association, 1983.

Howard, Dick and Wead, James. *Periodic Reappraisal of Real Property: The Utah Approach.* Lexington: Council of State Governments, 1976.

Hunt, Joseph E. "Practical Considerations When Contemplating A Computer-Assisted Mass Appraisal System." *Property Tax Journal* 3 (June 1984): 91-105.

Improving Real Property Assessment, A Reference Manual. Chicago: IAAO, 1978.

Index of Computer Hardware and Software in Use in North Carolina and Local Governments. Chapel Hill: University of North Carolina, Institute of Government, 1983.

Jackson, Nathaniel A. and Smit, Gerald J. "A Data Collection Experiment in the Town of Ramapo." *Assessors Journal* 11 (June 1976): 75-90.

James, Franklin J. "Assessment Procedures, Community Characteristics, and the Accuracy of Property Tax Assessments." In *International Property Assessment Administration 8, Proceedings of the 41st International Conference on Assessment Administration*, pp. 237-253. Chicago: IAAO, 1976.

Jensen, David L. *Alternative Modeling Techniques in Computer-Assisted Appraisal.* Monograph #83-5. Cambridge: Lincoln Institute of Land Policy, 1983.

Jensen, David L. "Application of Bayesian Regression for a Valuation Model Update in Computer Assisted Mass Appraisal." Paper presented at the Colloquium on Stability of Annual Value Estimates as Related to Valuation Methodology, Lincoln Institute of Land Policy, Cambridge, Mass., May 1983.*

Jensen, David L. "The Use of Multiple Linear Regression in Residential Land Valuation." Paper presented at the Colloquium on Econometric Approaches to the Valuation of Vacant and Improved Land, Lincoln Institute of Land Policy, Cambridge, Mass., January 1983.*

Johnson, Toni M. "A Network that Works: Using Computer Graphics as an Aid to Environmental Assessment." In *The Changing Role of Computers in Public Agencies,* edited by Rolf R. Schmitt and Harlan J. Smolin, pp. 480-492. McLean: Urban and Regional Information Systems Association, 1984.

Johnston, Kevin J. et al. "Restricted Interest Deductibility - A Treatment Using the Computer-Based Discounted Cash Flow Approach to Valuation." *Appraisal Institute Magazine* 26 (May 1982): 10-14, 19.

Kentucky. Department of Revenue. *CREAL, A System for Computerizing Real Estate and Land Records Systems.* Springfield: National Technical Information Service, 1977.

Killen, James E. *Mathematical Programming Methods for Geographers and Planners.* New York: St. Martin's Press, 1983.

Kinzer, Lydia G. and Moltz, Shirley W. "A Longitudinal View of Sales Data for a Computer-Assisted Appraisal Program." *Assessors Journal* 10 (October 1975): 41-56.

Kirk, William H. "Computerized Assessment Ratio Study: a "Big City" Technique Adapted for Small City Use." *Assessment Digest* 1 (March/April 1979): 12-14.

Koelsch, James P. "Computers: a Cost-Benefit Analysis." *Appraisal Journal* 51 (April 1983): 305-309.

Kohlhepp, David B. "Computers in Appraising: Applications, Problems, and Possible Solutions." *Real Estate Appraiser and Analyst* 48 (Winter 1982): 22-25.

Land Valuation Methods: Rural and Transitionary Land. Monograph #80-2. Cambridge: Lincoln Institute of Land Policy, 1980.

Land Valuation Methods: Urban Land. Monograph #80-1. Cambridge: Lincoln Institute of Land Policy, 1980.

Lester, Horace B., Sr. "Computer Assisted Valuation of Lands for Purposes of Taxation." In *The Changing Role of Computers in Public Agencies*, edited by Rolf R. Schmitt and Harlan J. Smolin, pp. 271-277. McLean: Urban and Regional Information Systems Association, 1984.

Lima, Robert J. "Interfaces Between Man, Machine, and the 'System,' or 'Hairy' Tales of Computerized Applications in Planning." In *Practical Applications of Computers in Government*, edited by Rolf R. Schmitt and Harlan J. Smolin, pp. 14-21. McLean: Urban and Regional Information Systems Association, 1982.

Lukens, Reaves C. *The Dictionary of Real Estate Appraisal.* Chicago: American Institute of Real Estate Appraisers, 1984.

McDonough, Wallace J. and Fisher, Roy R., Jr. "Computers and Statistics." *Real Estate Appraiser and Analyst* 47 (First Quarter 1981): 17-24.

McGill, Frank "Using Computers for Environmental Assessment, Orange County: Identifying Problems and Solutions." *Planning* 49 (September 1983): 18-20.

McKenzie, James. "The Computer and Rural Appraisal." *Appraisal Institute Magazine* 19 (Autumn 1975): 23-36.

McMullin, Scott G. "Simple Computer Data Processing for Appraisers." *Real Estate Appraiser and Analyst* 49 (Fall 1983): 31-37.

Madziya, R.G. and Dandy, Kathy. "OMIS: the Metamorphosis of a Planning and Development Department." In *The Changing Role of Computers in Public Agencies,* edited by Rolf R. Schmitt and Harlan J. Smolin, pp. 315-323. McLean: Urban and Regional Information Systems Association, 1984.

Mass Appraisal of Residential Property: A Programmed Course. Chicago: IAAO, 1979.

Mazursky, Jerome. "The Future of Assessed Valuation in New York City." *Assessment Digest* 1 (July/August 1979): 16-19.

"Microcomputers and Urban Design." *Urban Land* 43 (January 1984): 30-31.

Montgomery, David and Tait, James. "Development of a Simplified Market Data Approach for Mass Appraisal." In *International Property Assessment Administration 8, Proceedings of the 41st International Conference on Assessment Administration*; pp. 151-173. Chicago: IAAO, 1976.

Morton, T. Gregory. "Factor Analysis, Multicollinearity, and Regression Appraisal Models." *Appraisal Journal* 45 (October 1977): 578-588.

Müller, Anders. "The Effect of Using Valuation Estimates by Computer at the General Valuation in 1981 in Denmark." In *Proceedings of the 6th International Symposium on the Property Tax*, May 3-9, 1982, London, pp. 143-149. Chicago: IAAO in cooperation with the Lincoln Institute of Land Policy, 1983.

Müller, Anders. "Separate Models for Computer Calculations of Land Values and Building Values of 1.3 Million Residential Properties in Denmark." Paper presented at the Colloquium on Econometric Approaches to the Valuation of Vacant and Improved Land, Lincoln Institute of Land Policy, Cambridge, Mass., January 1983.*

Müller, Anders. "Valuation Estimates by Computer." In *Proceedings of the 5th International Symposium on the Property Tax*, May 8-14, 1980, Amsterdam-Paris, pp. 29-35. Chicago: IAAO in cooperation with the Lincoln Institute of Land Policy, 1980.

Mulready, Robert J. "Computer-Assisted Assessment System: Farmington, CT." In *International Property Assessment Administration 8, Proceedings of the 41st International Conference on Assessment Administration*, pp. 229-236. Chicago: IAAO, 1976.

Need for a Multipurpose Cadastre. Washington: National Academy Press, 1980.

New Jersey. Division of Taxation. Local Property and Public Utility Branch. *The New Jersey Property Tax System, Mod IV: Computer Applications in Tax Administration.* Trenton: Division, 1983.

O'Connor, Patrick M. "Making One MRA Model Behave Appropriately Across the Whole of a Large County." Paper presented at the World Congress on Computer Assisted Valuation, Lincoln Institute of Land Policy, Cambridge, Mass., August 1982.*

Peltzer, Kenneth. "Computerized Analysis of a Joint-Venture-Investment Office Building." *Appraisal Journal* 50 (October 1982): 537-563.

Proceedings of Colloquium on Computer Assisted Mass Appraisal Potential for Commercial and Industrial Real Property. Monograph #77-10. Cambridge: Lincoln Institute of Land Policy, 1977.

Reese, Louie. "Mass Appraisals: Raffle or Racket?" *Real Estate Appraiser and Analyst* 44 (May-June 1978): 16-20, 33.

Reinmuth, James E. "Innovative Techniques for Measuring Assessment Performance. In *International Property Assessment Administration 8, Proceedings of the 41st International Conference on Assessment Administration*; pp. 175-185. Chicago: IAAO, 1976.

Schafer, Robert. "A Comparison of Alternative Approaches to Assessing Residential Property." *Assessors Journal* 12 (June 1977): 81-94.

Schneider, Devon M. and Syed, Amanullah. *Computer-Assisted Land Resources Planning.* Chicago: IAAO, 1979.

Schott, L. Ried and White, Fred C. "Multiple Regression Analysis of Farmland Values by Land Classes." *Appraisal Journal* 45 (July 1977): 427-434.

Selected Bibliography on Land Valuation Methods. Monograph #77-9. Cambridge: Lincoln Institute of Land Policy, 1977.

Shenkel, William. "Using Advanced Appraisal Data Systems." *Appraisal Institute Magazine* 19 (Summer 1975): 43-62.

Shlaes, Jared and Young, Michael S. "Evaluating Major Investment Properties." *Appraisal Journal* 46 (January 1978): 101-111.

Skaff, Michael S. "Automation in Small Taxing Jurisdictions: A New Alternative." *Assessors Journal* 12 (September 1977): 157-170.

Skaff, Michael S. "Documentation: The Assessor's Computer Insurance Policy." *Assessors Journal* 15 (June 1980): 77-83.

Smith, David V. "An Appraiser Looks at Multiple Regression." *Appraisal Journal* 47 (April 1979): 248-252.

Spiegel, Robert J. "The Appraiser, the Computer and the 1981 Economic Recovery Tax Act." *Real Estate Appraiser and Analyst* 49 (Spring 1983): 43-50.

Spivak, Melton L. "The Future for Computers in Real Estate Valuation." *Appraisal Journal* 43 (January 1975): 80-89.

Standards on Mass Appraisal of Real Property. Chicago: IAAO, 1984.

Stevenson, D.R. "The Valuer, the Computer and the Future." *New Zealand Valuer* 22 (March 1975): 359-362.

Stevenson, Donald R. "Financing and Time in Multiple Regression Applications to the Assessment of Single Family Residential Properties." *Assessors Journal* 12 (September 1977): 171-205.

Stockman, Robert. "What's New in Microcomputer Applications." *Planning* 50 (August 1984): 21-24.

Swett, Hollis A. and Whalen, Jo Ann. "The Use of Multiple Regression Analysis to Select and Adjust Comparable Sales." *Assessors Journal* 12 (March 1977): 17-33.

Taggart, Joseph J. "The New York State Real Property Information System." In *International Property Assessment Administration 8, Proceedings of the 41st International Conference on Assessment Administration*, pp. 187-200. Chicago: IAAO, 1976.

Tchira, Arnold. "Comparable Sales Selection - A Computer Approach." *Appraisal Journal* 47 (January 1979): 86-98.

Thompson, John F. and Gordon, Jack. "Constrained Regression Modeling in Conjunction with the MRA Comparable Sales Approach." Paper presented at the Colloquium on Stability of Annual Value Estimates as Related to Valuation Methodology, Lincoln Institute of Land Policy, Cambridge, Mass., May 1983.*

Trippi, Robert R. and Spiegel, Robert J. "Computer Asisted Appraisal of the Regional Shopping Mall." *Real Estate Appraiser and Analyst* 44 (September-October 1978): 23-27.

Vieux, Ken. "Guidelines for a Successful Computerized Appraisal System." *Assessment Digest* 5 (Jan./Feb. 1983): 10-12.

Wachs, Peggy. "Implementation of Computerized Real Estate Assessment." *AIP Journal* (January 1978): 60-67.

Ward, Richard. "Residential Land Valuation Techniques Developed in Ramsey County, Minnesota." Paper presented at the Colloquium on Econometric Approaches to the Valuation of Vacant and Improved Land, Lincoln Institute of Land Policy, Cambridge, Mass., January 1983.*

Wilcox, James P. "Implementation of a Computer-Assisted Appraisal System: Multnomah County, Oregon." *Assessors Journal* 14 (December 1979): 179-191.

Wilson, Frank D. and Nielson, Donald A. "Mini-Computer Applications to Appraisal Analysis." *Real Estate Appraiser and Analyst* 41 (March-April 1975): 27-32.

Wisconsin. Bureau of the Property Tax. *Computer Assisted Mass Appraisal: A Technical Overview for Data Processing.* Madison: Department of Revenue, 1980.

Wisconsin. Bureau of the Property Tax. *Questions and Answers About Computer Assisted Assessment.* Madison: Department of Revenue, 1980.

Woolford, William A. and Cassin, Steven G. "Multiple Regression Analysis: A Valuable Tool for Mass-Land Appraisal." *Appraisal Journal* 51 (April 1983): 213-224.

Yeatman, John M. et al. "The In-House Development of a Computer-Assisted Appraisal System: Fairfax County, Virginia." In *International*

Property Assessment Administration 8, Proceedings of the 41st International Conference on Assessment Administration, pp. 217-227. Chicago: IAAO, 1976.

Zerbst, Robert H. and Eldred, Gary W. "Improving Multiple Regression Valuation Models Using Location and Housing Quality Variables." *Assessors Journal* 12 (March 1977): 1-15.

* These papers are available from the International Association of Assessing Officers, Education Department, 1313 East 60th Street, Chicago, IL 60637.

BIBLIOGRAPHY — LEGAL

"Computer-Assisted Property Tax Appraisals: Admissibility of Computer-Generated Evidence"

Carlisle B. Roberts, Senior Judge, Oregon Tax Court

Selected Bibliography

David Bender: *Computer Evidence Law: Scope and Structure*, 1 Computer/Law Journal 699-723 (1979). (This article is a revision of a paper presented at the ABA National Institute on Computers and Litigation, February 1-2, 1979. Computer/Law Journal's address is P. O. Box 54308 TA, Los Angeles, California 90054.)

John Hardin Young et al, Editors: *Use of Computers in Litigation* (Copyright 1979 by the ABA. Published by Professional Education Publications, 1155 East 60th Street, Chicago, Illinois 60637.)

Anno., *Proof of Public Records Kept or Stored on Electronic Computing Equipment*, 71 ALR3d 232 (1976).

Anno., *Admissibility of Computerized Private Business Records*, 7 ALR4th 8 (1981).

Corusy & Gossett, *Defending Computer Evidence in Assessment Appeals*, 15 Assessor's Journal 199-204 (No. 4, December 1980).

Computer Law Service Reporter (cited "CLSR") Vols. 1-7. Published by Callaghan & Company, 6141 North Cicero Avenue, Chicago, Illinois 60646, edited by R. P. Bigelow, Esq., of the Massachusetts Bar, beginning in 1972; terminated by the publisher about October 1981.

Selected Law Review Articles

Note, *Appropriate Foundation Requirements for Admitting Computer Printouts into Evidence*, Wash Univ L Q, (Vol 1977, No. 1, Winter) 59-93. [Note 9, at 60, states: "The correct spelling of the word is printout." The thrust of the Note is that "traditional foundation requirements of the business records exception to the hearsay rule are ineffective to ensure the reliability of a computer printout." At 62.]

J. J. Roberts, *A Practitioner's Primer on Computer-Generated Evidence*, 41 Univ of Chicago L Rev 254 (Winter 1974). [A sketch on computer mechanics to provide understanding of potential evidentiary problems.]

Colin Tapper, *Evidence from Computers*, 8 Ga L Rev 562 (Spring 1974).

Comment, *Computer Print-Outs of Business Records and Their Admissibility in New York*, 31 Albany L Rev 61 (Jan 1967).

Outline and Citations

I. The changing scene in property tax appraisals, indicated in judicial decisions:
(a) Courts are less permissive in approving four- to six-year reappraisal cycles. Oldman, 13 Assessor's Journal 34-35 (No. 1, March 1978). At the same time, judges, in greater numbers, are mandating annual assessments at 100 percent of true cash value.

> *Town of Sudbury v. Comm. of Corps and Tax*, 366 Mass 558, 321 NE2d 641 (1974).
> Hellerstein v. Assessor, Town of Islip, 37 NY2d 1 (1975), *modifying* 42 AD2d 689 (1974).
> 12 Assessor's Journal 106 (No. 2, June 1977).

(1) When a court held a proposed 1961 assessment roll in Springfield, Massachusetts, was inequitable and unconstitutional, the court ordered a wholly new assessment, noting: "It should be possible to accomplish such a new assessment rapidly through the use of the city auditor's electronic machines." *Bettigole v. Assessors of Springfield*, 343 Mass 223, 178 NE2d 10, 19 (1961).

(b) Computer-based appraisal of real property for tax purposes is now common throughout the United States and questions of the admissibility of computer-generated evidence have been raised.

II. Forms of Computer Evidence Offered in Court.
(a) The input in the computer process is derived from original records,

the work product of many individuals, stored in the computer for future use and disgorged ("the computer printout") in a form which is immediately understandable or in a code form or possibly as a computer-generated graph or chart.

(b) The cases presented to the courts generally involve business records, routinely stored in the machine and printed out in a readable form *or* results of compiled and edited business records, showing summaries and trends *or* results of compiled and edited nonbusiness records offered to show summaries or trends.

III. Acceptance by Judges of Computer Evidence.

(a) In *Bronson v. Consolidated Edison Co.*, 350 F Supp 443, 444 (SD NY 1972), the court states: "The facts as set forth by plaintiff suggest an Orwellian nightmare of computer control which breaks down through mechanical and programmers' failures and errors." This is an unusually strong statement. Judges, properly, have accepted computer evidence with caution, recognizing the danger of error in all business record systems and noting that "[t]he computer is a marvelous device that can perform countless tasks at high speed and low cost, but it must be used with care. This is because it can also make errors at high speed." *Neal v. U.S.*, 402 F Supp 678, 680 (D NJ 1975), 5 CLSR 913, 914. A sprightly comment on *computer language* is found in *Honeywell, Inc. v. Lithonia Lighting, Inc.,* (DC ND Ga 1970), 317 F Supp 406.

> *Perma Research & Development Co. v. Singer Co.*, 542 F2d 111, 121 (2d Cir, 1976), 6 CLSR 98 (dissenting opinion)
> *Harned v. Credit Bureau of Gillette*, 513 P2d 650, 5 CLSR 394 (Wyo 1973)
> *Sears Roebuck & Co. v. Merla*, 142 NJ Super 205, 361 A2d 68, 5 CLSR 1370 (1976)
> *Dept. of Mental Health v. Beil*, 44 Ill App3d 402, 357 NE2d 875, 880 (1976)

(b) Generally, the courts have accepted computer evidence, recognizing the questions raised are merely variations of familiar evidential questions; i.e., the laying of a proper foundation; the best evidence rule (and its exception for "voluminous writings" or "voluminous records"); the rule against hearsay and its exceptions (business records, official records, declarations against interest, judicial notice, treatises and trade publications, ancient documents, admissions and stipulations, photocopy statutes). Pretrial conferences on evidence are recommended. *Harned v. Credit Bureau of Gillette, supra.*

IV. Relevance of Computer Document.

(a) The witness must be able to testify as to the relevance of the offered document by showing his familiarity with the events which
led to the recording and the production and use of the records
to be introduced. At this juncture, the custodian of the document
or the head of the department responsible for the event which
has been recorded is probably a better witness than a computer
technician. (Abstracts of judicial decisions, stating qualifications
for nontechnical witnesses who testify from computer records,
can be found in the General Digest (West Pub Co., Sixth Series)
under "Evidence," Key No. 373(1).)

V. Reliability of the Computer Document.

(a) Reliability is established by demonstrating the accuracy of the
data used for computer input, establishing that the method of inputting was accurate and demonstrating that the computer program was accurately designed and coded. This calls for an explanation of the system controls regularly followed to ensure accuracy. A computer technician is a proper witness.

> *Transport Indemnity v. Seib*, 178 Neb 253, 132 NW2d 871, 1
> CLSR 368 (1965)
> *King v. State ex rel Murdock Accept. Corp.*, 222 S2d 393, 2
> CLSR 180 (Miss 1969)
> *United States v. Russo*, 480 F2d 1228 (6th Cir, 1973), 5 CLSR
> 687

(b) It must be recognized that problems will arise when manually kept
business records must be changed in form to some degree
because of the mechanics of computer input, with the result that
the printout will not conform to the original record. The witness
in this instance must be able to testify exactly as to the original
records, the method of change and the verification of input. He
must prove that there has been no distortion in the effect of the
printout because of the computer process. Most judges will in-
sist that the underlying information be admissible and that it be
properly qualified.

> *Pearl Brewing Co. v. Jos. Schlitz Brewing Co.*, 415 F Supp
> 1122, 1134-1140 (DC SD Texas 1976), 7 CLSR 1164 (an an-
> titrust suit; procedural question as to right to discover struc-
> ture of computer model)

VI. Hearsay Rule.

(a) Like other written documents, computer printouts are hearsay and, unless they fit within one of the exceptions to the hearsay rule, are inadmissible as testimony at trial.

(b) The Uniform Business Records Act is deemed by most courts to be broad enough to admit computer-generated evidence if all the conditions of the act are met. *Monarch F.S. & L.A. v. Genser*, 156 NJ Super 107, 383 A2d 475 (1977) (an exceptionally studious opinion).

    (1) Federal Rules of Evidence, Rule 803(6) recognizes the admissibility of computerized records by its reference to "data compilation."

    (2) Many states and federal courts have approved the introduction into evidence of computer output under the business records exception. For example:

State v. Veres, 7 Ariz App 117, 436 P2d 629, 1 CLSR 918 (1968)

Cotton v. John W. Eshelman & Sons, Inc., 137 Ga App 360, 223 SE2d 757, 5 CLSR 1287 (1976)

People v. Chicago and North Western Railway Co., 28 Ill2d 205, 190 N.E2d 780 (1963) (assessor's public records; also "voluminous documents")

Sears, Roebuck & Co. v. Merla, 142 NJ Super 205, 361 A2d 68, 5 CLSR 1370 (1976)

Ed Guth Realty, Inc. v. Gingold, 34 NY2d 440, 358 NYS2d 367, 5 CLSR 880, 71 ALR3d 224 (1974)

In re Matthews Est., 47 Pa D & C2d 529 (1969)

Texas Whse. Co. of Dallas, Inc. v. Springs Mills, Inc. (Civ App Texas 1974), 511 SW2d 735

State v. Smith, 16 Wash App 425, 558 P2d 265 (1976)

United States v. Fendley, 522 F2d 181 (5th Cir, 1975)

(c) Common Law Shop Book Rule. Where there is no business records statute, computerized business records have been found admissible under the hearsay rule following the Common Law Shop Book Rule.

Sears, Roebuck & Co. v. Merla, supra

King v. State ex rel Murdock Accept. Corp., 222 S2d 393, 2 CLSR 180, 183-184 (Miss, 1969)

(d) Official Governmental Records.

United States v. Farris, (CA 7, 1975), 517 F2d 226

State v. Loehmer, 159 Ind App 156, 304 NE2d 835 (1973)

VII. Best Evidence Rule (requiring the original document).
  (a) In *United States v. Russo*, 480 F2d 1228 (6th Cir, 1973), 5 CLSR 687, the court held that in that case the printout was the "original."

  Plyler v. City of Pearland (CA Texas 1972), 489 SW2d 459

  (b) In *King v. State ex rel Murdock Accept. Corp.*, 222 S2d 393, 398, 2 CLSR 180 (Miss 1969), the court stated: "Records stored on magnetic tape by data processing machines are unavailable and useless except by means of the printout sheets * * *" and, although holding that the original entry was *in* the machine, the court allowed the printout in evidence.
  (c) Federal Rules of Evidence, Rule 1001(3) provides: "If data are stored in a computer or similar device, any printout or other output readable by sight, shown to reflect the data accurately, is an 'original'."
  (d) The "voluminous writings" exception to the best evidence rule permits the admission of summaries of voluminous records or entries where, if it is requested, the party against whom it is offered is given access to the original data. *Ed Guth Realty, Inc. v. Gingold*, 34 NY2d 440, 358 NYS2d 367, 5 CLSR 880, 71 ALR3d 224 (1974); *Harned v. Credit Bureau of Gillette*, 513 P2d 650, 5 CLSR 394 (Wyo 1973); *State v. Smith*, 16 Wash App 425, 558 P2d 265 (1976).

VIII. Privilege.
  (a) The two privileges most pertinent to computer evidence are the trade secrets privilege and the government secrets privilege. (Bender, 1 Computer/Law J 721.)

  A. H. Robins Co. v. Fadely, 299 F2d 557, 561 (5th Cir, 1962)
  Baker v. Proctor & Gamble Co., 17 F.R. Serv. 30b.352, Case 1, at 460 (SD NY 1952)
  Grumman Aircraft Eng'r Co. v. Renegotiation Board, 425 F2d 578, 580-81 (DC Cir, 1970)
  Mead Data Central, Inc. v. U.S. Dept. of the Air Force, 402 F Supp 460 (D DC, 1975), *remanded* 566 F2d 243 (DC Cir 1977), *aff'd* 575 F2d 932 (DC Cir 1978)

IX. Simulation by Computer.
  (a) A different problem, from the evidential standpoint, is the use of a computer to reflect the behavior of some actual or proposed process, system or event, to be used in courtroom presentation. Simulation by computer is widely used in the appraisal process for the updating of property values in an inflated economy. The

simulation is evidence only to the extent that it is a valid and accurate representation. Simulation models accept data which are representative of actual events, manipulate this data according to sets of rules which represent how the world works, and present results which are an approximation of the actual results. Examples of admission by courts of computer simulations are found in:

Perma Research & Development Co. v. Singer Co., supra
United States v. Dioguardi, 428 F2d 1033 (2d Cir, 1970), 2 CLSR 647
Pearl Brewing Co. v. Jos. Schlitz Brewing Co., 415 F Supp 1122 (DC SD Texas 1976), 7 CLSR 1164
State v. Rella Verde Apts., Inc., 25 Ariz App 458, 544 P2d 675 (1976)
Jenkins, Computer-Generated Evidence Specially Prepared for Use at Trial, 52 Chicago-Kent L Rev 600, 605 (1976)
Eastin, The Use of Models in Litigation: Concise or Contrived?, 52 Chicago Kent L Rev 610 (1976)

(b) See Note, Computer Simulation and Gaming: An Interdisciplinary Survey With a View Toward Legal Applications, 24 Stanford L Rev 712 (April 1972), for background on computer simulation for resolution of legal problems.
(c) The use of computer simulations comes within the rules of expert testimony, which must be based upon facts, education, skill and experience and allow for opinion.

Perma Research & Development Co. v. Singer Co., 542 F2d 111, 123 (2d Cir); cert denied 429 US 987 (1976), 6 CLSR 98, a landmark case with strong dissent
NLRB v. Bogart Sportswear Mfg. Co., Inc., 485 F2d 1203 (5th Cir, 1973), 5 CLSR 1427
Hi-Lo Tariff, 55 FCC2d 224, 6 CLSR 355 (1975)

X. Credibility of Witness; Probative Value of Testimony.
(a) In the law of evidence, the "credibility" of a witness is that quality which renders his evidence worthy of belief. The judge must contend with a special computer jargon. He or she must not permit the glamour of a novel machine to afford an excuse for sloppy work or overcomplexity. See Bender, 707 et seq; and Use of Computers in Litigation 338 (listed in Selected Bibliography, supra).

GLOSSARY

Adaptive Estimation Procedure: A computerized process for estimating the relation between a dependent variable (selling price) and several independent variables by applying an equation to a succession of parcels and adjusting the coefficients each time in light of the difference between actual and estimated values. Also called feedback.

Algorithm: A well-defined and well-ordered set of instructions for performing a task such as sorting, searching, or calculating.

Alphanumeric: Any alphabetical, numerical, or special character acceptable for use in a computer.

Alternative Hypothesis: The hypothesis which is accepted if the hypothesis being tested is rejected.

ALU: Arithmetic and Logic Unit; the part of the computer hardware which performs the arithmetical and logical operations. The ALU is part of the CPU.

Analog Computer: A computer in which data is represented in magnitude form (e.g., pressure, temperature, voltage) rather than in digital form.

Bar Chart: A popular type of chart for presenting data. A bar chart shows a value as the length of a horizontal bar or the height of a vertical one. Usually, bar charts show multiple series of comparative values on a single chart. Popular types include clustered, stacked, three-dimensional, and flat.

Beta Coefficient: The standardized regression coefficient.

Biased Sample: A sample which does not represent all elements of a population in proportion to their actual occurrence.

Binary: Having just two values, 0 or 1, on or off.

Binary Variable: A data item which may only be represented by either 1 or 0. For example, a residential property record might contain a factor indicating whether a swimming pool is (1) or is not (0) included.

Bit: A binary digit (0 or 1). A series of bits constitutes the binary representation of a number or character to the computer.

Boolean Logic: A set of rules for performing logical operations such as "and," "or," and "not." These rules have been used as the theoretical basis for computer operations. Named for its developer, George Boole.

Byte: A group of adjacent bits treated as a unit and usually shorter than a word; in some computer systems, a group of adjacent bits that represents one alphanumeric character.

CAMA: Computer Assisted Mass Appraisal; refers to the use of computers in appraising large numbers of properties.

Chips: Small rectangular objects of semiconductor material containing micro-miniaturized electronic circuits.

Coefficient: (1) A term multiplying another term in an equation; (2) in statistics, any of several indicators of data performance, such as the Coefficient of Variance, Coefficient of Dispersion, etc.

Coefficient of Correlation: A number in the range -1 to + 1 that indicates the extent to which an independent variable accounts for the variability in the dependent variable. The further the coefficient is from zero, the greater correlation. If the coefficient is positive, it indicates that as the independent variable increases the dependent variable increases, and vice versa. If it is negative, it indicates that as the independent variable increases the dependent variable decreases, and vice versa.

Coefficient of Determination: The square of the product-moment correlation between two variables. It expresses the proportion of the variance of one variable, Y, given by the other, X, when Y is expressed as a linear regression on X. More generally, if a dependent variable has multiple correlation R with a set of independent variables, R^2 is known as the coefficient of determination.

$$R^2 = \frac{\text{Explained variation in Y}}{\text{Total variation in Y}}$$

Coefficient of Dispersion: A statistic used in the assessment industry to indicate levels of equity of estimated values as compared to sales prices; usually calculated as the mean absolute deviation divided by the sample mean and expressed as a percentage.

Confidence Level: The chance that a result may be due to random fluctuation rather than a significant difference. The value is usually expressed either as a percentage or as a decimal fraction. In drawing inferences from sample data, a value of less than 5% is considered significant, meaning that there may be as much as 1 chance in 20 that the results are due merely to random variation.

Constant: A number, characteristic, or item that does not vary in value or amount.

Correlation: The likelihood of one particular event or state, given the occurrence of a second. Correlation between two or more events does not necessarily imply causation. Sometimes known or unknown external factors may be the cause of all the observed events.

Covariance: Characteristic of two or more variables that change together rather than independently.

CP/M: Control Program for Microcomputers; the operating system used on many 8-bit microcomputers.

CPU: Central Processing Unit; the part of a computer that controls overall system operation.

Crossproducts: Numbers produced by finding the difference between single observations and average values for dependent and independent variables, and multiplying these quantities together. An intermediate step in multiple regression analysis, performed prior to an MRA run.

CRT: Cathode Ray Tube; the video screen used in monitors and terminals.

Damping Factor: In feedback, a number between 0 and 1 that determines how much information will be contributed to coefficient adjustment by each current provisional value computation.

Degrees of Freedom: The amount of latitude in computing the regression line. It decreases as more explanatory variables are included.

Dependent Variable: The variable which is determined by the explanatory or predictor variable(s).

Deviation: The difference between a single observation in a sample of values and the mean of those values; distance between any plotted variable and the regression line.

Digital: Representing quantities by means of digits (symbols), rather than physical analogs. A digital computer calculates by using signals representing digits.

Digitize: Convert an image, usually a map, into a list of digital coordinates using a device called a digitizer.

Disk: A magnetic recording device for storing programs and other information.

Diskette: A thin, flexible platter coated with magnetic material, used for storage with microcomputers. Available in 8-inch, 5 1/4-inch, and 3 1/2-inch sizes.

DOS: Disk Operating System; a computer operating system/program designed to be used with disk drives.

Dummy Variable: A variable that does not mean anything in itself but is required by the form of an expression.

EDP: Electronic Data Processing; the automatic manipulation of data and information by an electronic computer system and its operators.

Error Analysis: The branch of numerical analysis concerned with studying the error aspects of numerical analysis procedures. Includes the study of errors that arise in a computation because of the peculiarities of computer arithmetic.

ESP: Estimated Sales Price as calculated by regression analysis; essentially the equivalent of market value as used by appraisers. May also be termed "most probable sales price" (MPSP) or the "computer-estimated value" (CEV). Also used to denote the process or method of using regression to obtain this value.

F-test: A statistical "overall" test for goodness of fit of the regression equation.

Factor: A characteristic (as of a piece of property) that can be given a name and a value for storage in a database.

Field: The space allowed for a group of characters in a word or block which, taken together, form a unit of information - for example, a person's name.

File: A collection of related data records, organized as a unit to permit systematic access, maintenance, and modification.

Frequency Distribution: Consolidation or summarization of observations into groups according to their frequency of occurrence; an orderly arrangement of data to show the number of times an event occurs or a value is noted in a sample of observations, as a number of comparable sales. It is usually used for analytical or communication purposes and can take the form of an array, a table, a graph, or a curve.

Generic Software: Computer software that provides great flexibility for user input in a specific application category such as word processing, graphics, databases, etc.

Goodness of Fit: The accuracy with which data points fit a function.

Hard Copy: Computer-generated output that can be kept as a permanent or semipermanent record (like a printout).

Hard Disk: Solid magnetic recording device that rotates at very high speeds; can store considerably higher volumes of data than diskettes.

Independent Variable: A variable whose value determines the dependent variables and is not determined by them.

Interactive Terms: Terms (in an equation) whose values may influence each other.

I/0: Input/Output; the transfer of data into and out of the computer.

Language: A set of representations, conventions, and rules used to convey information. Programming languages include BASIC, COBOL, and FORTRAN.

Mean: A measure of central tendency for a number of observations or items. Obtained by adding the values of all the items and dividing by the number of items; often denoted by $\overline{x}$, read "x bar."

Median: A measure of central tendency for a characteristic; the value associated with the middle item or observation, when all the items or observations are arranged according to size. The median is that value of the variate that divides the total frequency into two halves.

Memory: The faculty of retaining a symbol which can be retrieved. Also, the device in the computer enabling this faculty.

Modem: MODulator/DEModulator; a device that permits computers to talk to each other over communications media. It changes digital symbols to audio signals and audio signals to digital symbols.

MRA: Multiple Regression Analysis; a statistical process for estimating the relation of several independent variables to a dependent variable, on the basis of a series of observations of each variable.

Multicolinearity: In statistics, a situation in which several independent variables are highly correlated.

Null Hypothesis: A negative statement asserting the opposite of the hypothesis to be verified. An instance that refutes the null hypothesis supports the true hypothesis.

Operating System: An organized collection of techniques and procedures for operating a computer; a part of a software package designed to simplify housekeeping.

PROM: Programmable Read Only Memory; a type of computer memory that can be programmed initially with a desired set of instructions or patterns by the user rather than the manufacturer. Once programmed, it is permanent.

R^2: A measure of closeness of fit and linearity of a regression equation.

RAM: Random Access Memory; a type of computer memory that users and programs can change. Any address location can be accessed as easily as any other. These elements of memory lose their contents when the power is turned off.

RCN: Replacement Cost New; calculated from the summation cost approach.

RCNLD: Replacement Cost New Less Depreciation.

Record: A document or unit of computer information containing information regarding one property or observation.

Residual Analysis: The process of examination oriented toward improving valuation model performance. Residuals (i.e., differences between estimated and actual values) are analyzed to determine data or model structure deficiencies.

ROM: Read Only Memory; a type of computer memory whose contents will not change when the power goes off. It is generally set at the factory and cannot normally be altered or erased by computer programs.

RS-232: The industry standard for the serial transmission of data to peripheral devices like printers or modems.

Sales Ratio Analysis: The process of examining the accuracy and equity of estimated appraised values in relation to actual selling prices of properties.

Standard Error of the Estimate: A measure of the accuracy of the regression estimating the dependent variable; expressed in units of the dependent variable.

Standard Deviation: The most widely used measure of dispersion of a frequency distribution. It is equal to the positive square root of the variance. The square root of the average of the squares of the deviations in a sample (the root-mean-square of the deviations) is found by (1) squaring the deviations, (2) summing the squares, (3) dividing the sum by the number of values, and (4) extracting the square root.

Standard Error: The positive square root of the variance of the sampling distribution of a statistic; a measure of the distribution of an estimate of a parameter.

Variance: A measure of the dispersion of data about the mean of a variable; a statistical tool for determining the strength of a central tendency in a collection of data.

INDEX